Ireland's Tragic Comedians

JOHN FITZGIBBON

*From the picture by Hugh D. Hamilton in the National Gallery of Ireland.
By kind permission of the Board of Governors and Guardians.*

Ireland's Tragic Comedians

by

JOHN CHARTRES MOLONY

Essay Index Reprint Series

 BOOKS FOR LIBRARIES PRESS
FREEPORT, NEW YORK

First Published 1934
Reprinted 1970

INTERNATIONAL STANDARD BOOK NUMBER:
0-8369-1933-5

LIBRARY OF CONGRESS CATALOG CARD NUMBER:
73-134117

PRINTED IN THE UNITED STATES OF AMERICA

FOREWORD.

THE four men whose careers I shall follow were connected, though in different ways, with the attempts of England to govern Ireland towards the close of the eighteenth century. All four were intelligent : at least one was gifted with intelligence far above the common measure of man. All were brave ; and, now that the whirlwinds of passion which raged about them in their lifetimes are laid, it may be admitted that all were sincere. They lived and they died ; and this was the manner of their several deaths. One was hanged ; one was shot like a dog in a scuffle with the officers of the law ; one escaped the gallows by cutting his own throat (very inexpertly) with a penknife. One died full of honours if not of years : the inward satisfaction which his outward honours brought to him may be judged from his own words uttered in the last years of his life : " Happy would I be if I could go to my bedchamber without entering an armoury ; could I close my eyes without the apprehension of having my throat cut before morning, of seeing my wife and children butchered before my eyes."

In the lives of these Irishmen of yesterday Irishmen of to-day may read a lesson. In the troubled religions and politics of Ireland no one ever was, no one ever is, wholly right or wholly wrong. Cannot all Irishmen unite at last to work for the good of Ireland, cease at last from

Fightin' like divils for reconciliation,
An' hatin' wan another for the love o' God ?

CONTENTS.

JOHN FITZGIBBON

(1748-1802)

"The Irish peasant never had a truer friend, nor Ireland a nobler patriot."—FROUDE.

"Although a native of the soil he evinced no *amor patriæ*, and sought his own advancement at the expense of his country."—O'FLANAGAN.

CHAPTER I.

BARRISTER-AT-LAW.

JOHN FITZGIBBON, son of a Dublin lawyer, was born in Dublin almost exactly at mid-point of the eighteenth century. In the twenty-eight years of his working life he was to become Member of Parliament for Dublin University, Attorney-General for Ireland, Lord Chancellor of Ireland, Vice-Chancellor of Dublin University, Baron Fitzgibbon of Lower Connello, Viscount Fitzgibbon, and Earl of Clare. He drained the cup of worldly success to the dregs. Yet the general verdict of his fellow countrymen has been that he devoted his short life, his great talents, his iron will, his insatiable ambition, to the holding together of a fabric built up of English oppression, Irish corruption, economic stupidity, religious intolerance ; that his last and most significant political act was to destroy the political independence of his country. As a statement of fact the verdict may be in some degree correct ; as an inference of the man's intentions drawn from his acts it may be mistaken.

He was born in a conquered country, and in a country badly governed by its conquerors. The facts of conquest and of misgovernment it is useless to explain or to deny. These are facts of history ; and in the end the facts of history justify themselves. If the Normans conquered the English, if the English conquered the Irish, it is probable that English and Irish deserved to be conquered. If the Normans governed England well, if the English governed Ireland badly, it is possible that England and Ireland got the government which each deserved.

The governing of England by the Normans was not in the beginning a gentle business. "North of the Humber a stern Wilhelmus Conquæstor burned the country, finding it unruly, into very stern repose. Wild fowls scream in those ancient silences, wild cattle roam in those ancient solitudes, the scanty, sulky Norse-bred population all coerced into silence . . . feeling that under these new Norman Governors their history has probably as good as ended." In truth, the great history of England was just then beginning. What the Norman offered, the Norse-bred man accepted, and added to. The fusion of the two races came in time and for a season wellnigh to dominate the world. But in the fusion all conscious element of Norman disappeared. For no nation can for ever or for very long govern, or be governed by, another, if the two remain consciously distinct.

The English and Irish in Ireland either could not or would not unite with one another. Half-heartedly the English at times seem to have considered the idea of exterminating the Irish : "Truly," said an English bishop, "this is the most godly way of reformation, and most profitable and commodious if it might easily be brought to pass." Queen Mary drove the Irish from

4

Leix and Offaly to fill their places with English settlers in King's County and Queen's County; Cromwell endeavoured to segregate the Irish in one corner of their own island. In later days English misgovernment drove the Irish in swarms from their own country, and made the existence of those who remained behind wellnigh impossible. But the attempts, conscious or unconscious, at extermination failed. Perhaps they were not carried through with sufficient resolution, perhaps the Irish have in them a faculty of survival. In any case the Irish survived : survived to be, in the words of Froude, the reproach and torment of England. Froude died in 1894 : what words would he use had he been born half a century later than 1819, and were he living still ?

In sum, this was the position of Irish affairs when John Fitzgibbon was born. The country was in a large measure a desert. The land of Ireland was owned for the most part by absentee proprietors resident in England; it was tilled by a race of starving savages, whose food was the potato, to whom meat was practically unknown, whose drink was water, to whom milk was a costly medicine only to be used on rare and emergent occasions. The manufactures of the country and her commerce had been heavily fettered or wholly destroyed. The great Government Offices of dignity and profit were the monopoly of Englishmen ; the revenues of Ireland provided pensions for the mistresses of English Kings. The religion of the vast majority of the Irish people was a thing proscribed : an Irish Judge was to declare from the Bench that the

Law recognised the existence of no such person as an Irish Catholic. The ' Penal Laws ' forbade an Irish Catholic to vote at an election in his own country, to sit in the Legislature of Ireland. No Catholic might sit on the Irish Judicial Bench or practise at the Irish Bar ; no Catholic might serve as an officer in the Army or Navy ; enter the University of Ireland or conduct a public school ; own freehold land or carry arms. And the word ' Catholic ' was then wellnigh synonymous with ' Irishman.'

It is a miserable picture, a picture before which a fair-minded Englishman may feel ashamed. Yet a fair-minded Irishman will not at once assert that all the fault was on the side of the English. The Irish brood overmuch on the memory of past wrongs ; they are slow to accept the hand of apology and friendship. At no time have they shown themselves especially amenable to orderly, progressive, peaceful government, whether by men of another race or of their own. And people who will not stand up and co-operate with a government which may be good, are likely to find themselves prostrate under the heel of a government which undeniably is bad.

And the words of to-day will not alter the facts of two hundred years ago.

Fitzgibbon sprang from the soil : he was the grandson of Edward Fitzgibbon, a working peasant farmer of the County Limerick. The date of this Edward's birth we do not know, but it is not unreasonable to assume that it was about 1680. And the date, if we attempt to visualise its meaning, calls up a strange picture. From the old men about him young Edward must have heard tales, as of an actual living fact, of the great rebellion of 1641 : it may be that some greybeard who had played a part on one side or the other of the struggle had strayed south, and that the boy heard wild stories of mutual savageries from his lips. Cromwell's invasion, the sack of Wexford, these were the realities of yesterday for his father : it may be that his mother lulled him or frightened him to sleep by the threat that the Puritan ogre prowled by night to eat naughty little boys who would not say their evening prayer, and sink into sleep and into the protection of a Saint. By the cottage door flowed the Shannon, a grim reminder of the choice between Connaught and Hell offered to the Irish who had withstood the power of the English Parliament. For the order had been that all Irish liable to transportation, a phrase which may be translated as all Irish who professed the Catholic faith and who possessed anything which their Protestant neighbours coveted, must remove themselves west of the Shannon by May 1, 1654. The strife of the two kings, William and James, the battlings of Ginkel and Sarsfield for the possession of Limerick, these were well-remembered incidents of his boyhood. As a child he must have trodden Thomond bridge, and gazed open-mouthed at the shot-holes in the walls of the Irish town of Limerick. Perhaps he was wandering, a bewildered urchin, in the muddy streets of the ' city '—Limerick was then but a provincial town of some 12,000 souls—when grim soldiers signed and sealed the articles of surrender : ere he grew at all to man's estate he must have sensed how shamelessly these articles had been disregarded by the conquerors. Patrick Sarsfield, no doubt, was the hero of his boyish daydreams : as he squatted by the cabin fire of turf he must have heard whispered stories of the ' Wild Geese ' winging their flight from Ireland to find sometimes honour, more often a soldier's death, in foreign lands. And as he took up the burden of his life's work, the Penal Laws, the " ferocious acts of Anne," slowly tightened their grip on him.

For the English reader perhaps the most vivid, though possibly not the most truthful picture of an English farmer's life in those days in England is found in the pages of Blackmore's ' Lorna Doone.' It is the picture of a happy life. The Ridds owned their farm of Plover's Barrow in freehold. There is little mention of money ; but of the good things which money can provide there was no lack. When Tom Faggus, the highwayman, paid a friendly call, the widow Ridd apologetically remarked that she could not set before him the fine fare to which he was accustomed at the lordly inns on the road. Nevertheless she could offer a ham, some deer collops, abundance of rashers and fresh eggs, a woodcock on toast. Ale and cider were plentiful and good ; and by some strange mistake the ' good people,' who had borrowed the farm horse Smiler, had left in Smiler's stall a little keg of choice French brandy.

We see the great kitchen with the great open fireplace by which Mr Faggus sat and smoked his *cigarro :* by the same fireplace ' girt Jan Ridd ' bewilderedly listened to the casuistry of that unconscionable old rascal Counsellor Doone and hospitably plied the visitor with schnapps and tobacco. In the summer the parson, chanting in his gown and bands, led the reapers to the fields for the beginning of the harvest : at night there was the jolly harvest supper with plentiful plain cheer for all.

The life of the working farmer in Ireland was very different. The farmhouse was a four-walled hovel : it is computed that nine-tenths of the Irish farm homes of that day lacked chimneys. Tom Faggus, the highwayman, probably would have scorned to stable his roan mare Winnie in Edward Fitzgibbon's home. The Irish farmer might work as he pleased ; but the opportunity to earn much was denied to him, and the little that he did earn was filched from him. He might fatten stock or grow a crop : the sale of these in England was either totally forbidden or checked by heavy duties. Did he make a hundred pounds in the year from his holding, he must pay two-thirds of this to a landlord usually an absentee. Freehold in land, the power to transmit to his children the land to which his labour had given value, freedom to educate his children in their own faith and in their own land ; all these things were denied to the Irish Catholic peasant. Such were the conditions of the life to which Edward Fitzgibbon found himself committed.

Yet purposefulness, tenacity, courage, these qualities which we mark in their full flower and fruition, can now and then be traced back to the seed from which they have sprung. There was smouldering in the soul of Edward Fitzgibbon that fire which was to burn brightly in his son and blaze to heaven in his grandson. He would set his children higher than himself, he would free them from the slavery to which he stood condemned. And as a means to this end he would educate them.

Educate them in his own country he could not. Bits and scraps of Latinity the Catholic Irish lad might pick up, often did pick up in surprising quantity, in hedge schools; but in the face of such the gate leading to a formal, systematic education was banged, barred and bolted. Such boy, if he would learn, must go abroad, usually to Paris, where the piety of Catholic benefactors had established foundations for the instruction of Irish Catholic youth.

It was, no doubt, a hardship, an injustice that the Irish boy could not be educated in Ireland. Yet the mere fact of going abroad at once gave him a measure of education better than any that he could have received at home. He saw that there was a world wider than Ireland or even England; in the most impressionable years of his life his eyes were turned away from the unending, miserable squabblings of Englishman and Irishman, of Protestant and Catholic. And the measure of material inconvenience and hardship may not have been so very great. To-day we time our crossings of the channels, English and Irish, in minutes : at the beginning of the eighteenth century the traveller was at the mercy of the winds and waves. Granted a favouring wind, the journey from Limerick to France may have taken no longer than the journey from Kingstown (not yet so called) to Holyhead against the wind. And the conditions of the journey by sea from Limerick to France may have been easier than those of the journey by land from Limerick to Dublin. The poor scholar bound for France walked aboard his ship, and on his ship he remained until the journey's end was reached. Bound for Dublin he must trudge afoot across the breadth of Ireland.

So to France and Paris Edward Fitzgibbon despatched his sons : with what sweat and toil he must have amassed even the little sum needed for the great adventure. The eldest son, Edward, his father, typical Irish Catholic, devoted to the service of the Church. Edward was educated, and in due course ordained : he returned to Ireland as one of those priests whom Lecky has thus described : " no subsequent generation of Irish priests have left so good a reputation as the better class of those who were educated at the seminaries of France, Italy, and Flanders. They brought with them a foreign culture and a foreign grace which did much to embellish Irish life. They came to their ministry at a mature age, and with a real and varied knowledge of the world. They had the manners and feelings of cultivated gentlemen, and a high sense of clerical decorum." Father Edward, good man, is henceforth swallowed up in his calling,

11

and for our present purposes interests us no more.

His younger brother, John, born in 1708, followed him abroad. There was a story that John, too, was destined for the priesthood, but the story is improbable. The Irish peasant desires ardently a priestly son ; but he desires no less ardently a son to continue his name. And so he does not willingly devote two sons to celibacy.

The history of his life shows this John Fitzgibbon to have been a sober, cautious youth. Yet on two occasions, without his own intention and probably much against his own will, he brought himself surprisingly to the knowledge of Authority. The first occasion was his first day in Paris. He had wandered forth to see the sights ; and as evening closed in he found himself in the Cathedral of Notre Dame. Perhaps he was weary with walking, perhaps he was bored by a sermon in a tongue which he did not then understand. Anyhow, he fell asleep in a corner ; and when he awoke the church was deserted, the great doors closed. He groped about and found a bell-rope : he pulled lustily, and the result surprised him. For this particular bell gave the alarm of fire, riot, sedition : the Irish boy in all innocence had 'turned out' all the officialdom of the great city.

Even if he had been destined for Holy Orders, young John Fitzgibbon speedily changed his mind. He resolved to be called to the Bar, and to practise law. But there was an obstacle in his way : no Catholic could appear as a barrister

in the Courts of Ireland. So John 'turned':
he became a Protestant. We should not judge
too hardly his conversion or perversion for the
avowed purpose of gain. Philosophic theologians
have recognised that a man may sometimes
embrace a lesser evil to avoid a greater ; and
'turns' such as that of John Fitzgibbon were
not uncommon in eighteenth century Ireland.
As a Catholic could not hold or transmit land,
it was not uncommon for one member of a family
to profess Protestantism, and to hold the family
property in trust for all members of the family.
And it is said that there is no record of such
trust being abused. Similarly, it is probable
that quite fifty per cent of the nominally
Protestant barristers in Ireland at that day were
in their hearts devout Catholics. So possibly
young John's 'turn' gave no great offence to his
Catholic father or priestly brother.

He returned to England, to the Temple, and
to the study of law. A young man of his ability
found no difficulty in passing the required ex-
aminations ; but once more he collided with
Authority, and the collision came within an ace
of shipwrecking his hopes by preventing his
call to the Bar.

He was very poor : obviously his peasant
father could give him little help. So, perhaps
to earn a little money, perhaps to bring himself
into some notice, perhaps to improve his legal
knowledge, he conceived and carried out the
project of publishing a volume of Law Reports.
The Reports are said to have been fair, the points
at issue clearly set forth ; but, said an angry

Judge, " Mr Fitzgibbon makes the Judges, and especially myself, talk nonsense wholesale." Young John, it seems, was innocent of any intention to offend ; for an English lawyer, who looked into the matter, has left it on record that Mr Fitzgibbon put into the mouths of the Judges exactly the words which their Lordships used. But it is ill for a recruit to offend, however unwittingly, a company of Generals ; and in the end only John Fitzgibbon's Irishry saved him. He would not have been called to the English Bar : he was called, and allowed to depart to Ireland, where presumably it was a matter of small importance whether Judges talked, or were represented as talking, sense or nonsense.

So to Ireland he came, qualified and free to take up work in the Courts. The peasant Irish of the south are wont to style a barrister ' Counsellor.' The name seems to fit John Fitzgibbon, and it serves to distinguish him from his famous son. So as ' Counsellor ' let us henceforth know him.

The Counsellor had no money, no family influence at his back. If the briefs flowed in, it can only have been because he showed that he had ability to handle them. And flow in they did : the man had brains and tact in abundance. By the time that he was middle-aged the Counsellor had his town house in Dublin and his country house in the adjoining village of Donnybrook. By the evening of his days he had purchased the fine estate of Mount Shannon in his own County of Limerick. Let us hope that his old father lived long enough to see his son's good fortune, and to share it.

14

There is no portrait extant of the Counsellor ; but from imagination one may construct some likeness of him. Perhaps he was a short man, stocky but not stout. He may have had the typically florid complexion of the southern Irishman, and the typical black hair that at an early age is plentifully streaked with grey. In his tastes he may have resembled his contemporary of fiction, the lawyer of ' Catriona.' Probably he enjoyed his bottle of good wine, a well-drawn plea, a shoppy talk with his brother lawyers. He is said to have been avaricious : it is related that once he was offended by the smallness of a fee proffered, but mollified when he learned that the fee represented all that his client possessed. But this tale has been told of many a lawyer, and has been appropriated to himself by at least one eminent lawyer still living. Possibly in the Counsellor's day it was a jest related of some gentleman of the long robe practising in the Courts of Strongbow.

The Counsellor played some nominal part in politics, and in this maze he trod a cautious path. Owing to the peculiar Constitution of the Government of Ireland a man in those days could enter politics by just two roads. He could enter by the road of service to Government, or by the road of perpetual and sterile opposition to Government. The latter road was the more ' popular,' the former much the more profitable. The Counsellor chose the first road. He rose in time to be Attorney-General for Ireland ; but the office as he held it probably was little more than a glorified Crown Solicitorship. Indeed in politics he seems to have shown little interest ; nor does he seem to have harmed any man, to have cherished rancour against any man. There have been many Irishmen more eminent, and there have been very many much less useful.

The Counsellor married. To his firstborn son he gave the very unusual name of Ion ; was this some faint reminiscence of his days of classical study in Paris ? Ion did not live long ; and in 1748 the Counsellor was presented with his second son and ultimate heir. To this boy he gave his own name of John. If a metaphor and a change of sex be permitted, we may picture the Counsellor as a worthy old barnyard hen that unexpectedly hatches out a fierce young eaglet.

The boy is father of the man ; and the first story told of the boy John Fitzgibbon is prophetic of the man that John Fitzgibbon was to be. When he was but twelve or thirteen years old he incurred his father's displeasure, and the Counsellor sent a servant to order the boy's attendance in the study. " Order," said the boy, stamping his foot, " such language suits me not. I will not come. *Decretum est.*" The Counsellor was equal to the situation. He did not storm or rave ; he did not, though he might very well have done so, go in search of his offspring with his riding-whip. With a shrewd grin—one can still see him grinning—he indited a formal letter in which Mr John Fitzgibbon, senior, craved the honour of some moments' interview with Mr John Fitzgibbon, junior, and the tablets of wrath were dissolved in laughter.

Yet the tale is curious ; so curious that it can

scarcely be an invention. What schoolboy, unless he be a monster of literary precocity such as John Mill or Thomas Macaulay, speaks Latin in his anger ? Precocious, mature beyond his years, John Fitzgibbon always was ; but even in the great set speeches of his manhood there is no trace of literary taste, of a love for ' the humanities.' He was cold, clear, logical, incisive. His natural good sense saved him from the flatulent absurdity which often passed for eloquence in the Ireland of his day. But he had nothing of Grattan's splendour, of Duigenan's humour, of Curran's wit. And when provoked to sudden anger he could sink not only very far from the quality of a scholar, but also very far from the quality of a gentleman. As for example : " The politically insane gentleman has asserted much, but he only emitted some effusion of the witticisms of fancy. His declamation, indeed, is better calculated for the stage of Sadler's Wells than the floor of a House of Commons. A mountebank with but one-half the honourable gentleman's theatrical talent for rant would undoubtedly make his fortune. However, I am somewhat surprised he should entertain such a particular asperity against me, as I never did him a favour." Thus Fitzgibbon addressed himself to John Curran across the floor of the House. It is pitiful, from the fishwife vulgarity of the opening to the inept insolence of the ending.

From one disability which had attended his father young John Fitzgibbon was free. He was a Protestant : he could be educated in his own country. ' This freedom ' may have been for him something of a disadvantage and something of an advantage. It would have done him good had he been compelled to spend a few years of his early manhood in a foreign country, to learn that there were practicable forms of government other than the form which obtained in Ireland. He grew up in an atmosphere of senseless sectarianism : it would have been to his lasting benefit to live for a time in a country where sectarianism was practically non-existent, and where the religion of the dominant class was other than his own. He might have learned, what he consistently denied, that a Catholic can be trusted to exercise authority "with temper and with justice." On the other hand, reared in a liberal environment he might never have made the mark in the world that he did make. His intellect was extraordinarily powerful, but at the same time narrow. He resembled a spring, which reaches its greatest power at the point of maximum compression, an explosive which is most effective in a narrow chamber.

He was educated at Dublin day schools, and thence passed into Trinity College, Dublin. This is his formal University record :—

FITZGIBBON, JOHN, second son of John, of Dublin. June 6, 1763. B.A., Vern. 1767; LL.D. (*honoris causa*) Vern., 1779 ; Vice-Chancellor, 1791.

The most noticeable entry is the honorary degree of Doctor of Laws. In Trinity this degree can be won in the ordinary way by examination. It is also the degree which the University confers *honoris causa* on men whom she desires to honour. In modern days the degree has been conferred on men eminent in such very different ways as Henry Irving, Joseph Chamberlain and Cardinal Mercier.

It does not appear that the abilities of young Fitzgibbon attracted particular notice in his undergraduate days. One curious judgment, indeed, remains on record : " That little fellow will deceive you all," said some shrewd observer. Presumably the speaker meant that those who thought lightly of the young man would yet find themselves mistaken. Deceitfulness, in the ordinary sense of the word, could never be charged against John Fitzgibbon. Perhaps some comparison had been drawn between Fitzgibbon and two undergraduates who were his contemporaries. These were Henry Grattan, the great patriot leader of the Irish people, and John Foster, later Speaker of the Irish House of Commons.

Men then entered and left the University at a much earlier age than they do to-day. John Fitzgibbon was but fifteen years old when he entered Trinity, and he graduated at nineteen. Evidently the ' Arts Course ' was then a preliminary to the ' Professional Course,' not concurrent with it. John Fitzgibbon studied Law, and in 1772 was called to the Irish Bar. He chose the Munster Circuit ; and there he found among his competitors Barry Yelverton (eight years his senior), who became Chief Baron of the Exchequer, and his life-long adversary John Philpot Curran, who in 1806 was appointed Master of the Rolls. These men forged to the front in the race of life ; but ' the little fellow ' far outstripped them.

We may pause for a moment to recall the man as he appeared to those about him. Physically and mentally he changed but little throughout his life. He was a small man, so slightly built as to suggest physical delicacy. The portrait of him by Hamilton greatly exaggerates his height. His face was pale ; but it could flush with sudden anger. It was a handsome face : the features were intellectual and finely cut. His eyes were steely grey ; they were, perhaps, his most noticeable feature ; they pierced through men. On one point all observers are agreed : the young man's demeanour was markedly haughty. Many have described it as insufferably arrogant. This is interesting ; for the haughtiness or arrogance may have been in a measure but a ' defence reaction.'

Shrewd, successful, and wealthy though the Counsellor was, it is probable that he neither took up nor greatly desired any considerable position in the social world of Dublin. In his profession he was the servant of his clients and of his solicitors ; in politics he was the servant of the Government. He was one who would accept an order, and carry it out carefully and competently. " Orders," his son, aged thirteen, had said, "such language suits me not." Young John Fitzgibbon might be but the grandson of a humble working farmer. But he would show the aristocracy of Ireland and of England that he obtempered to no man. On Viceroys, Lords and Dukes the old Counsellor probably looked with reverence and respect, though in the respect and reverence there may have been mingled

some element of quizzical humour. The Counsellor's son would show to such that it was his
part to issue orders, their part to obey.

As the son of the Counsellor the young man
must have started his career at the Bar under
favourable auspices. The solidly established
reputation of the father would divert at the
outset a measure of ' junior business ' to the
chambers of the son. But the prizes of the Irish
Bar have never been open to family influence
alone, available for the first advantageously
connected fool who chooses to stretch out a hand
and gather them in. As with father, so with
son : if the current of business flowed steadily
in the direction of young John Fitzgibbon, it
flowed because he, like his father, showed that
he had ability to handle the business that came
his way. We can follow in detail young Fitzgibbon's professional career. For his first act—
it was rather characteristic of him—was to open
an account of his fees : this has been preserved
and handed down. In his first year he earned
£340, an uncommonly good start ; and over
seven or eight years he averaged about £800.
His ' peak year ' was £1600. To-day in England
these figures seem paltry ; but even a hundred
years after John Fitzgibbon's death £1600 would
have been no bad income for a ' junior ' in busy
practice at the Irish Bar.

In the last few years of this preliminary period
earnings show a marked decrease : Fitzgibbon
has left a note that in the very last year he
seldom attended Court. It is not in the least
likely that he had failed to give satisfaction to

his clients and solicitors : it is still more unlikely that he had grown lazy and satisfied with
the prospect of accession to the Mount Shannon
estate. The eaglet's wings had begun to beat
the air : they were never to be folded until they
were folded in the repose of death. Possibly
the Law, as such, had no great attraction for
Fitzgibbon : more probably it offered no sufficient
fuel wherewith to feed the flame of his ambition.
The way to greatness lay through politics ; and
to understand Fitzgibbon's political career it is
necessary to understand the political Constitution
of the Ireland of his day.

The Government of Ireland was then a curiously
limited autocracy. The Viceroy was not then,
as later, a mere figurehead representing the
Sovereign : he was the man charged with carrying
into effect the intentions of the English Cabinet
with regard to Ireland. His instructions were conveyed to him by letter : some of these letters were
to be shown to the coadjutors of his task ; some,
marked 'most secret,' were for his eye alone.
The Viceroy might be, as Froude pleasantly
described one holder of the Office, a "fluttered
imbecile"; he might be a dexterous and dishonest
party manager like Townshend; he might be an
honest but indiscreet reformer like Fitzwilliam.
He might enjoy the task imposed on him : he
might, as many Viceroys did, openly and un-
disguisedly loathe it. But he had to fulfil it.

To aid him in his task the Viceroy had his
Secretary, a gentleman appointed in England,
and seemingly invested with much more authority
than usually falls to a Secretary's lot. Some

Secretaries appear to have enjoyed the privilege of direct communication with the English Cabinet ; and some letters preserved make quaint reading. They impart a vividness, an intelligibility to the phrase 'Satan's invisible world displayed.' The Viceroy had also by his side the Lord Chancellor of Ireland, the Protestant Primate, and, in a measure, the Speaker of the Irish House of Commons. This junta possessed no power of law-making : what they desired should be the law of the land they must get enacted as law by the Irish Legislature. And that Legislature was a strangely constituted Body.

From the franchise and from seats in the House of Commons Catholics were wholly excluded. Dissenters, though not wholly excluded from the franchise in theory, had little hope of representation or of enforcement of their opinions. An estimate of the membership of the several sects in Ireland gave : Catholics, 3,000,000 ; Dissenters, 900,000 ; Episcopalians, 450,000. The House did not represent even the Episcopalians in general. At one time out of 300 Members 201 were returned at the bidding of 101 persons. Until the Octennial Bill of 1768 the Irish Parliament sat indefinitely or permanently. One Irish Parliament sat for thirty-three years.

The result might have been foreseen from the outset : there was no attempt to conceal it when the system was in full swing. The Executive Government 'managed' the Members and their patrons ; the Members and patrons 'undertook' that the King's Government should be carried on. The 'undertaking' was not given for

nothing. Colonel John de Blaquiere, a famous
' Secretary,' writing to England about a proposal
starkly iniquitous in the interests of Ireland,
observes : " You must by pension or place sink
a sum of not less than £9000 per annum. I have
been obliged, with my Lord Lieutenant's leave,
to promise additional salaries or pensions to "—
here follows a list of ten names—" most of whom
were wavering in their faith." Comment is needless. It was into this witches' cauldron that
John Fitzgibbon proposed to plunge : no doubt
he was confident that his strength would keep
his head above the boiling scum.

He sought the suffrages of Dublin University.
The seat was at once a difficult one and an easy
one. ' Difficult,' for the candidate must first
secure the approval of the grave Heads of the
University. Fitzgibbon's honorary Doctorate in
1779 is an obvious indication that his candidature
was approved. The seat was ' easy,' for there
were no meetings to address, no hecklers to
subdue. Nevertheless a constituent did inquire
Fitzgibbon's views on some burning questions of
the day. The questions, and Fitzgibbon's answers
to them, are interesting : they reveal the character
of the man that was Fitzgibbon.

These were the questions : What did Mr
Fitzgibbon think of the claim of the English
Parliament to legislate for Ireland ? What did
he think of Poynings' Law ? And what of that
perpetual bone of contention, the Perpetual
Mutiny Bill for Ireland ?

Mr Fitzgibbon was quite clear that the English
Parliament was incompetent to legislate for

Ireland. But he would not abruptly repeal Poynings' Law. By this Law, passed in 1495, all " causes and considerations " for the summoning of a Parliament in Ireland, the heads of all legislation to be proposed to such Parliament when summoned, must first be approved under the Great Seal of England. Perhaps the difference between the power of England to legislate for Ireland and the power of England to decide what laws an Irish Parliament should be permitted to pass was speculative rather than practical. But Fitzgibbon was then, as ever, a saviour of things as they are rather than a constructor of things as they ought to be. Poynings' Law did offer some practical solution of the difficulty attendant on the existence, cheek by jowl, of two independent Parliaments within the United Kingdom. The Law had worked, on the whole, well enough for a good many hundred years : Mr Fitzgibbon would not precipitately mar what was made already well enough. No doubt on reflection some working compromise could be found.

But in answering the third question Fitzgibbon struck the keynote of his character. He would have none of a Perpetual Mutiny Bill: " It lays the foundation of a military despotism in the country."

Hard things have been said of John Fitzgibbon. He had his faults, serious faults and many of them. But from a fault characteristic of his fellow Irishmen he was entirely free : there was no trace of servility in him. No people have ever shouted more passionately than the Irish their defiance of Law : no people have ever shouted more unashamedly with the village ruffian, truckled more abjectly before force superseding Law. John Fitzgibbon would enforce the law of the land ; but no other compulsion than that of the Law would he recognise. He never quailed before the anger of a mob, or turned his back on an armed man.

He was duly elected a Member for the University : his fellow member was Walter Hussy Burgh. Burgh lives in history by the words with which he threw down his office of Prime Serjeant of Ireland : " Talk not to me of peace. England has sown her laws like dragon's teeth : they have sprung up as armed men." Burgh was also the natural father of William Dowdall, a man who exercised a very unfortunate influence on Robert Emmet.

For a time Fitzgibbon sat in silence : then opportunity came to him to show the stuff that was in him.

Passionately though the Irish protested against the misgovernment of Ireland by England in the eighteenth century, they showed at all times an ungrudging readiness to support England in the defence of the United Kingdom against a foreign invader. The drain on England's resources due to her war with the American colonies practically denuded Ireland of troops ; left her defenceless against attack by any enemy of England. The Irish Volunteers sprang into being to undertake the task of defence.

They proved themselves to be an efficient and well-disciplined force. But as the immediate danger of invasion grew less and less, the Volunteers began to busy themselves with internal politics, to call for reform of the Irish Parliament. No doubt reform was needed ; but Parliamentary reform is not best brought about by the threats of armed men. The Volunteers called on the people of Ireland " to rise in support of the violated rights of Ireland, and of the privileges which their treacherous representatives had basely sold to the infamous administration of Great Britain."

Strong language, language not wholly un-justified it may be, but language not to be tolerated by any Legislative Assembly which retained any shred of self-respect. The Irish House of Commons declared the resolution of the Volunteers to be " false, scandalous, libellous and calculated to raise sedition."

This was early in 1781. The Irish Parliament had asserted its dignity, and for nearly a twelve-month the Volunteers restricted their energies to their legitimate military duties. But by the autumn of 1781 the American War had practically ended in disaster for England, and there remained but for England and for her Administration in Ireland to wind up the bad business as best might be. Among the proceedings was a vote of thanks proposed in the Irish House to the Irish Volunteers for their services. Ere the proposal could be discussed, Mr John Fitzgibbon, Member for Dublin University, requested the Clerk of the House to read aloud the censure which the House in its last session had passed on the Volunteers.

The cat was now among the pigeons. Nevertheless the vote of thanks was passed; and undoubtedly fear of the Volunteers, combined with gratitude for their services and with the depression resulting from the American adventure, won the first instalment of Irish Parliamentary Reform from England. There is a considerable measure of truth in the lines of Thomas Davis :—

> When Grattan rose, none dared oppose
> The claim he made for freedom.
> They knew our swords, to back his words,
> Were ready, did he need them.
>
> Remember still, through good and ill,
> How vain were prayers and tears ;
> How vain were words, till flashed the swords
> Of the Irish Volunteers.

By the Constitution of 1782 the English Parliament formally renounced its pretensions to legislate for Ireland ; Poynings' Law was repealed ; the authority of England to decide what laws Ireland should pass for herself was ended. A biennial Mutiny Bill was conceded ; and so Mr Fitzgibbon's earlier fears of " a military despotism in the country " may have been assuaged. *Esto perpetua,* cried Henry Grattan to the Irish Parliament now liberated from its shackles.

A corrupt but fettered Legislature might be a bad thing ; a Legislature corrupt but unfettered was likely to prove a thing decidedly worse. The cart of freedom had been placed in front of the horse of reform, and the Volunteers, resurgent, bent their energies to getting cart and horse into their proper places.

They made an imposing show of the business. They held a Convention in Dublin; in their thousands they marched through the streets clad in brilliant uniforms and carrying guns, swords, battle-axes. Napper Tandy commanded their artillery: with more wit or piety than one would have expected from him he adorned his cannon with the inscription, "Open Thou our mouths, O Lord, and our lips shall show forth Thy praise." To preside over the deliberations came Frederick Augustus Hervey, Earl of Bristol and Protestant Bishop of Derry; before the Bishop and commanding his bodyguard rode George Robert Fitzgerald, who at one point in his career shut up his own father in a cave in the company of a muzzled bear, and who at the end of his career was hanged for murder. "We shall have blood, my Lord, we shall have blood," said the Bishop pleasantly to a friend. It seemed not at all unlikely.

The Volunteers presented their proposals for reform to the House of Commons. Henry Flood proposed that these be embodied in a Bill, and he found a seconder. Barry Yelverten, opposing, essayed methods of peaceful persuasion. Tempers and terrors waxed high: Mr Flood declared that the Parliament and the Volunteers might yet find themselves committed against one another. And the Volunteers had arms in their hands, and they had gentlemen of the kidney of George Robert Fitzgerald to be their leaders.

Mr Fitzgibbon rose in his place. "I do not think life worth having at the will of an armed demagogue," he said; "gentlemen may call

this liberty ; I call it the worst kind of tyranny.
I am for putting an end to it at once." He moved
curtly that permission to introduce the Bill be
refused.

The Irish as a leaderless mob will quail before
a threat. Given a leader, they will laugh at the
hosts of Satan. The little man with the pale
face, the delicate features, the piercing grey eyes,
the arrogant mien, carried the House with him.
Permission to introduce the Bill was refused by
155 votes to 77. And in 1783 Mr John Fitzgibbon
was appointed His Majesty's Attorney-General
for Ireland. He was but thirty-five years old :
verily the eaglet had spread its wings and soared.
Mr Fitzgibbon's first act was to open a new
account book of his fees. In the succeeding six
years he earned £37,000.

CHAPTER II.

MR ATTORNEY-GENERAL.

IT is a common proceeding, but a very foolish one, to pass judgment on men and on their actions in the light of after knowledge. Policies, actions which by their results men of no more than average intelligence to-day *know* to have been misguided, may have suggested, and suggested quite reasonably, very different possibilities to the minds that first shaped the policies, determined on the actions. It is easy now to *know* what was amiss in the Irish body politic in the eighteenth century, to assert that a mind so acute, so clear as John Fitzgibbon's mind, should have diagnosed the disease, prescribed the remedy. It is easy to say that Fitzgibbon chose servitude to England rather than service to Ireland, that he sacrificed the interests of his country to his personal ambition. But surely it needs no great exercise of human charity to reflect that these easy assertions are absurd. In how many matters will posterity judge the best minds of to-day to have been hopelessly mistaken.

And indeed could John Fitzgibbon rise from his tomb to-day, he might put to his detractors some questions which they might find it very difficult to answer. " Good friends," he might say, " I did my best. Grant me this poor justice.

I grant you that I was mistaken ; I accept the verdict of my fellow countrymen who hurled dead cats at my coffin, as at the coffin of the man who would have held them in bondage. But more than a hundred years later two Irishmen —their names were Collins and O'Higgins—at the cost of blood, tears, crime, won what they and others considered to be the freedom of Ireland. Their fellow countrymen murdered them.

" But I might have tried some wiser policy, I might have left behind the name and fame of a far-sighted statesman ? Again, I did my best ; I grant that I did not find the answer to the riddle. But since I first took part in politics men have tried every device of which I ever heard, and a few devices of which I never dreamed, for the better ordering of Ireland. There has been an independent Irish Parliament, there has been a Parliamentary Union of Ireland with England, there has been full Catholic emancipation, there has been disestablishment of the hated Irish Protestant Church, there has been a practical extinction of the tyrannous landlord class, there has been disseverance of Ireland from England, there has been severance of the Protestant North from the Catholic South, there has been formal recognition of two independent governments in Ireland. And at the end of it all, are the Irish people appreciably nearer to political sanity and political satisfaction than they were when I lived and strove to govern them ? "

We must take John Fitzgibbon as he was, not as he might have been. He is now setting foot on a path that is to lead him very far, farther than any Irishman yet has trodden. The grandson of the poor Irish farmer will take his place among the Peers of England, the son of the foxy, cautious old Counsellor will practically govern Ireland. He is ambitious ; and he knows that there is no place that he cannot fill, no great employment for which he is unfitted.

We might say that Fitzgibbon was a narrow man, that he seldom lifted his eyes from the Irish scene. He visited England a few times, usually to ' drink the waters ' at Bath ; but of England, the English people, the statesmen of England, he seems to have known little. It must be remembered that for an Irishman in those days England was indeed ' a far country ' : a man much occupied then with Irish affairs might quite understandably know as little of England as an Englishman occupied to-day with English affairs knows of the internal politics of France. And a life in Ireland then was not necessarily a narrow, provincial life.

Perhaps with the passing of the Act of Union, more probably with the coming of the steamship and the electric telegraph, Dublin sank to the level of a second-class provincial city. But the Dublin that John Fitzgibbon knew was the second city in the British Empire, and a city not markedly inferior in all that really mattered to the first. It was spreading out in handsome buildings : the Irish Parliament House was not inferior in architectural beauty to the Parliament House of England. Dublin University was far smaller than the Universities of Oxford and

c

Cambridge, but the stately pile of Trinity College fronting Dame Street need take no shame before any English College. Fitzgibbon had his house in Ely Place hard by St Stephen's Green : there was, perhaps there is, no nobler city square in Europe.

And because they were physically separated far from England, because they are a nation different from the English, the Irish developed a culture of their own, and a not unworthy culture. What Irishmen of Fitzgibbon's day might have claimed for their city as a whole may be made clearer to English readers by a suggestion of what Irishmen of a hundred years later might have claimed for their city in its parts. An Irish undergraduate, an Irish lawyer, of the late eighties of the nineteenth century might have boasted that Dublin University and the Bar of Ireland were no whit inferior to the Universities and Bar of England. On the teaching staff of Dublin University then were George Salmon, John Mahaffy, Robert Tyrell, George Fitzgerald, and John Bury. The world, not any one country, passes judgment on them as men of learning. On the Irish Bench sat Christopher Palles ; at the Irish Bar were practising John Atkinson, Edward Carson, James Campbell, Timothy Healy, Stephen Ronan. These names are not unknown nor lightly held in the legal world of England.

Letters of English travellers in that far away day bear testimony to what the fashionable, the intellectual world of Dublin then was. " A man," writes Arthur Young, " may go into a vast variety of families, which he will find actuated by no other principles than those of the most cultivated politeness and the most liberal urbanity." Booksellers abounded ; and the shops of the best-known booksellers were centres of literary society. Garrick played ' Hamlet ' in Dublin before he played the part in England, Handel's ' Messiah ' was sung for the first time in Dublin. It is a curious fact that the actor's calling was then much more highly regarded in Ireland than in England. A famous Irish actor of the period refused all inducements offered to him to play before the London public. In England, he said, he would be but a rogue and vagabond ; in Ireland the house of every intellectual man was open to him.

And Dublin in these days of John Fitzgibbon had a real Court, possibly the most brilliant Viceregal Court that Dublin has ever known. The Duke of Rutland was the Viceroy : he was young, clever, gay, perhaps a little dissipated. His Court was a passing show of balls, routs, theatricals. By his side stood his beautiful young Duchess, Mary Isabella : at her feet statesmen sighed, and to her wits addressed their sonnets. And young Mr Fitzgibbon, for all his ambition and industry, was no dullard with his nose eternally buried in briefs and Statutes. He was a handsome man ; the costume of the day must have set off his slight figure to perfection. At his house in Ely Place he entertained their Excellencies ; and undoubtedly he awakened a more than passing interest in the heart of the Duchess of Rutland. A perfectly proper interest : Fitzgibbon was never the man to play Buckingham to Anne of Austria. Perhaps the interest did as much of honour to the Duchess as of compliment to the Attorney-General. She had the wit to see where worth lay ; later in the sad days of her widowhood she was to serve John Fitzgibbon well.

Opportunity soon came Fitzgibbon's way to prove his worth to the Duke of Rutland and Lord Lieutenant of Ireland. But was it that opportunity always came his way, or was it that the man created opportunity, was quick to seize any semblance of opportunity that offered ? And it is strange that his adversaries wellnigh always attacked him on the side on which he was least vulnerable. Subtlety might have baffled him : his was no subtle mind. But threats, defiance, fell from him as pebbles from the mail of an armoured knight.

He had crushed the claim of the Irish Volunteers to dictate to the existing Parliament of Ireland. Now in the first year of his Attorney-Generalship an attempt was made to set up a parallel Parliament in Ireland. The attempt has been made again in Ireland and in other countries under English rule : it has not always been met with the same resolution.

At the suggestion of certain politicians the High Sheriffs of the Irish Counties proposed to call on the King's lieges in Ireland to elect representatives to a Congress of three hundred persons chosen by the Irish nation, at which Congress " the majesty of the people would resume its proper influence." The Duke of Rutland declared that such action would be illegal : he left the execution of his policy in the hands of his Attorney-General. Mr Fitzgibbon addressed the Sheriffs by letter. Their proposal, he informed them, was in his opinion " so highly criminal " that, should they persist in it, he would proceed against them with the utmost rigour of the law. For practically all this warning was sufficient. But Mr Stephen Reilly, High Sheriff of Dublin, showed himself defiant. He would have representatives elected to the Congress ; and the citizens of Dublin assured him of their support with their lives and fortunes.

Mr Reilly had convened his meeting, he was about to take the chair for the despatch of business, when into the meeting walked Mr John Fitzgibbon. There were yells and hootings : they produced singularly little effect on the visitor. Mr Reilly, he observed coldly, had broken the law ; and now Mr Reilly would pay for breaking the law. Mr Fitzgibbon then left the meeting : most of the assembled patriots, unostentatiously, and as if they were scarcely conscious of what they were doing, followed his example.

It was a notable moral victory, a triumph of courage backed by complete self-confidence. It has been charged against Fitzgibbon for vindictiveness that he did not rest content, that he haled Mr Reilly before the Courts and secured his conviction. But the charge is scarcely just. As chief law officer of the Government Fitzgibbon had given his opinion : now he confirmed that opinion, established its correctness by a formal judgment of the Courts. And in another way the action was characteristic of him. If it be permissible to borrow a cue from melodrama, it may be said that anyone who started to play a game with John Fitzgibbon must play it to the end. Yet once and again at the end of a game which left him triumphant Fitzgibbon did not show himself rancorous, implacable, vindictive.

Assuredly this proof of courage and capacity could not fail to attract attention in the highest quarters. Mr Fitzgibbon in due course received a letter from "your most obliged and faithful humble servant," the Duke of Rutland. The Duke had wished to thank Mr Fitzgibbon for "the manly and spirited part which you have played in upholding the Constitution of the country"; but the Duke would not have ventured to obtrude on Mr Fitzgibbon, recuperating from his labours at Mount Shannon, had he not "received the King's commands to express to you his entire satisfaction with every part of your conduct." On perusing this letter Mr Fitzgibbon must have felt that he had well and truly laid the foundation of his fortunes.

Moral courage is a noble quality. But in those Irish days something more was needed : a gentleman not only *might* but *must* defend his honour with his own right hand. Most men found cause for duelling in wine, women, cards : John Fitzgibbon found cause in the subject of 'Commercial Propositions.'

The renunciation by England of the right to legislate for Ireland was, no doubt, a salutary reform. But, as was not unusual in Irish affairs, theory had somewhat outstripped practice. How, for example, was trade legislation, as between the two countries, to be adjusted ? Undoubtedly the balance had been tilted hitherto somewhat heavily against Ireland.

As a basis of discussion eleven Propositions were drawn up in Ireland and transmitted for the consideration of the English Parliament. They came back in the shape of twenty Articles for a Treaty of Commerce. And the original Propositions had been altered much to the disadvantage of Ireland. Fitzgibbon defended the Articles in the House ; but clearly his heart was not in the business ; his defence was laboured and unconvincing. Yet he spoke some words on which later Irishmen might well ponder : " I say that if Ireland seeks to quarrel with England, she is a besotted nation. I say that she has not the means of trading with any country on earth without the assistance of Great Britain. I say that Ireland cannot exist one hour without the support of Great Britain."

When Fitzgibbon sat down, John Curran spoke to him in an undertone. What he said is not known : it must have been something pretty strong if it was more offensive than the remarks which the two men now and then addressed to each other in open debate. Mr Fitzgibbon promptly sent ' a friend ' to wait on Mr Curran. They met at dawn ; the weapons were pistols ; they tossed for first shot. Curran won, and fired in the air. Fitzgibbon took long and careful aim at his opponent, fired, and— missed. Curran, as he left the ground, called out sarcastically, "It was not your fault, Mr Attorney, if you missed : you were deliberate enough."

The story to-day reads horribly : we might say that Fitzgibbon came on to the ground with murder in his heart. But the ethics of the eighteenth century in Ireland were not the ethics of the world in the twentieth ; and here, as ever, Fitzgibbon showed himself consistent. Any work that he had undertaken he would do his best to finish.

There was a comment on the affair, too cynically witty to deserve oblivion, made by a contemporary of the two men. Said William Plunket, later Lord Chancellor of Ireland, " Fitzgibbon and Curran fought : unluckily they missed each other."

What the Government thought of its Chief Law Officer's readiness with his pistol is not known. Possibly in its secret heart Government was pleased. Here was a man in a sense *teres atque rotundus*, a man whose courage, moral and physical, would be found equal to any test. Indeed at no period of his career did Fitzgibbon manifest the slightest reluctance to look down the barrel of a pistol. As Lord Chancellor he received a ' message ' which he declined on the score of his official position. But the ' friend ' who brought the message carried away an impression of the Chancellor's dauntless courage.

We may turn from politics and the duelling ground to an episode of Fitzgibbon's private life. He married. Why, it is not quite easy to say : in the matter of women his seems to have been a very cold nature. Perhaps he desired an heir, perhaps he felt that the mansion in Ely Place at which he had entertained Their Excellencies *en garçon* needed a mistress, perhaps he reflected that sensible men usually do marry. And if not pre-eminently a marrying man, he certainly was eminently marriageable : he may well have been the desire and the despair of dowagers and débutantes at the Viceregal Court. He was a handsome man ; the golden stream of barristerial fees flowing towards him was plain for all to see ; there was the Mount Shannon estate, with its reputed rent-roll of six thousand a year. Assuredly some whisper of Majesty's ' entire satisfaction ' with Mr Fitzgibbon's conduct must have reached the ear of the outer world. Who would be the lucky girl ? Miss Anne Whaley carried off the prize : in the summer of 1786 she was married to Mr John Fitzgibbon.

It was not a marriage of romance, a union of two hearts that beat as one, a rushing together of two strong souls. In the pages of history Miss Anne Whaley, Lady Fitzgibbon, the Countess of Clare, is a singularly pale and elusive ghost. She married her remarkable husband, she duly provided his heir, she found herself, somewhat inexplicably, in straitened circumstances after her husband's death. That is all that we know of her : perhaps no woman married to John Fitzgibbon could be much more than John Fitzgibbon's wife. Married to someone else Miss Whaley might have been a more distinctive personality. For she must have had some spirited blood in her veins. She was the daughter of one Richard Whaley, who by his anti-Catholic activities had earned the pleasing sobriquet of ' Burn-Chapel Whaley.'   Her brother was a noted ' buck ' and gambler of the day : his most famous wager was that in a given time he would journey to Jerusalem, play a game of ball against the walls of the Holy City, and return to Dublin. He won his wager.

And yet in telling the story of this marriage some have professed to draw aside for a moment a curtain which veiled a secret sanctuary of Fitzgibbon's soul.   It is whispered that he had loved and had been rejected by one Miss Swete. She married another, Henry Sheares, then a briefless barrister.   It is said that she eloped with him : they were an affectionate couple, and between them they added six citizens to their country.   It may be that Mr Fitzgibbon sought surcease of passion's raptures and torments in the respectable arms of Miss Whaley.

If this story be true, it was to have a grim sequel.

Political opportunity soon knocked again at John Fitzgibbon's door.   And, as ever, he was not slow to welcome the visitor.

The matter in which he now found his account was this.   In 1788 King George III. was smitten by the first onset of that malady which was to cloud his later years and render him incapable of his kingly office.   The English Parliament proposed to appoint by Bill his son, Prince George, to be Regent of the United Kingdom, and by Bill to define and restrict his authority.   The Irish Parliament resolved to invite Prince George to assume the Regency of Ireland untrammelled by any restrictions which the Parliament of England might impose on the Regent of England. In strict Constitutional theory the Irish Parliament probably was within its rights : this, it is interesting to note, was the opinion of the sagacious gentlemen afterwards known as George IV. The Act (George I., 6) in virtue of which the English Parliament presumed to pass laws affecting Ireland had been specifically repealed. But from the standpoint of plain common sense a situation had arisen which no man could have been expected to foresee. Conciliation, a spirit of reasonable give-and-take on both sides, would have provided an easy way out of the dilemma.

But of reasonableness the proud Irish Parliament would not hear. The Parliament of Ireland was independent ; it would do as it listed ; that was the end of the matter. Fitzgibbon's words of warning fell on deaf ears : " The only security of your liberty is the connection with Great Britain ; *and gentlemen who risk breaking that connection must make up their minds to a Union.*" In other words, Ireland under any Constitutional name can exist quite comfortably in amity with England. If she will not be contented so to exist, England may be forced to experiment with measures for making existence tolerable or possible for both countries. When Fitzgibbon spoke Ireland was an independent country. She is an independent country to-day. But were Fitzgibbon's words uttered in the eighteenth century prophetic for the twentieth ?

The Irish Parliament passed its address to Prince George, and sent the same to the Viceroy for transmission to His Royal Highness. Parliament made an impressive business of the sending : the Lords and Commons, headed by the Chancellor and the Speaker, walked in procession to the Castle. The Viceroy was Lord Buckingham : Rutland had died in 1787. Lord Buckingham refused to transmit, even to receive, the address, "under the impression which he felt of his official duty." The wrath of Ireland boiled over : was the independent Parliament of an independent nation to be flouted by the simulacrum of Majesty ? If Lord Buckingham would not transmit the address, the Irish Parliament would arrange for its transmission. The Duke of Leinster, Lord Charlemont, Messrs Conolly, O'Neill, and Ponsonby were chosen to proceed to England, and to place the Address in the hands of the Prince of Wales, Heir Apparent to the Throne of the United Kingdom.

Foolishness, if prompted by a genuine though mistaken pride, men will not judge hardly. But here the pure flame of Irish patriotism sprang from a very dirty kindling. The Prince of Wales was on no good terms with his old, half-cracked father : did son but succeed to father there would be "a dripping roast to carve" for those who had the prescience to worship the rising sun. The great offices of Ireland, even the Viceroyalty itself, had been distributed in advance. Then, as ever, Irishmen were sharing the lion's skin ere the lion was dead. But the sordid inner history of this affair belongs to another place.

Perhaps Fitzgibbon's coldness saved him from this Irish weakness. Perhaps he saw that the gratitude of 'the first gentleman in Europe' would prove a sandy foundation whereon to erect a lofty structure of expectation. Perhaps the cupidity, the time-serving of his fellow Irishmen, disgusted him. He spoke fiercely, contemptuously, in the Irish Parliament. But, as usual, he spoke words of hard sense : " There is a feature in this proceeding which, independent of other objections to it, does in my mind make it highly reprehensible. I consider it a formal appeal from the Parliament of England to that of Ireland. Though I do not desire the Parliament of this country to follow implicitly the Parliament of England, I should consider it a wise maxim for this country always to concur with that Parliament, unless for very strong reasons we are obliged to differ from it. If it is to be a point of Irish duty to differ from the Parliament of England to show its independence, I very much fear that the sober men in this country will soon become sick of independence."

Ireland is independent to-day. Sober Irishmen may not as yet be sick of their independence ; but it is a question whether they are entirely satisfied with it.

The deputation sailed to England, but found cold comfort there. The unexpected had happened ; and King George III. had come to his wits, or was visibly coming to them. The deputation met with perfect civility, nothing more, from the Prince of Wales whose cause they had so hotly espoused. And they returned to Ireland with the sickening feeling that the Viceroy now held them in the hollow of his hand. And by the side of Lord Buckingham stood Mr John Fitzgibbon, and the Viceroy's messages would be delivered by the mouth of his Attorney-General.

There is believed to be safety in a multitude. Practically all who had flouted the Viceroy in this matter were placemen, pensioners, men of influence in Irish affairs. Now all bound themselves together by an oath : did the Viceroy dare to punish one, all would withdraw from the Viceroy their support. There was still some hope ; they might yet make things impossible for Lord Buckingham. A very obvious first step was the voting of a short supply. For, did Parliament but grant a full supply, Lord Buckingham, following Lord Townshend's example, might prorogue and govern without Parliament.

Now the winding up of this business has been made the basis of a slur on Fitzgibbon's memory. And the slur is the more serious in view of the source from which it emanates.

The standard historians of eighteenth century Ireland are J. A. Froude and W. E. H. Lecky. Froude was a superb *writer*, but if his historian contemporaries, notably Professor E. A. Freeman, are to be believed, he was quite careless and untrustworthy in regard to *facts*. One may indeed admit that Froude's unceasing eulogy of John Fitzgibbon is overdone : in the end it becomes wearisome. Lecky takes a different and much less favourable view of Fitzgibbon ; and Lecky's name has come to connote exact scholarship and scrupulous impartiality. Condemnation by Mr Lecky is condemnation indeed. In the index to his ' History of Ireland in the Eighteenth Century ' Mr Lecky, under the heading *Fitzgibbon (Earl of Clare)*, wrote or allowed to be written these words : " Theory that corruption should be the normal form of government." He gives a reference to his own pages, and at the page specified cites proof of his assertion : " in one of the debates in the Regency he [Fitzgibbon] openly avowed that half a million had on a former occasion been spent to procure an address to Lord Townshend, and intimated very plainly that the same sum would, if necessary, be spent again."

Now if words have any meaning, these words imply that John Fitzgibbon had been privy to the corrupt spending of half a million pounds during the Viceroyalty of Lord Townshend. Townshend was recalled from the Viceroyalty in 1772 : only in that year was Fitzgibbon called to the Bar. He did not enter Parliament as a private Member until eight years later. Fitzgibbon then or later may have *known* of this transaction—there was never much secrecy about Irish political corruption—but to assert that he was *privy* to it is surely absurd as well as unjust. It is impossible to suppose that the Viceroy admitted to his inmost confidence a youth just looking eagerly to any solicitor for his first employment. Mr Lecky, indeed, makes some curious mistakes in respect of the dates of John Fitzgibbon's life. He adds a dramatic touch to his account of the debate on the Union by stating that Fitzgibbon's heir, Colonel Fitzgibbon, refused to support his father's policy, and walked out of the House without recording his vote. John Fitzgibbon was married in 1786, and so his heir at the date of the Union cannot have been more than, and may have been less than, thirteen years of age. Influence and money would buy rapid advancement in eighteenth century Ireland, but scarcely advancement so rapid as this.

To corroborate his statement Mr Lecky refers his readers to the actual words of John Fitzgibbon recorded at page 181 of Volume IX. of the Official ' Irish Parliamentary Debates.' Fitzgibbon was speaking on the Vote of Supply, and these were his words : " I recollect the event referred to by the honourable gentleman. I recollect Lord Townshend proroguing Parliament, and I recollect that when they met they voted him an address of thanks, which address cost this nation half a million of money. I hope to God that I shall never again see such effects from Party. I hope to God that I shall never again see half a million of the people's money employed to procure an address from their representatives. I have ever attempted to defend the people, and shall ever oppose measures which may tend to an address that will cost half a million."

Fitzgibbon told the Irish Members of the Irish House of Commons, in words the plainness of which was justified by their truthfulness, that he considered them to be an Assembly pitiable, cowardly, corrupt. They had roared defiance before ; and they had come tamely to heel when an opportunity was offered to them of filling their pockets. He " hoped to God " that he would not see this performance repeated : he scarcely disguised his belief that the " honourable gentlemen " would be only too glad to repeat it were the chance of repeating it offered to them. That a man expresses a savage contempt for those who take bribes scarcely justifies the accusation that he himself is prepared to offer bribes.

The end of the business was never in doubt. Fitzgibbon was always formidable : when he had a cast iron case he was irresistible. The patriotic mutineers in due course crawled before the Viceroy. " They lay themselves at His Majesty's feet with every expression of duty, and of their humble hopes by their future support to remove every unfavourable impression from His Majesty's mind."

John Fitzgibbon had proved himself. The years of apprenticeship were ended : there was no reward to which he might not fittingly lay claim. The prize of his profession, the greatest official position in Ireland, was the Lord Chancellorship. Hitherto no Irishman had carried off that prize.

Politically there was no difficulty. The Viceroy in Ireland, and Mr Pitt in England, were only too ready to reward the man who had served them so well. But the legal conscience of England was queasy. John Fitzgibbon might be a supremely able man ; but, after all, he was but an Irishman. Lord Thurlow, Lord Chancellor of England, was adamant in his refusal.

The affair had a half-comic termination. Mary Isabella, the beautiful widowed Duchess of Rutland, had not forgotten John Fitzgibbon. Where the authority of the Prime Minister of England proved impotent, the tears and cajoleries of a beautiful woman prevailed. And John Fitzgibbon stepped forward, the first Irishman to indue the robes of Lord High Chancellor. He was at once created Baron Fitzgibbon of Lower Connello : in 1793 he was made Viscount, and in 1795 Earl of Clare. Leaving the Bar he bequeathed his brief-bag to a bitter political opponent, George Ponsonby ; and he dropped a hint that solicitors who hitherto had briefed him would find in Mr Ponsonby an eminently capable successor. The action does not betoken a small-minded man.

Lord Thurlow, departing defeated, loosed a Parthian arrow. He wrote to his " Dear Lord " a letter of congratulation. This letter has been preserved and may be read. It is a most singular mixture of fulsome civility and covert insolence.

CHAPTER III.

LORD CHANCELLOR.

A LORD Chancellor has a twofold function or capacity. He is the head of the Judiciary and of the legal profession in his country; he can also, if he so desires, make himself heard on political issues either in the Cabinet or in the House of Lords. Ordinarily the first capacity far transcends the second : in the case of John Fitzgibbon the order of importance was reversed.

On Fitzgibbon in his purely legal capacity it would be presumptuous on the part of one not technically skilled in law to express a confident opinion. This much, at least, may be said. The man had a splendidly efficient intellect, and the whole training and practice of his life must have tended to make of him a competent lawyer. But it does not seem that he takes rank with the great Judges, with those who by their interpretations made some positive contributions to the science of Law.

Assuredly he was diligent. In one of his private letters he pleads the weight of business resting on his shoulders in his Court as an excuse for not undertaking a kindly office. This office, it may be mentioned, he did undertake ; and even at the cost of a slight digression the tale is worth telling. It throws some light on the character of the man whom most men have considered hard, pitiless, unforgiving.

The matter concerns one Arthur Hamilton Rowan, whose story may be more fittingly related in another place. Here it is sufficient to say that Rowan had personally affronted the Lord Chancellor : he had had the incredible effrontery to deliver to him a challenge from a barrister practising before him. Rowan had also blundered into treasonable conspiracy ; he had received the sentence of the law, and he was at the moment a fugitive from the law. He was a man of considerable wealth, and the sentence passed on him automatically entailed forfeiture of his estates. Fitzgibbon intervening saved the estates for the benefit of Mrs Rowan and of her children. Later he was asked to use his influence on Rowan's behalf. He wrote to Rowan some excellent advice, and undoubtedly bestirred himself to ensure that Rowan's fault should be forgotten, his sentence annulled.

One serious charge was made against Fitzgibbon : if proven it would reflect gravely on his memory. John Curran alleged that the enmity of the Lord Chancellor had cost him some £30,000 in professional fees. In other words, he could not hope for success before the Lord Chancellor, whatever the merits of his case ; and therefore no Chancery business came his way. But there is another side to the story.

Admittedly Curran hated Fitzgibbon, and Fitzgibbon reciprocated the feeling. Possibly in Fitzgibbon's hatred there was an element of cold contempt. Curran was an accepted wit, the darling of the public and of his fellow barristers. But he would joke at all times seemly or unseemly ; and many of his applauded and recorded witticisms strike us to-day as in bad taste, as personal, cruel, offensive. He had no small conceit of himself. He availed himself of his first appearance before the Lord Chancellor to make a veiled but violent personal atttack on John Fitzgibbon. Fitzgibbon's contribution to the scene was but a cold expression of surprise that a lawyer of Mr Curran's eminence should persist in introducing wholly irrelevant matters into his argument. It is quite possible that solicitors felt that their clients' business could not most advantageously be entrusted to a barrister who would go out of his way to attack the presiding Judge. If Mr Curran lacked business before the Lord Chancellor, he may have had only himself to thank for this.

Fitzgibbon was punctilious in the routine administration of his office, and his punctiliousness, his absolute refusal to brook defiance, are illustrated by a tragic tale. This had to do with Mr Justice Power, a Baron of the Exchequer. With his judicial office the Baron held some administrative post in the Court of Chancery, and was responsible for the receipt and disbursement of monies. He had received an order from Fitzgibbon's predecessor in respect of a certain sum, and he had disregarded the order. There was no question of dishonesty : the sum was comparatively small, and Baron Power was a wealthy man. But Fitzgibbon would endure no slight affecting the Chancellor's office :

he sent a stern order to the Baron to appear at the Bar of his Court and there explain his disrespect. Baron Power, aghast, protested against this indignity offered to a brother Judge : he received a cold reply that the Lord Chancellor had addressed himself to a subordinate of his own Court, not to a brother on the Bench. The wretched Baron Power could not face the ordeal : on the day before that appointed for his appearance he put an end to his own life.

It is pleasant to turn from this tragedy to some scenes which exhibit the stern Lord Chancellor in a softer light. Not, indeed, that there was much softness in John Fitzgibbon : that element known as ' Irish humour ' was altogether wanting from his composition. But now and then his aspect is grimly humorous.

He had accepted the office of Vice-Chancellor of Dublin University; and undoubtedly there were matters there which required his attention. ' Old Trinity ' towards the close of the eighteenth century was a veritable nursery and breeding ground of sedition. The Vice-Chancellor descended like a hawk from a clear sky. He held a visitation ; he examined many witnesses ; he demanded that the Board enforce certain disciplinary measures. Among the victims of his displeasure was the well-known Dr Whitley Stokes, who in Wolfe Tone's amusing ' Journal ' figures as ' the Keeper of the College Lions.' But among the trembling boys haled before the Inquisitor was a personality better known at a later date to the popular world. This was Tom Moore, poet of the ' Irish Melodies.'

Young Moore—he was then but seventeen
years of age—has left a spirited and amusing
account of the interview. By the Vice-Chancellor's side sat his assessor, Dr Duigenan, a
man who aped his master, and who, says Froude,
resembled his master very much as the buzzard
resembles the eagle. Mr Moore at first was
reluctant to be sworn. He was prepared to argue
the point, but was cut short by a stern admonition
that the Vice-Chancellor did not visit the College
to bandy words with undergraduates. So Mr
Moore was duly sworn ; and thereafter he gave
his answers candidly. That ' United Irishmen '
societies existed within the College was a matter
of common knowledge ; but Mr Moore could
declare quite truthfully that he had never joined
any such society, and was entirely ignorant of
any business there transacted. One crucial
question was not asked : Had Mr Moore ever
been invited to join any such society ? It is
extremely unlikely that Fitzgibbon's astuteness
missed this very obvious point : it is more probable that he had no wish to embarrass or to
prejudice an obviously harmless boy.

Parcere subjectis et debellare superbos. If Fitzgibbon could deal lightly with the lowly, he
could hold another conduct towards the mighty
in their seats. The Dons of Dublin University
at that time led double lives in a quite peculiar
sense. In private they were patterns of virtue ;
in public they paraded a flaunting immorality.
By the Statutes of the University they were
forbidden to marry on pain of losing their academic emoluments : being human and unfettered

by sacerdotal vows they did marry. They safe-guarded their material interests by labelling their wives as their mistresses. Invitations issued bidding guests to the table of ' The Reverend Mr X and Miss Y ' : that the maiden shared the board of the Clerk in Holy Orders was obvious, and usually there was not wanting tangible evidence that she also shared his bed.

Mr Vice-Chancellor Fitzgibbon was not a man who suffered gladly either fools or foolery. He drew up a Statute permitting the Dons to marry, if they so desired, without fear to themselves or amazement to others. He sent his Statute to England for formal sanction ; and the answer tarried. Apparently the Duke of Portland, charged in England with Irish affairs, disliked the proposal and was minded to let it expire of inattention. Mr Vice-Chancellor took pen in hand : he addressed himself to Lord Castle-reagh, but his words were for the eye of the Duke of Portland. Mr Vice-Chancellor could not under-stand " why the Duke of Portland should interfere with me on a subject so peculiarly within my province, and which he would not have the means of understanding." And His Grace, even if he could not understand Irish University affairs in general, was asked " fully and explicitly to understand " that Lord Fitzgibbon, Lord Chan-cellor of Ireland, would continue in the office of Vice-Chancellor of Dublin University only on the conditions which he felt that he had a right to demand. It was the story of the Volunteer debate, of Mr Stephen Reilly, all over again. The imperious little man with the cold grey eyes spoke : the man to whom he addressed himself hastened to obey. And the Misses Y of Trinity forthwith were made ' honest women.'

But it is on Fitzgibbon's political work in Ireland during the last ten years of the century that his fame or infamy (he has had his share of both) must rest. His position has been well stated by Lecky : " In the House of Lords and in the Privy Council he appears to have attained an influence which was little less than despotic. He was by far the ablest Irishman who had adopted, without restriction, the doctrine that the Irish Legislature must be maintained in a condition of permanent and unvarying subjection to the English Executive ; and in order to secure that end there was no measure either of force or corruption from which he would recoil."

That Fitzgibbon from the date of his appointment as Lord Chancellor up to the Act of Union did dominate the Government of Ireland is unquestionable. But Lecky's description can only be accepted subject to qualification. Reasons have already been given for holding to be unfounded Mr Lecky's charge that Fitzgibbon was prepared to connive at corruption. The charge of ' force ' presumably implies brutality, revengefulness. Now Lord Cornwallis came to Ireland just after the terrible rebellion of 1798, at a time when the worst passions of men on either side of the Irish question had been inflamed.; and by his own admission he came prepared to dislike the overbearing Chancellor. He has testified that he found Fitzgibbon to be " by far the most moderate and right-minded man in the kingdom." It must also be remembered that at times force must be met by force, that a public official is not *entitled* tamely to yield to threats. A plot unravelled about 1794 had for its principal feature the hanging-in-state of John Fitzgibbon on Stephen's Green ; another and later plot announced, somewhat prematurely, that he *had* been hanged. The manners of those days were not the manners of to-day.

It is true that Fitzgibbon would have had the Irish Legislature amenable to the wishes of the Executive appointed by England to govern Ireland. This was the system which obtained when he entered on his political career, and he strove to continue it. But ' permanent and un-varying subjection ' is too strong a phrase. Evidently Fitzgibbon did not see the social and political faults which vitiated the whole system of government in Ireland. The social fault was that the Government of Ireland did not represent the general interests of the people of Ireland : it represented, in the main, the private interests of a few great families. The political fault was that the Government was at once independent of Parliament, because irremovable by a vote of Parliament, and yet dependent on Parliament for financial supply and for the enactment of its policies into law. Had Fitzgibbon seen these faults, had he essayed to reform them, the tremendous force of his character probably would have enabled him to carry any reform which he desired. But to ask why he did not do these things is but to ask why he was not other than he was. His powerful intellect was administrative rather than creative ; it differed from the intellect of the ordinary man in *degree* rather than in *kind ;* it is extremely probable that in *quality* of intellect Grattan and many of his contemporaries were Fitzgibbon's superiors.

And there is a good deal to be said on Fitzgibbon's side of the argument. The working, the practical effects of the social and political system had not been entirely bad. The great Irish families may have been overbearing, dishonest, nepotic ; but they produced a remarkable number of really able men. The Parliament which they constituted or ruled really did effect a good deal for the benefit of Ireland. Could it have been purged of its capriciousness and jobbery, it might have become a very efficient instrument of government in the hands of an entirely competent permanent official. And Fitzgibbon was the supreme type of permanent official.

Again, it is a well-known adage that a man should not change horses while crossing a stream. And a man riding across a raging, swirling torrent has quite enough to do with keeping his horse on its feet without thinking of changing mounts. Throughout Fitzgibbon's period of power England was struggling for her life. Why Ireland in 1796, on the occasion of Wolfe Tone's attack, did not fall into the hands of France is a question which can never be answered. In 1797 England would have accepted peace on any reasonable terms ; but the terms offered by France were so outrageous that England clenched her teeth and fought it out. That is England's way. Eighteen years later she prevailed completely and finally.

But the end was not until long after Fitzgibbon's death, and during his lifetime the end was not even in sight.

And throughout these stormy years Fitzgibbon had his full share of personal anxiety. Of 'fear' we can hardly say; because John Fitzgibbon never feared anyone or anything. It has been mentioned that a conspiracy announced that he had been hanged. The story of this conspiracy may be told: it contains the sequel to the supposed romance of Fitzgibbon's early years.

It is the story of Henry Sheares, whom Miss Swete preferred to John Fitzgibbon. Sheares seems to have been by no means a bad sort of man: he was a good husband, a kindly father. Unfortunately he had the Irishman's love of flamboyant 'patriotism,' the Irishman's greed of cheap applause, the Irishman's disregard of danger up to the moment when regard and disregard alike avail not.

In 1794 Henry Sheares addressed a most amazing letter to the Lord Chancellor. Mr Sheares had perused a speech delivered by the Chancellor in the House of Lords; and this speech, in Mr Sheares' opinion, contained " a grave and infamous calumny " directed against himself. Mr Sheares found it incumbent on him to address the Chancellor " prior to taking any steps towards the punishment of the author." Fitzgibbon, as might have been expected, took no notice of this impertinence. The Society of United Irishmen presented Mr Sheares with a complimentary address; and Mr Sheares, no doubt, strutted and preened himself.

The spring of 1798 found Henry Sheares and his brother, John, members of a Committee whose purpose it was to free Ireland. The freeing was to be accomplished by the seizure of Dublin Castle and other strategic points, and by the hanging of certain enemies of the people, notably John Fitzgibbon, Earl of Clare. But in their enthusiasm the Committee forgot common prudence in the enlistment of recruits; and they poured their designs into the ear of one Captain Armstrong, an officer of the armed forces of the Crown. Possibly they expected him to swing his soldiers to their side. Whether the Committee were utter fools, or whether Captain Armstrong was an astute secret service agent, are questions of small importance : suffice to say that the Government of Ireland in general, and the Lord Chancellor in particular, speedily knew all that there was to be known about the conspiracy. The Chancellor, indeed, seems to have gone out of his way to drop a hint to the Sheares brothers that children who play with fire are likely to get their fingers burned. The hint was disregarded.

On May 21, 1798, the officers of the law forced an entrance into the house of the Sheares in Dublin. John and Henry Sheares were arrested : among their papers was found evidence ample to convict them of high treason. On July 12 they were brought to trial; on July 13 they were condemned to die. And now Henry Sheares' courage failed him : on the evening of July 13 he addressed himself through Sir Jonah Barrington to the Earl of Clare : " Tell the Chancellor that I will pray for him for ever, and that the

Government shall ever find me what they wish. On my family, my wife, my children, my mother. Let them throw themselves at the Chancellor's feet."

Poor wretch! Let Barrington continue his story.

"By some unfortunate delay this letter was not delivered to me till eleven o'clock of the morning after the trial. I waited on Lord Clare. He read it with great attention: I saw that he was moved. He said: 'What a coward he is! But what can we do?' He paused: 'John Sheares cannot be spared: do you think that Henry can say anything which can warrant the Viceroy in making a distinction?'

"I hastened to the prison, and arrived at the moment when the executioner was holding up the head of my friend, and saying, 'This is the head of a traitor.'"

Fearless himself Fitzgibbon had only contempt for a coward. And yet he would have saved poor Henry Sheares.

So much is, in a sense, the negative aspect of Fitzgibbon's character. The positive principle of his policy was a refusal to allow any political liberty, privilege, responsibility to any person professing the Roman Catholic faith. His anti-Catholic bias was wholly political: in his own words he "meddled not with the speculative opinions of any man." It is impossible to suppose that he had any admiration for the Protestant Church established in Ireland in his day. That Church was an iniquity: it had been bitingly described by Swift as administered by highway-

men who had murdered bishops en route from
England to their Sees, and who personated their
victims in Ireland. That no great change for
the better was effected during Fitzgibbon's lifetime may be judged from a letter written by the
Protestant Primate of Ireland with reference to
a nomination to a bishopric in the year after
Fitzgibbon's death. Said the Archbishop :
" Emolument is the only object of this young
man, whose character is indisputably infamous."

Fitzgibbon based his policy on two reasons.
The first is startling in its blunt brutality : " The
Act by which most of us hold our estates is an
Act of violence, an Act subverting the first
principles of the Common Law." The right of
the English Parliament to legislate for Ireland
had been renounced ; a Catholic electorate presumably would elect a Catholic Legislature ;
and a Catholic Legislature might bring the whole
structure of Protestant landlordism in Ireland
toppling to the ground. Fitzgibbon undertook
no general defence of Irish landlordism : " I
know," he said, " that it is impossible for human
wretchedness to transcend that of the miserable
tenantry of Munster. I know that the unhappy
tenantry are ground to powder by relentless
landlords."

This much may be said for Fitzgibbon : he
did not parade himself as an exception to his
own rule. Mount Shannon he had lawfully
inherited from his father, old Counsellor John ;
and the Counsellor had lawfully purchased Mount
Shannon with his lawful professional earnings.
Fitzgibbon was reputed to be a just and con-

siderate landlord : the tenantry of Mount Shannon trusted and respected him. But he essayed no special pleading in his own favour.

Apart from inherent morality or immorality, was Fitzgibbon's argument a correct foretelling of an effect that would inevitably follow from a cause ? A Member of Parliament at that day observed that landed title in Ireland was forfeiture, and that old proprietors kept alive the memory of their claims. Arthur Young wrote that the dispossessed heirs to an Irish estate were always known : "They regularly transmit by testamentary deed their right to those estates which once belonged to their families." It is true that the Irish have long memories, that they love to brood over lost rights, real or imaginary. But that an Irish Legislature, of whatever creed and however elected, would have enacted a wholesale reconfiscation without compensation might have seemed to a reasonable man impossible, were it only because of the sheer impossibility of deciding between conflicting claims.

His second reason was no less startling : "No man who acknowledges the Spiritual supremacy of the Pope can exercise the legislative power of a Protestant State with temper and justice."

Fitzgibbon reminded his hearers of " the horrid excesses " due to Catholic bigotry which had marked more than a century of Irish history. History might repeat itself. This was one way of looking at the matter : in a Protestant Legislature there was no one to point out that the matter might be viewed from a different angle. If Protestants in eighteenth century Ireland really had cause for fear, what they had to fear were reprisals by no means unprovoked or undeserved. What was the rebellion of 1641 but an illustration of the saying that the worm will turn? If the Catholic peasants of Fitzgibbon's day houghed cattle, carded tithe-proctors, murdered landlords, need these facts surprise anyone who remembered Fitzgibbon's own description of the condition of the Catholic peasants of Munster? An opponent of the Earl of Clare might have admitted that religious bigotry had produced ' horrid excesses ' in Ireland. He might have gone on to ask which side began the bigotry, on which side had the excesses been more horrid!

There may have been some deeper thought underlying Fitzgibbon's words. The Catholic Church, according to the words of one of its prelates, " claims not only to judge infallibly on religious questions, but to advert on opinion in secular matters which bear upon religion, and it demands our submission to her claim. It claims to censure books, to silence authors, and to forbid discussion. It must be obeyed without a word." But who is to decide between secular matters which "bear upon religion" and secular matters which do not? Can a man who yields to this tremendous claim be expected to judge "with temper and with justice," to judge according to his own conscience and according to the law of the land in which he lives?

Fitzgibbon, at least, was consistent : to him the motto of the Church of Rome might be applied : *semper, eadem, ubique.* At the end of his life he stood where he had stood at his life's beginning.

E

He spoke against Catholic emancipation in 1793 : he must have had a very considerable share in defeating proposals for full Catholic emancipation in 1795. And this business of 1795 was one of the two significant acts of his political life, and possibly the one for which his countrymen have blamed him most bitterly.

In 1795 Lord Fitzwilliam came to Ireland as Viceroy, to all seeming authorised by Mr Pitt to make an end, once and for ever, of the long-standing grievances of the Catholics of Ireland. He "would leave not a point of distinction between Catholics and Protestant." Parliament, the highest offices in the State, should be open to all : ability, character, not speculative religious opinion, should be the test of a man. In less than two months Fitzwilliam had received notice of recall, and the policy of Catholic emancipation was as chaff scattered by the wind. What was the reason of this amazing performance, and what was Fitzgibbon's part in it ?

An utterly fantastic explanation has gained wide credence. It is suggested that the minds of Pitt and Fitzgibbon were already set on a Parliamentary Union of Ireland and England. By the announcement of Catholic emancipation the hopes of the Irish Catholics, that is, of the vast majority of the Irish people, had been raised to the highest pinnacle : by the sudden reversal of policy these hopes were hurled into the lowest depths of despair. Could it be made apparent that the generous intentions of England had been frustrated by the selfish bigotry of the Irish Protestant Oligarchs, then the Irish people might turn their eyes, once and for all, from the Parliament of Ireland to a Parliament in England. In fact, and for this reason, the Irish Catholic Hierarchy, in the main, favoured the Union. But the explanation is too subtle, too far-fetched. A much simpler explanation is possible.

Shut up in their lonely island the Irish have always been apt to imagine that questions of the utmost interest to them are also of the utmost interest to everyone else. It is not so. Probably Pitt's preoccupation with Irish Catholic disabilities was very much less than the Irish imagined. Brutal though it may seem to say so, it is possible that Pitt looked on the Irish, Catholic and Protestant, as little better than savages. A certain number of these savages desire some politico-religious rearrangement : let them have it. But it appears that certain other savages strongly disapprove, that the King of England himself has qualms about the matter : very well then, let the matter drop. And Lord Fitzwilliam, " that infatuated man " Fitzgibbon styled him, certainly was not a prudent agent of a great reform. Ten days after his arrival in Ireland he dismissed John Beresford, chief of the Protestant ' oligarchs,' from his offices and emoluments, and at once the hand of every ' oligarch ' was turned against him. Fitzwilliam himself did not attribute his recall to any Machiavellian policy of Pitt and Fitzgibbon : he avowed his belief that he might have continued in office had he not meddled with John Beresford. And continuing he might have carried through Catholic emancipation. But if his first act was to bring a nest of hornets buzzing about Pitt's ears, Pitt's first reaction may have been to get rid of Fitzwilliam, and, incidentally, of the policy which he represented.

To say this is not to excuse Pitt. Whatever be the real truth of the matter, there is no doubt that the whole business was disgracefully muddled, bungled, confused. Fitzgibbon's part in the affair is plain. He opposed Catholic emancipation then as he had opposed it before, as he opposed it to the last day of his life. Had Pitt and the Government of England really been determined on Catholic emancipation in Ireland, it was their obvious duty to remove Fitzgibbon from the position of Lord Chancellor. This would have been an unpleasant duty. But the unpleasantness of a duty is not for a statesman sufficient excuse for refusing to undertake it. It is simply absurd to send to an army a Commander-in-Chief with orders to advance, and to retain under him a Chief-of-Staff whose avowed determination is to remain immovable in his trenches. Pitt's conduct in this matter leaves a slur on his reputation.

The rather dreary history of Ireland between 1795 and 1800 can best be told with reference to Tone, Fitzgerald, Emmet. It is a sorry tale of conspiracy, rebellion, repression. But it does not touch Fitzgibbon very nearly. Indeed throughout the last ten years of his life the man somewhat recedes into his office ; he is for us a power rather than a person. We may pass to the Act of Union, to the enforcement of a policy for which Irishmen have reviled John Fitzgibbon as the betrayer of his country.

One charge against his memory is easily rebutted. Men have said that in the Union he sought his own profit. He had already received every honour that could be granted to him : in point of power he stood to lose, not to gain, by a union of the kingdoms. Before the Union he was the controlling force, wellnigh the dictator in an independent kingdom : the coming of the Union must necessarily reduce him to the position of a servant of an alien kingdom and of an alien Legislature. It is unlikely that against his opposition, whether he were in office or out of office, the Union could have been carried ; and by opposition he could have won for himself popularity, the one reward which he had always lacked—and despised.

How soon Fitzgibbon's mind envisaged Union as a possibility or necessity it is difficult to say. There is a letter from him to Lord Westmoreland, written so early as the spring of 1795, which contains this passage : " I do most strongly suspect that this idea was drawn out from the Duke of Portland by Lord Fitzwilliam's representation of a conversation which I had with him upon the subject of his Popish projects, in which I stated to him my opinion that a union with the Parliament of England was the only measure which could give Great Britain a chance of preserving this country as a member of the Empire." But a man's speculative thoughts expressed in private conversation are scarcely the measure of his practical politics. If the purpose was really, practically, in Fitzgibbon's mind so early as 1795, it is strange that Sir Jonah Barrington only ' smelt a rat ' so late as 1799. Barrington was the Chancellor's enemy (he described Fitzgibbon as " the greatest enemy Ireland ever had "), he was not particularly scrupulous, he was a lobbyist and self-seeker, and he had the keenest of ears for political rumour. Yet only in 1799 did he become aware that Fitzgibbon had Union in mind. He was (as usual) seeking his own advancement : he was a candidate for the office of Solicitor-General. His antipathy to John Fitzgibbon was not so intense and honourable as to debar him from seeking favours from the Lord Chancellor. He interviewed the Lord Chancellor's secretary ; and the secretary indirectly and discreetly inquired whether Barrington would support a proposal for a Legislative Union of the two kingdoms. " Never," said Barrington, by his own account aghast. He did not get the Solicitor-Generalship, and so had no occasion to forswear himself.

Fitzgibbon stated the reasons for his policy in a speech of many hours' duration in the Irish House of Lords. A man of his immense ability could always find reasons plausible, even cogent, in support of any cause which he advocated. It is unnecessary now to recapitulate these arguments : the verdict of time has gone against Fitzgibbon. Perhaps this much may be said in his favour : he had honestly striven to save the society which he found about him, to use to best advantage the strangely made political machine which he found ready to his hand. Society would not be saved ; the machine could not be made to do its work. Fitzgibbon's intellect was not creative ; he had no capacity to make what was absolutely new. He turned for aid to an instrument already made, and, as he fancies, perfected.

IRELAND'S TRAGIC COMEDIANS

He was mistaken, as many a statesman or politician before him and after him has been. The Union came about. Some words which Fitzgibbon used in his advocacy have been held by Lecky to support the charge that Fitzgibbon accepted corruption as a normal instrument of government. These were Fitzgibbon's words : " It is vain to expect, so long as man continues to be the creature of passion and interest, that he will not avail himself of the critical and difficult situation in which the Executive Government of this kingdom must ever remain under its present Constitution to demand favours of the Crown, not as the reward of loyalty and service, but as the stipulated price to be paid in advance of discharge of a public duty." A hundred years and more of history testified to the truth of those words. To recognise, sadly, it may be, that corruption had been rife in Irish politics, to point out that the Irish political system had always produced, and must inevitably produce, corruption, is not to avow a belief that the corruption or the system which has produced it ought to continue.

One charge lies against Fitzgibbon from which he cannot escape. The Act of Union was carried through the Irish Parliament in a veritable orgy of bribes, threats, political profligacy of every conceivable sort and kind. Of this Fitzgibbon in his station must have been aware, and to this, willingly or unwillingly, he must have consented. We may reproach him now ; but certainly the Irish parliamentarians of his day had long since forfeited the right to do so.

By the Union Fitzgibbon did lose, as a man so

71

clear-headed must have foreseen that he would lose. With the Union his political career was at an end. He spoke a few times in the English House of Lords, but ineffectively. In truth for all his gifts he was a narrow man, no great statesman or politician in the true sense of the words. And he had been master for too long to undergo willingly a new apprenticeship.

One piece of useful work remained for him to do in Ireland. The shameful misuse of Irish revenues for the benefit of Englishmen had allowed the office of Master of the Rolls in Ireland to be held by Englishmen who had no capacity, who had no pretence to discharge its duties. At the moment the office was held conjointly by *two* Englishmen who shared its emoluments. Fitzgibbon secured the appointment of a competent Irish lawyer.

He died in 1802. The seeming delicacy of his youth was not a delusive appearance; there was to be no great length of days for him. The Government which he had served so well could not avert insult from his dead body. He was laid to rest in the burying ground of St Peter's Church in Dublin: that cemetery has been filled up with earth, abandoned. His peerage was extinct by the time that the new century had half run its course. Of the great Earl of Clare no memorial in life or in stone remains; wellnigh every principle for which he stood has gone the way of dusty death. He sprung from nothing; and to nothingness he has returned.

THEOBALD WOLFE TONE

1763-1798

" We have come to the holiest place in Ireland, holier to us even than the place where Patrick sleeps in Down. Patrick brought us life, but this man died for us. Let us not pledge ourselves unless we mean to keep our pledge, holding fast to the memory and inspiration of Tone."—PATRICK PEARSE.

" Of all the United Irishmen, of all the Irish rebels of whom the history of that country contains a record, Wolfe Tone is the least offensive.' —J. A. FROUDE.

CHAPTER I.

For Patrick Pearse, as he walked through the valley of the shadow of death, Tone was a guide and stay : all that Froude could see in Tone was that he was slightly less contemptible than others of his day who thought and acted as he did. There cannot have been two such very different sides to Tone's character : the difference was in the men who judged him. And the difference is instructive. It is the difference between Irish and English mentality, between Irish and English upbringing.

For most Englishmen Patrick Pearse, inspirer of the Dublin rebellion of 1916, is a scoundrel who stabbed England in the back at a moment when England was fighting desperately for the freedom of the world. For very many Irishmen Pearse is a hero-martyr. Of him, and of some who suffered death with him, Mr Yeats has written :—

> We knew their dream ; enough
> To know they dreamed and are dead.
> And what if excess of love
> Bewildered them till they died.

For most Irishmen Froude is a liar, the maligner of the Irish race, the fanatical hater of the faith which most Irishmen profess.

In fact, Pearse declared—and there is no reason to doubt his sincerity—that he felt no enmity to England or to the English people, that he only desired the freedom of Ireland. Froude's whole life shows him to have been an honourable man, incapable of deliberate falsehood, far above the meanness of petty spite against a person or a people.

Pearse was an Irish schoolmaster. He may have had some genius in his composition ; but probably he had little real education. He saw the Irish story from only one side : there is much wrongdoing in it, but the wrongdoing was not altogether on one side. Pearse was a sentimentalist, a dreamer ; the Ireland in which he lived spiritually was the Ireland of the eighteenth, not of the twentieth century. Froude was the product of his remarkable elder brother, Hurrell, of Oxford, of the great world. His brother ' hardened him '—it is said by holding him head downwards in an icy stream—Oxford and the world polished him. He had in his soul something of a diamond's glitter and coldness. He could make no allowance for Irish ' harum-scarumry.' A shudder runs down his spine when he lights on a passage such as this in Tone's ' Journal ' : " Walk out and see M'Cracken's new ship, the *Hibernia*. *Hibernia* has an English crown on her shield. We all roar at him. Dine with Neilson. Generally drunk. *Vive la Nation*. Damn the Emperor of Russia. Bed, God knows how." Prejudiced by these artless confessions Froude cannot view Tone's accomplished work : he does not care to brush aside the froth of words and see the current of purpose flowing strongly and silently underneath. Tone could not help being a playboy. But he was not a ' bladdering ' (his own word) stage Irishman.

There is a point of resemblance between Pearse and Tone. A certain type of fanatic, of martyr, is not only willing to die for his cause, but in the end will be satisfied with nothing else save death. At the end neither Tone nor Pearse sought or desired to live.

If it be not unchristian to wish for the earlier demise of any man, one could wish that the life of Mr Peter Tone had ended before the morning of November 12, 1798. On that morning, supported by the great advocate John Philpot Curran, Peter Tone appeared in the Court of King's Bench, Dublin, swore an affidavit that his eldest son, Theobald Wolfe Tone, had been illegally condemned to death by Court Martial, and prayed for a writ of *Habeas Corpus* whereby, pending the judgment of a properly constituted Court, execution might be deferred. If the souls of just men survive, and from Heaven look down on the perplexed traffic of the world, we can picture Peter Tone and Counsellor Fitz-gibbon watching from Heaven the ' goin's on ' of their offspring, and holding converse in a rich Dublin brogue. " Begor you're lucky, John, to have had but the wan o' them out o' the way," old Mr Tone might have said ; and as probably old Counsellor John, shaking his head, might have replied, " 'Tis thrue for you, Pether ; the childhren can be a heart-scald." If Counsellor John was a hen that hatched out an eaglet, Peter Tone was a hen that hatched out a clutch of demented ducklings.

Peter Tone was to his trade a builder of coaches in Stafford Street, Dublin, and not an unprosperous man. Unfortunately for himself he inherited what in Ireland was called an estate, and what in England would be called a farm of moderate size. He leased this farm to a younger brother, and was utterly ruined by the legal proceedings which are the usual sequel to friendly business arrangements between relations. Nevertheless, despite business and legal worries he found time to marry a Miss Lamport ; and Miss Lamport, after the dreadful fashion of the day, found time to present her husband with sixteen infants. Dreadful, for death rate trod on the heels of birth rate. Of the sixteen Tones but five survived infancy, four sons and a daughter. In whatever order one views the brood it is possible to hold that anyone was more extraordinary than any other.

Theobald Wolfe was the eldest, and for the moment he may be shoved aside. Next came William : at the age of sixteen he ran away from home and enlisted as a private soldier in the service of the East India Company. He set sail for India ; but some freak of Fortune diverted him to Elba, where (without the company of Napoleon) he passed the next six years of his life. Returning to England he volunteered for India again, and persuaded his elder brother (by this time a husband and father) to join him in his application for re-enlistment. That Wolfe Tone did not then and there disappear from the scene of Irish history is due simply to the fact that the brothers were late in making their application—the recruiting season had closed. However, India seems to have had an irresistible attraction for William, for in 1792 he again applied, and in due course reached Madras. *En route* he had assisted in quelling a mutiny, and his services were rewarded by the Directors with a grant of £50 and discharge from his military obligations. Free and with money in his pocket William made his way to Hyderabad, where we find him an officer in the Nizam's service under a French Commandant. For some reason or other his fortunes did not thrive at Hyderabad ; he is next heard of at Calcutta ; and from Calcutta he disappears into Mahratta service. He is said to have fallen in battle as an officer of the Maharajah Holkar.

Matthew Tone was the Sobersides of the family : " In the family we called him the Spectator from his short face and his silence." Nevertheless by the time that he was twenty-five years of age Matthew had visited England, America and the West Indies. He next took a look at Germany, and thence passed once more to America. He returned to France to bear a hand in the Revolution, and, suspected of being a royalist in disguise, he was promptly clapped into a revolutionary prison. He must have satisfied his captors as to the purity of his republican principles, for in 1798 he accompanied the expedition of General Humbert to Killala. He was taken prisoner, tried by court-martial, and hanged.

Arthur Tone, like the wild boy of story books, ' would go to sea.' So to sea he went at the tender age of twelve ; and he liked the sea so well that after his first voyage he was formally bound apprentice to the profession. But meeting his eldest brother at Belfast shortly afterwards he accompanied him to America, and by his brother he was sent back to Ireland as confidential emissary to the party of armed rebellion. This astonishing child, who at the time was under fourteen years of age, seems to have discharged his commission with perfect discretion : of a voyage across the Atlantic under eighteenth century conditions and at a time of confused and general war he probably thought nothing at all. Arthur Tone later became an officer of the Dutch Navy, and as such he passes out of sight.

Miss Mary Tone accompanied her eldest brother and his family from Ireland to America. From America she escorted Mrs Wolfe Tone to France ; and while resident in France she married a Swiss. Perhaps she infected or inspired her husband with the spirit of the Tones ; for the good Swiss instead of decorously keeping a hotel or making watches set out with his bride for San Domingo. What there became of them is not known. But what a family !

Proceeding backwards we reach Theobald Wolfe, the eldest of the flock, and its flower.

He was born in 1763, and ere he was twelve years old he had impressed his first schoolmaster as a lad of parts. It was the dominie's proposal that young Wolfe should be educated for a

Fellowship in Trinity College, which promised "a noble independence besides the glory of the situation." It is interesting to note the respect which even then Dublin paid to the Dons of her University. Possibly because learning is less widely spread, though perhaps more loved, in Ireland than in England, possibly because the stately University buildings of Dublin reflect some measure of their stateliness on those magisterially occupied within, possibly because it has been the general habit of the Trinity Fellow to live aloof from the profane herd, a Fellow of Trinity has usually enjoyed in Ireland a consideration greater than that accorded to a Fellow of an English College in England. For the average Irishman a Fellow of Trinity is *ex officio* a sage, a man versed in mysteries, one walking easily in an atmosphere too rarefied for the breathing of the ordinary man. And the simplicity of life which he as a matter of course adopts still renders his none too extravagant emoluments ' a noble independence.'

In preparation for his great career young Tone was promoted to a more advanced school and to the study of Greek. Unfortunately in no long time he became conscious of his own abilities, and discovered that with three days' work a week he could easily keep pace with his class. The remaining three days were his ' lawful prize,' and he spent them in part on the harmless amusements of walking and swimming, in a greater part in attendance at reviews, parades, military functions of each and every kind. There was a ' call of the army ' in Tone's blood :

God knows whence it came. And he loved to peacock : for him a red coat, a cockade and gold epaulets were ecstatic visions.

Had old Mr Tone been wise, he would have acceded to his son's prayers, allowed the boy to give University life the go-by, and ' follow the gleam.' But the old gentleman showed himself to be an obstinate old hen : he *would* scare away the duckling from the duck-pond, with the inevitable result that in the end the duckling plunged madly into the mill-race. To Trinity young Tone went, and, although his career was in sum fairly creditable, there can be no doubt that he owed his distinctions much more to his ability than to his application. His course was interrupted by an extraordinary incident, and practically ended by another wellnigh as extraordinary. Before he was twenty years of age he ' went out ' as second to a fellow student who shot his opponent, also a student, through the head. No actual penalty was incurred by principal or second ; but both judged it prudent to withdraw themselves for a time from Trinity. Returning, Tone took the first of the many precipitate steps of his career. Aged about twenty-one he made the acquaintance of Miss Witherington, "not sixteen years of age and as beautiful as an angel." He loved and was beloved : the pair walked out together one fine morning and were married. An imbecile performance, to be sure ; but one illustrative of Tone's precocity. Seemingly a young fool had married in haste, and had before him a lifetime of leisure in which to repent. As a matter of

fact Tone never did repent : there are few love
stories more beautiful than the life story of
Wolfe and Mary Tone. Romeo and Juliet were
lovers still when, thirteen years later, Romeo's
brief life ended abruptly. The extravagances of
the ' Journal ' were for the eyes of his " Dearest
Life," and the eyes of " Dearest Life " probably
were more percipient than the eyes of Mr Froude.
The feather-headed youth was either extraordinarily lucky or extraordinarily mature in
perhaps the most important of his judgments ;
the scatter-brain in other things was the very
perfect knight and true lover of his mistress.

But Romeo must needs provide for Juliet
and for a little Juliet (" my little Fantom ")
who in due course made her appearance. Old
Mr Tone, to give him his due, accepted the
situation philosophically : the knot was tied,
and there was no untying it. The family of young
Mrs Tone, perhaps understandably, were less
amenable to persuasion and conciliation. It
was decided that Wolfe should study for the Bar ;
and so to London and the Middle Temple he was
despatched, while young Mrs Tone and her little
daughter found food and shelter at her father-in-
law's charges. And again the curious contra-
dictoriness of Tone became apparent. He had
won (or run away with) his Mary ; the coming
of " little Fantom " had but increased his love
" a thousandfold " ; one would have expected
him to bend his back to his obvious duty, to work
for the two human beings for whom he professed
quite sincerely an extravagant affection. As a
matter of fact he proved incorrigibly idle ; the

profession of the law he "particularly disliked" at the commencement, and later declared to be "an illiberal profession both in its principles and practice." After his first month of study he never opened a law book, and he did not attend the Courts more than three times during his whole stay in England. That he lived is clear, but how it is difficult to say. His father seems to have provided for him to some small extent, he earned a trifle now and then by contributions to periodicals of the day. His literary efforts were purely mercenary : literary fame, he tells us, had no attraction for him. This, again, is strange. For a man who wrote so surpassingly well as Tone a few years later wrote must have shown at least promise in his early essays, and a man so able can scarcely have been unconscious of his own ability.

One *magnum opus* Tone at this time did attempt. He drew up a plan for a colony in the South Seas, took it to Downing Street, and handed it to Mr Pitt's butler. Mr Pitt, much to his chagrin, made no reply ; but perhaps the performance was not quite so silly as a bald narration makes it appear to be, for a few years later Tone revised his plan, and sent it to the Duke of Richmond. This essay by a wholly unknown youth must have differed strikingly from the general run of such compositions, for the Duke sent it on to the Secretary of State for Foreign Affairs, and the Secretary wrote to Tone a letter which was far more than a formal official acknowledgment. A young Irishman of twenty-seven who could thus engage the attention of a great

English Minister must have had in him some quality of constructive statesmanship.

Allusion has been made to Tone's crazy attempt to enlist in the service of the East India Company. He was desperately poor, and he felt that he was making little headway in a profession which he disliked. For the first and only time in his life he showed himself consciously, despairingly, selfish, unmindful of the duty which he owed to " Dearest Life " and to " little Fantom." Blind chance saved his memory from this reproach, and in due course he was admitted to the Bar. He returned to Ireland, by courtesy learned in the Law, by his own account knowing exactly as much of Law as he did of necromancy. This ignorance need not necessarily have proved a barrier to success : great legal learning is not invariably part of a successful barrister's equipment. Unless common repute has sadly maligned them, some of the greatest advocates of modern days have been by no means distinguished by their accurate knowledge of the textbooks. But the Bar in itself was distasteful to Tone, and the Bar combined with politics even still more distasteful. " A profession," he says, " which I always disliked, and which the political prostitution of its members (though otherwise men of high honour and of great personal worth) had taught me sincerely to despise." A prescient judgment on the Irish Bar of even a hundred years later. Then the Irish barrister was learned, eloquent, the very soul of honour in his personal and professional conduct. But politics in nefarious combination with religion were the stepping-stones from Bar to Bench, and as such politics and religion were shamelessly exploited.

There may have been an element of 'sour grapes' in Tone's poor estimate of the legal profession. That shrewd judge of men, Sir Jonah Barrington, has left on record a very unfavourable estimate of the newcomer to the Irish Courts. "He was too light and visionary, and, as for law, was quite incapable of mastering that species of science. His person was unfavourable, his countenance thin and sallow, and he had in his speech a harsh guttural pronunciation of the letter R. It is my belief that Tone could not have succeeded in any civil profession. He was not worldly enough ; nor had he sufficient common-sense for his guidance." This is harsh, and Tone's history shows it to be in a measure true. But there are higher callings in life than the Bar or any other 'civil profession.'

Yet Fortune seemed to smile on Tone at the outset of his barristerial career. It is a curious incident, and an informative one : it gives in some degree the measure of the man that was Tone. Eternally interested in and dabbling in politics he joined the newly-founded Whig Club. On this institution he soon came to look with contempt : its "peddling with petty grievances instead of going to the root of the evil" he despised. But the Whig Club sported a uniform—an irresistible attraction. In the first enthusiasm of his membership Tone wrote a pamphlet, 'A Review of the Last Session of Parliament,' and his pamphlet attracted the favourable notice of Mr George Ponsonby, the barrister to whom

John Fitzgibbon had bequeathed his brief-bag, and a member of one of the great ' undertaking ' tribes which then practically governed Ireland and quite as practically fleeced her. Mr Ponsonby was pleased ; and the immediate and visible result of his pleasure was a brief marked one hundred guineas for Mr Wolfe Tone.

For the ' client ' of an immensely powerful political family there were then boundless possibilities in Ireland. Tone thought otherwise. He did not fling back the brief after the fashion of a Communist rejecting an invitation to a Royal tea-party. He accepted and discharged the task ; and he considered that, while the fee was undeniably handsome, he as undeniably gave full value for money received. Thereafter he spoke civilly to Mr Ponsonby when he happened to meet him ; but he never manifested the slightest inclination to attach himself to Mr Ponsonby's political or professional coat-tails. Mr Ponsonby showed himself equally civil and equally distant. He may have expected some advance from Tone ; he may have come to think Tone less able than he had first imagined ; anyhow he restricted his conversation to indifferent topics. And Tone telling the story without the smallest semblance of ill-will remarks that in politics confidence between individuals is essential, and that " on this footing only would I consent to be treated."

There is nothing more remarkable in Wolfe Tone than his power of winning men's confidence, of inducing men to do his will. He never hectored, blustered, presumed ; he never essayed the rôle of strong silent man, a rôle to which a man who dies at thirty-five has scarcely time to adapt himself. On the other hand he never cheapened himself. Metaphorically Tone was a coachman gifted with perfect courage and perfect hands : he could drive the most unruly team with the craziest of tackle. John Fitzgibbon's courage was as flawless, but his hands were heavy. For control he relied on the strength of his harness, the power of his bits, and the tautness of his curbs.

Tone's next effort in political pamphleteering is worthy of notice because of a criticism which it evoked. The pamphlet was an attempt to prove that Ireland as an independent nation was in no way bound by England's international engagements ; that, should England declare war, Ireland would be entirely within her rights in declaring her neutrality. The critic was a Bishop : " Sir," he said, " if the principles contained in that abominable work were to spread, do you know that you would have to pay for your coal at the rate of five pounds per ton ? " The remark reads comically, but it goes straight to the heart of an economic problem as urgent now as then. Could Ireland in the eighteenth century exist independently of England, and can she now so exist ? Geography is a factor in economics which cannot be altered or abolished by political enthusiasm.

Drifting farther and farther on to the stormy political ocean Tone formed the undying friendship of his life. This was with Thomas Russell, immortalised in the ' Journal ' as " P.P., Clerk of this Parish." The friendship is at once sincere

and inexplicable. " I think the better of myself,"
says Tone, " for being the object of the esteem
of such a man as Russell ": did he achieve
success in any purpose Tone's first thought was
" my dearest love and Russell will be glad of
this." Tone's later diary during lonely months
of racking labour and anxiety in Paris is full of
longing for the company and counsel of " P.P."
Russell enjoyed in equal measure the esteem and
affection of Mrs Tone ; this is one of the few
instances in which a handsome young bachelor
and an attractive young married woman have
been brother and sister, and nothing more.
And yet it is difficult to see *what* in Russell so
attracted Tone, so excited his admiration. The
frank outpourings of the ' Journal ' suggest that
Russell was a thoroughly decent fellow, perhaps
something of a boon companion, perhaps a little
of a buffoon, perhaps something more than a
little of a blockhead. An army officer at the
beginning of the friendship, he was able to present
himself at the Irish town cottage of the Tones
" all clinquant, all in gold." And the Tones turned
him on to help in cooking the dinner ! A fine
figure of a man, maybe, but a man immeasurably
Tone's intellectual inferior. A comparison between Tone and Newman perhaps is possible.
Newman found the guide and stay of his later
life in the friendship of the worthy but not over
intellectual Father Ambrose St John. Manning
observed acridly that Newman loved the adula-
tion of his intellectual inferiors : the reproach,
be it applicable or inapplicable to Newman,
cannot fairly be levelled against Tone. A more

cynical critic has suggested that for Newman
Father St John served the purpose of 'foolometer,' of an instrument by which the reactions
of average stupidity to the proposals of exceptional
intelligence might be calculated. Possibly Russell,
without Tone's consciousness, served as Tone's
foolometer.

Pamphleteering now and then, strutting in
Whig Club uniform, lounging on Irishtown beach
and talking politics with Russell, endeavouring
to found a political society of his own and attract-
ing to its ranks such men as Drennan, Burrowes,
and Whitley Stokes ('Keeper of the College
Lions'), Tone reached the conviction which
informed the rest of his life. " The influence of
England was the radical vice of our Government,
and consequently Ireland would never be either
free, prosperous or happy until she was independent, and independence was unattainable
while the connection with England existed."
It is impossible to say that, granted the circumstances of his day, in the first part of his conviction Tone was mistaken. It is Mr Froude's
view that the native Irish were a race of turbulent, untrustworthy savages, insusceptible of
civilisation and incapable of orderly self-govern-
ment. Mr Froude may have been right in his
view. But the fact that I am morally, intellec-
tually, culturally superior to another man does
not justify me in picking that man's pocket ;
nor is it likely that by picking the pocket of a
savage I shall conclusively demonstrate to that
savage the moral superiority of civilisation. It
seems to be Mr Froude's thesis that England

might have civilised and benefited Ireland, and his admission that up to the end of the eighteenth century England persistently robbed, misgoverned, tormented the unfortunate island and its inhabitants. It is idle to argue (the case is arguable either way) that the facts of the nineteenth century confute Tone's theory of the eighteenth. Tone died ere the nineteenth century opened, and he perforce based his judgment on the facts of past and present, not on the possibilities of a future which he could not and did not foresee. Tone's belief that Ireland freed entirely from English influence and control would rise balloon-like into the ether of prosperity was and still is much more assailable and controvertible.

Tone anticipated, though he did not utter in words, the saying of Abraham Lincoln, that a nation cannot exist half slave and half free. He looked about him, and he saw that the Catholics of Ireland, the vast majority of Ireland's population, were slaves. " There was no injustice, no disgrace, no disqualification, moral, political or religious, civil or military, that was not heaped on them. The system had reduced the great body of the Catholic peasantry of Ireland to a situation, morally and physically speaking, below that of the beasts of the field. The spirit of their few remaining gentry was broken, and their minds degraded ; and it was only in the class of their merchants and traders, and a few members of the medical profession, who had smuggled an education in spite of the penal code, that anything like political sensation existed." Ad-

mittedly by the year 1790 the rigour of the
Penal Laws had been very sensibly relaxed.
But the evil wrought by these Laws was in the
blood of the nation ; Catholic disabilities were
a canker in the body politic of Ireland. Fitzgibbon would have treated the disease with the
unguent of just administration : Tone saw that
the canker must be extirpated ere the patient
could even enter on a probably trying and
tedious process of convalescence.

It was the decisive step of Tone's life when he
joined the ' Catholic Committee,' and became its
Assistant Secretary.

CHAPTER II.

POLITICIAN.

WOLFE TONE was baptised into the Protestant
Church, and there is nothing in his writings
which suggests that he ever felt the slightest
admiration for or sympathy with the Church of
Rome, whether as a Church or as a social institution. On one of his propaganda tours in Northern Ireland he attended Mass: he found it
"foolish enough; too much trumpery." The
grimmest Ulster Presbyterian will scarcely suspect
Tone to have been a Papal Emissary in disguise
when he reads in the 'Journal' a passage such
as this: "Salicetti mentions in his letter to the
Directory that in the conditions granted pro-
visionally to the Pope Bonaparte did not neglect
to avail himself of the terror which the French
armies had inspired through Italy. I dare say
not, indeed; who doubts him? I am heartily
glad that the old priest is at last laid under
contribution in his turn. Many a long century
he and his predecessors have been fleecing all
Europe, but the day of retribution is come at
last; and, besides, I am strongly tempted
to hope that this is but the beginning of his
sorrows!" The Catholic priests of Ireland Tone
considers to be by no means solicitous for the
freedom of their country: "Mr Bride thinks,

what I fear is true, that the Catholic clergymen
are bad friends to liberty." And one remark by
Tone is striking in the light of after knowledge :
" The Catholic clergy have almost totally lost
their influence since the people have got arms ;
so fatal to superstition and priestcraft is even
the smallest degree of liberty." Whether the
Catholic priest is, or is not, a friend to political
liberty (the Papal States were not remarkable
for their liberalism !) is an arguable question.
But it is an indubitable fact that in Ireland the
influence of the priest has always waned pro-
portionately as the theories and acts of ' physical
force extremism ' have waxed. Of all theological
bias in favour of Rome Tone must stand acquitted
in his advocacy of the rights of the Irish Catholics.

In fact, sectarian or theoretical religion was not
a factor which entered into or influenced Tone's
calculations. He saw that a particular class,
the Roman Catholics of Ireland, were oppressed
and ill-treated, and his instinctive love of equal
justice for all was outraged. He saw quite clearly
that Ireland as a whole could never be contented
and prosperous so long as the majority of her
population were kept in the status of slavery.
He saw nothing in the Protestant religion which
entitled its few professors to domineer over the
multitude of their fellow countrymen. But it
would be unfair to suggest that Tone was in any
sense an ' irreligious ' man. There is no trace
in the frank outpourings of the ' Journal ' of
that rancour against all and any form of revealed
religion which in Tone's day was the first characteristic of the French Revolution, and which

in the present century has been a predominant characteristic of the Revolution in Russia. Tone's religion, so far as we can judge it, seems to have been that to which in the present day many men all over the world, weary of the windy, childish recriminations of ' The Churches,' are drawing near. He believed in doing what he honestly conceived to be his duty, quite irrespective of the consequences to himself ; in doing his duty so far as in him lay to those dependent on him ; in refusal of all favours or advantages which might lead him even unconsciously to tolerate that which his conscience condemned. The rest he left to whatever Power may judge men's actions on Earth. He was a well-living man : to blame him overmuch for his occasional and self-confessed convivial indiscretions is absurd. His was a convivial age, and the confessions of the ' Journal ' should be read and judged in the spirit in which " Dearest Life " probably read and judged the whimsical exaggerations of her husband. For example : " Nov. 1. Mr Hutton [Tone's name for himself] like the sun in the centre of the system, fixed, but everything about him moving in rapid rotation. Essays to walk across the room, but finds it impossible to move rectilineally from his having taken a sprig of watercress with his bread."

" Nov. 2. Propose to leave off watercress with my bread." This last entry, one feels, a sly promise of amendment to " Dearest Life."

No mercenary advantage accrued to Tone from the cause which he espoused. He received from the Catholic Committee a small salary for his services. He and his had to live; and, even allowing for the very different value of money a hundred and fifty years ago, the Tones must have exercised a very constant frugality.

The Catholic Committee was a body formed to advocate mildly and constitutionally the just political claims of the Catholics of Ireland. It was in the beginning, like most such bodies, self-constituted; a fact which allowed its detractors to allege that it spoke without authority from those whom it professed to represent. The Committee wisely recognised the formal truth of the allegation, and took steps to remedy the fault. A definite Constitution was planned, and the Committee became as fairly representative of its clients as any central political organisation can become or be. Its leading figures were John Keogh, Richard M'Cormack, and Edward Byrne. All three were shrewd and sensible men, and were recognised as such by Tone. Tone's respect, however, did not prevent him from bestowing on the three in the privacy of the ' Journal ' the names of Gog, Magog, and The Vintner. Had they known their names, they might have been offended : they also might have reflected that they had fared well in comparison with other friends of Tone who figure as ' The Hypocrite,' ' The Irish Slave,' and ' The Pismire.' Nor did Tone's respect prevent him from suggesting, perhaps unworthily, that the success of a brilliant subordinate was not over welcome to Keogh. " Gog has not strength of mind to co-operate fairly ; must do all, or seem to do all himself. Little mind ; paltry." Keogh, in Tone's opinion, was " vain as the devil " ; and in a most matter of fact way Tone sets himself to play on Keogh's vanity as a means of advancing the common cause. M'Cormick (' Magog ') was Secretary to the Committee, but the appointment was probably honorary and nominal, the real duties of Secretary being discharged by Tone. Byrne (' The Vintner ') was a very wealthy Dublin business man.

At the time of Tone's appointment the affairs of the Committee certainly were " in bad shape." However much the Irishman may declaim against England, he usually has a pathetic belief in the superior strength and efficiency of the Englishman ; and cynics have remarked that the Catholic places much more faith in the intercession of a Saint than in his own diligence for the accomplishment of any purpose. The Irish Catholic Committee looking about for a suitable agent or instrument of policy had lighted on a quasi-Englishman and a second-hand Saint. This was Mr Richard Burke.

Richard Burke was the son of the great and famous Edmund Burke ; and undoubtedly the Irish Committee hoped to appeal to the father through the intercession of the son, and to the English Government through the intercession of the father. Richard was a curious creature : a succinct summing up of him is to be found in a letter of Lord Hobart to a correspondent : " Every circumstance induces me to agree with you in thinking him entirely mad." He was, in fact, a parody of his father. He had mastered in a considerable degree the trick of Edmund's

sonorous eloquence : a passage added by him to
the ' Reflections on the French Revolution ' is
an imperceptible darn on a purple patch. But
the words of Richard were words and nothing
more, and his conduct entirely justifies Hobart's
description of him as a fool. He came to Ireland
as Agent to the Catholic Committee ; and within
a comparatively short period of time he had
quarrelled with most of the members, inspired
dislike of the Committee in English statesmen,
and rendered the Committee ridiculous in the
eyes of the Irish House of Commons. He drew
up on behalf of the Committee a flatulent petition
to that House ; and the reluctance of the Committee to allow the petition to go forward was
only equalled by the difficulty of finding a Member
of the House to take charge of it. However, the
petition was presented, and in an assembly of
wits it had an unkindly reception. The climax
of the business was an attempt by Richard Burke
to invade, and to speak in, the Chamber : he was
ignominiously chivvied out by the Serjeant-at-
Arms. The Committee presented him with two
thousand guineas (more than ten years of Tone's
salary !), and sent him packing. Tone in the
' Journal ' makes a very acrid comment on the
association of the Burkes, father and son, with
Irish Catholic affairs : " Edmund has Gog's
boys on a visit at Beaconsfield, and writes him a
letter in their praise. He wants to enlist Gog
on behalf of his son, but it won't do. Gog sees
the thing clear enough. Edmund wants another
two thousand for his son, if he can. Dirty work.
Edmund no fool in money matters. Flattering

Gog to carry his point. Is this Sublime or Beautiful ? "

Wolfe Tone was a man of very different calibre : the course of conduct which he sketched out for himself on joining his appointment suggests the suave dexterity beneath a guise of boyish frankness which was later to ensure his success in dealing with men of different nations and of different dispositions. " I determined to model my conduct with the greatest caution. I seldom or never offered my opinion unless it was called for, but contented myself with giving my sentiments in private to the two men who had the greatest influence on the Committee. I am sure that by my discretion I secured the esteem of the Committee, and consequently an influence in their counsels." Here is a diplomat—some might say a stage Jesuit or an authentic Monsignor Talbot—in the making.

Tone's first business was to get rid of Richard Burke. Mr Burke was " very desirous to resume his former station," and he wrote long letters on the matter. Mr Tone's answers were " concise and civil," but for all their conciseness and civility they must have been quite explicit and perfectly firm. For Mr Burke " soon found that the business was desperate, and gave it up accordingly." So effectively, indeed, did Tone dispose of this matter that shortly afterwards he records his conviction that Mr Richard Burke, should he presume again to intermeddle in the affairs of the Catholic Committee, would be ' rumped.' A delightful word, which unfortunately has not gained currency !

Established in his Secretaryship Tone set about the preaching of Catholic emancipation —and of other things.

In the course of his life Wolfe Tone wrote (usually with his tongue in his cheek) a good many papers and proclamations addressed to the public at large. But for serious business, for the accomplishment of any practical purpose, he relied entirely on personal contact, on the persuasive power of his conversation across a table ; and results achieved visibly justify his choice of method. Of the typical Irishman's faculty for and facility in oratory he seems to have been destitute. He gives a candid criticism of himself in this respect ; and Tone (when sober !) was a singularly clear-sighted critic of himself and of everyone else. "Mr Hutton no great orator at a set speech, though he converses well enough. Because he is not only modest, but sheepish ; which is a shame." We may agree that Tone was no speaker, but we should scarcely have noticed his unconquerable modesty had he not called our attention to it ! Tone on "Mr Hutton" is always delightful : "Nobody universally and at all times right except that truly spirited and patriotic character." He was not quite so tolerant of criticism and reproof from others. At a Committee meeting 'Gog' pointedly remarked that information supplied by Mr Hutton was but gossip heard at street corners. Whereupon "Mr Hutton taketh fire : he riseth in great heat." Friends compose the difference : 'Gog' explains that his words must be taken in a purely impersonal sense : Mr Hutton is appeased and " answers by a low bow." But there is a queer footnote. Had ' Gog ' not made the *amende*, " Mr Hutton would have sent a certain officer with a message which would have speedily brought him to a sense of his duty." Had the tragic meeting of the two Trinity lads (their names were Foster and Anderson) eleven years before passed wholly from Mr Hutton's recollection ?

Tone first turned his eyes to the Protestant North of Ireland. His reasons may be described as ' negative ' and ' positive.'

It is a waste of time to preach to those who are at once wholly converted and wholly indifferent. Outside Dublin the vast majority of the Catholics of Ireland—those dwelling in the South and West—assuredly could have no objection to Catholic emancipation, but quite as assuredly they could have extremely little interest in it. For the most part they and theirs were the prototypes of Teufelsdröckh's ' Poor Slave Household.' " There was a loft above, on which the inmates slept ; and the space below was divided by a hurdle into two apartments ; the one for the cow and pig, the other for themselves and guests. The Poor Slave himself our Traveller found broad - backed, black - browed, of great personal strength and mouth from ear to ear. Of their Philosophical or Religious tenets or observances no notice or hint." Miserable the Poor Slave's circumstances may have been, but the Penal Laws or specific Catholic disabilities *as such* added little to his miseries. Theoretically his religion might be proscribed, practically he had his priest to his hand, and ordinarily no one interfered with his attendance on the priest's ministrations. The Bench and Bar were closed to him : what personal interest had he in either ? He was debarred from the Army and Navy : probably the Poor Slave would have been devoutly thankful had the debarrment from the Navy been a little more thorough. For Irishmen were crimped in shoals, and sent to serve in the English Fleet. Later Tone founded (mistakenly) his hopes of armed attack against England on the possibility of seducing the huge mass of Irish sailors in the Fleet. It is an odd circumstance that Tone himself escaped naval conscription only by the skin of his teeth. Later, on the way to America, his ship was boarded by the officers of a British frigate, who forcibly impressed some fifty of Tone's fellow passengers. Tone himself was chosen, but the screams of his wife and sister secured his freedom. Had Mrs Tone and Miss Tone not been aboard, had they not screamed effectively and wept seductively, Able Seaman Tone might have fought the battles of His Majesty King George III. on the deep waters. Without a doubt he would have fought them exceedingly well.

From the Catholics of higher station in the Catholic provinces there was little to hope. They may have been no worse than the Protestant squireens, but assuredly they were no better. Tone made one tour to Connaught to spy out the land. Charles Lever later described in doggerel verse the *beau idéal* of those parts :—

> To keep game-cocks,
> To hunt the fox,
> To drink in punch the Solway ;
> With debts galore
> But fun far more,
> Oh, that's the man for Galway.

And " The man for Galway " was in no better case in Tone's day : " Dined with eight Galway bucks. Handicapping, wagers, horse-racing, swapping ! Never saw such a sight before, and hope sincerely I never may again."

And Tone, as already pointed out, though a passionate advocate for the freedom of all men (including Catholics) was no friend to the pretensions of any ecclesiastical institution. It is but sense, not sectarianism, to suggest that a curse of Irish politics always has been the deference paid by Irish politicians to the exaggerated claims of the Irish Catholic clergy. Does Whitley Stokes' principle, " What I would highly, that I would holily," mean for the Irish politician that no enterprise may be undertaken without a preliminary aspersion of holy water ? To clerical domination of any sort or kind Tone would not submit. " Busy all day folding papers for the Munster bishops. Damn all bishops. Gog not quite well on that point. Thinks them a good thing. Nonsense." Tone was quite impartial : when he attends a Church of his own faith at Belfast and hears a political exhortation to ' loyalty,' he christens the preacher Caiaphas.

He seems to have suspected that with ' the Church '
the interests of the Church came first, the interests
of Ireland lagging a long way in the rear. And
some of the words of the ' Journal' are prophetic : reading them to-day one recalls the
words of Newman written in the middle of the
nineteenth century : " There was an awful sim-
ilitude, more awful because so silent and so
unimpassioned, between the dead records of the
past and the feverish chronicles of the present."
It was Tone's ideal to unite the whole people of
Ireland, to abolish the memory of all past dis-
sensions, " to substitute the common name of
Irishman in place of the denominations of Protestant, Catholic and Dissenter." What means
better suited to this end than a liberal education
and free interminglement which would induce
mutual toleration, respect for another's point
of view ? The ideas of the Irish hierarchy were
different : " Drs Troy and Reilly, the Catholic
archbishop of Dublin and Catholic primate,
refuse to concur in a general system [of education].
Damn them : ignorant bigots." And again :
" Gog has been disgusted with Dr Bellew, Catholic
archbishop of Killala, on the subject of a national
college. The bishop wants to get money from the
laity to endow it, and exclude them from all
share in its management. Damned kind ! Gog
revolts like a fury, and tells Mr Hutton he begins
to see they are all scoundrels." Long years
afterwards Newman discovered that the orthodox
idea of a University in Ireland for the education
of all was a priest-ridden seminary. The mergence
of Catholic, Protestant, Presbyterian into the

common name of Irishman is no nearer to-day than when Tone wrote nearly one hundred and fifty years ago. Even then as regards Tone himself, Mr Lynch, whoever he may have been, thought that " it would be better if a Protestant were not to interfere in their business."

To understand Tone's positive reasons for his choice of Ulster as a pulpit or preaching ground it is necessary to understand the curious change in political thought—or in political labels—that a century brought about.

Tone went to Belfast in 1792. In 1892 no one, unless he were looking for a bang on the head, would have ventured to claim a Belfast Dissenter as a ' Home Ruler.' A hundred years earlier the Belfast Dissenters were the real Home Rulers in Ireland : perhaps without knowing it they have always been so. They fought the battles of King William because they disliked the tyrannical obscurantism of King James ; but in 1792 the Ulster Volunteers flatly refused to parade round the statue of King William. As a sort of counterweight Tone records maliciously that some Catholic pilgrims seeing a statue of Commerce in a Belfast square took it to be a Saint, and addressed a few prayers to it !

Loyalty to England, to the British Empire, this for the Ulsterman was academic theory. Restraints on Irish trade, diversion of Irish taxation to provide pensions for King's mistresses, permission to a few great families of the Established Church to plunder the community, these for the Ulsterman were facts which needed dealing with. And however intolerant in his religious principles the Ulsterman might be, he, like Tone, realised that Ireland as a whole could not thrive while three-quarters of her population were slaves and one-quarter free. Moreover, the Ulsterman was formidably ready to back his words by deeds. The revolution of '98 in the South caused the Viceroy (Camden) and the Chancellor (Fitzgibbon) no very great concern; but their eyes were fixed with genuine apprehension on the North.

Tone even then had passed beyond the ideas of his employers. The Catholic Committee would have been well pleased to accept emancipation from their religious disabilities (or even less than total emancipation), and to settle down contentedly under England's rule. Tone, had he been addicted to quoting the Scriptures, would have said, "Seek first the Kingdom of Heaven, and all these things shall be added unto you." In an Ireland free from England's control the Catholics would automatically be as free as anyone else, Ireland would make her own trade regulations, amend her agriculture, protect her industries, spend on Ireland the taxation paid by Irishmen. It might have been so—or it might not. Was Irishman ready to unite with Irishman, was the Catholic lamb (or lion) ready to lie down with the Protestant lion (or lamb)? Tone could not foresee the answer which a hundred years of history have given, and Ulster seemed to be a ground quite singularly fitted for the sowing of precious seed.

So to Belfast Tone fared forth; and the spirit in which he started on his journeys is indicated by the heading to the 'Journal' of the third embassy :—

" *Journal of the proceedings of John Hutton, Esq., on his third journey to the North of Ireland, including his artful negotiations with the Peep-of-day-Boys and sundry Peers of the Realm ; also his valorous entry into and retreat out of the city of Rathfrilan ; interspersed with sundry delectable adventures and entertaining anecdotes.* — VIVE LE ROI."

For a time the comedian in Tone was uppermost : no thought of political failure or personal danger cast a gloom over his spirits. The faithful Russell of course accompanied him ; and the pair had scarcely started ere Tone records " P.P. very drunk." On his second journey Tone took with him the grave Whitley Stokes (' Keeper of the College Lions '). Tone " proposed piquet ; played very fair ; doubt the Keeper is a blackleg." And once arrived, Tone's love of *panache* bursts forth. He hurries on his ' regimentals ' (to what regiment did he belong ?) ; he figures in reviews. " Drums beating, colours flying, and all the honours of war. Ride the Draper's mare. The review tolerably well." He buys " a fine sword of which he is as vain as the Devil ; intends to sleep on it to-night." A lamentably large proportion, it must be admitted, of the day's entries close thus : " God bless everyone. Generally drunk. Huzza." Next day's entry begins, " Wake drunk." Tone shakes his head on paper and sighs, " Bad, bad, sad." We may re-echo his sighs and self-reproaches. Still, he was not the only one : " The Hypocrite made the Keeper drunk ! "

Yet there is a demented truthfulness in an entry, already quoted, of the Journal : " Mr Hutton, like the sun in the centre of the system, fixed, but everything about him moving in rapid rotation." Certainly there was a deal of riotous tomfoolery about the Belfast proceedings, and certainly everybody was frequently and quite irrelevantly drunk. Here, for example, is the conclusion of a meeting which listened to a " long and accurate statement " by Mr Hutton on the Catholic question : " Damn the Empress of Russia. Success to the Polish arms with three times three. Huzza. Generally very drunk. Bed, God knows how." Yet in this whirligig of crapulous absurdity Mr Hutton *was* fixed : he was pressing steadily forward to the end which he had in view, and he was adapting means to ends with the cool sagacity of a grey-haired diplomat.

Tone's ends were, officially, to obtain Northern support for the Catholic claims, unofficially (one suspects), to promulgate ' nationalist ' doctrines much more extreme than his employers, the Catholic Committee, would permit. For both purposes circumstances seemed to favour him. So extremely liberal in its theology had Belfast for the moment become that Tone met " a hair-dresser, one Taylor, who has two children christened by the priest, though he himself is a Dissenter, merely with the wish to blend the sects." What was the result, one wonders, of this curiously compounded religious cocktail ? And among Tone's new political friends were H. J. M'Cracken (he who by inadvertence put the Crown on the shield of his new ship, *Hibernia*), and Samuel Neilson, founder of ' The Northern Star,' the first open advocate of the ' United Irishmen.' The tenor of these gentlemen's politics may be inferred from the facts that M'Cracken later was hanged for armed rebellion against the British Government, and that Neilson spent several years of his life (a considerable period without trial) in a British prison.

But the age-old, suspicious unfriendliness between North and South, between Catholic and Protestant, was not so easily to be conjured away by the speeches and toasts of enthusiastic young men. To demand political liberty for Catholics was all very well ; but what would be the practical result when political influence was conceded to the uneducated rabble which formed the majority of Ireland's population ? Revolution was admirable in Paris ; but Revolution with its practical consequences seemed much less admirable in Belfast. Mr Hutton was quick to see that his disquisitions on Irish Independence were prejudicial to the mission entrusted to him : with admirable sagacity he dropped republicanism in favour of religion, and seized an opportunity to do a bit of plain, practical work. His " valorous entry into Rathfriland " was a praiseworthy endeavour to compose the differences of two unreasoning mobs. These were the Peep-of-day-Boys and the Defenders.

The permutations and combinations of these

two bodies are curious. The Peep-of-day-Boys were Presbyterian, an offshoot of the United Irishmen, and republican. The Defenders, generally speaking, were Catholic and Conservative. But in no long time the Peep-of-day-Boys transmuted themselves into the Conservative Orangemen, while the Defenders were politically swallowed up by the Radical United Irishmen, and theologically swallowed up their swallowers. At the particular moment of Tone's interference just one thing was clear : the two hated one another, and were prepared on the slightest excuse to translate their abstract dislike into very practical violence.

In some measure Tone met with the reception usually accorded to a stranger who thrusts himself into an Irish faction fight. He descended with his fellow ambassadors (they were six in all) at ' Murphy's Inn ' ; and Mr Murphy, who by his name should have been a Catholic Celt, promptly kicked them into the street dinnerless. " He has cold beef and lamb chops, and will give neither, but turns off on his heel. Damned fine." And Mr M'Nally rode over from Newry with the cheering intelligence that the gentry of the town (presumably Protestant) proposed to duck the ambassadors in the horse-pond. Reversing the precept of Vergil, Tone, unable to move those below, called on those above. He visited Lords Downshire and Hillsborough : the faculties of the first were " quite gone," and the second informed Tone that " he will see that the laws execute themselves without our interference." It was not very cheering ; and Tone doubtless was thankful enough when he got out of the business with a whole skin. " Generally glad that we are back safe. Mug porter to a la:ౖ ౖ extent. God bless everybody." ' Generally ' was a favourite word with Tone : there was a large benevolence in the man !

A subsequent fact provokes a doubt as to the soundness of Tone's judgment in one case. Were Lord Downshire's faculties really " quite gone " ? Lord Downshire was the man to whom later Turner, one of the shrewdest of the Northern United Irishmen, betrayed the channel of communication between the United Irishmen in Ireland and their sympathisers on the Continent. A traitor who puts his own life in the direst jeopardy by his treachery does not ordinarily select as confidant a man whose faculties are wholly or even partly gone. Tone may have seen in Lord Downshire just what he desired to see. It is a fairly common mistake.

Still, something had been accomplished. Tone, before he got through with his pacifying, was able to note that in one place the Peep-of-day-Boys had chosen a Catholic commander, and that the Catholics had gracefully returned the compliment by lending some of their arms to the Peep-of-day-Boys. It may have been a reconciliation, or it may have been a sporting desire that the crash, when it did come, should provide a full and evenly matched afternoon's entertainment for everyone concerned.

It might be desirable that two Ulster rabbles should desist from breaking each others' heads. But this end achieved, though in itself highly commendable, was not likely to be of great importance to the larger politics of the Catholic Committee at Dublin. What that body desired, and what Tone had to obtain, was a public pronouncement by the Northern Radicals in favour of Catholic claims. Individual sympathy was plentiful, but a public and representative declaration was a different matter. There were the usual objections and tergiversations : "Danger of disunion—repulse would be fatal, and success of small consequence," and so on. Tone acted with admirable decision : "Let us look the question in the face, nor delude ourselves with the idea of support where no support is to be found." He held a council (in a potato-field) ; there were seven councillors, "all fools except the first and the last." The first was William Sinclair ('The Draper'), and the last (is it necessary to name him ?) was Mr Hutton. The spirited two swept the lagging five along with them. So to a great meeting in the Linen Hall, Belfast, where a resolution of sympathy with the Catholics was passed publicly and by acclamation. Only half a dozen sheep strayed sideways from the flock which Mr Hutton was driving triumphantly before him. "God bless everybody ! Stanislas Augustus, George Washington ; *beau jour*. Huzza. Generally drunk. Broke my glass thumping on the table. Home, God knows how or when. Huzza. God bless everybody again, generally."

For all his drinking, roaring, ' blatherumskiting,' Tone had accomplished the task laid on him by his employers. Assured of Northern support the

Catholic Committee now feels itself strong enough to disregard the Government of Ireland, to address Majesty direct. So five gentlemen are chosen to proceed to London, and to deliver into the reputedly anti-Catholic hands of George III. the petition of his loyal Catholic subjects of Ireland. As a *parergon* the Committee draws up a defence of the Catholics " against the malicious and unfounded charges of their adversaries." One adversary in particular is named : his name is John Fitzgibbon. " We know that man," declare two members of the Committee; " the road to his favours is through his fears." A remark which provokes a doubt as to the degree of the acquaintance of the two gentlemen with John, Baron Fitzgibbon of Lower Connello. The road to anywhere is not through a gateway which does not exist.

The five set forth ; they deliver the petition into the hands of Majesty ; Majesty is pleased to receive the same very graciously. And this is very curious.

At a later period Pitt excused his desertion of the Irish Catholics by the plea that George III. personally and absolutely vetoed any extension of privilege or liberty to the Catholics of Ireland. Now if George III. was prejudiced enough and felt himself strong enough unconstitutionally to reject the advice of his Prime Minister, why did he let slip the opportunity of administering quite constitutionally a rebuff to these delegates of the Irish Catholic Committee ? There is an order in doing all things ; and if individual Irish subjects desired to approach the Throne, the proper road of approach was quite clearly marked out for them. That road was through the chief officers of the King's Government in Ireland. George III. would have been perfectly within his rights in refusing to receive the deputation. Is it possible that the blind anti-Catholic prejudice of George III. was but a bogey set up by Pitt to excuse his own bad faith ? Or was old ' Varmer George ' prejudiced indeed, but much more subtle than men generally supposed in giving play to his prejudices ? Did he see that one can better avoid a blow by stepping back than by standing up and opposing a rigid guard to it ? Either supposition is possible.

In due course proposals for Catholic relief came over from England. Something was conceded, but much was refused. Skilfully the Catholic Committee was drawn on to the ground of negotiation and discussion. A bird in the hand is worth two in the bush ; why reject a certain *some* in the hope of gaining a problematical *all ?* And so on and so forth. The gist of the matter was that the vote was to be conceded to the Catholic rabble, the right to sit in the Irish Legislature was to be withheld from the Catholic gentry.

Tone, one may suppose, would have been for rejecting this delusive concession, which from the Catholic point of view was unjust, and from any point of view was utterly unwise. But Tone at the moment had other things to occupy his mind. His duties to the Catholic Committee discharged —and admirably discharged—his mind had turned once more to speculative republicanism, to Irish independence. And suddenly he became aware of a creepy sensation in his back, of a growing coldness in his toes. The steely-grey eyes of a handsome imperious little gentleman were following him as he took his walks abroad. In public meeting Mr Stephen Reilly had dropped his eyes before the eyes of Mr John Fitzgibbon; Mr Wolfe Tone found the eyes of Lord Fitzgibbon fixed on the small of his back to be no less disconcerting. Tone was the bravest of men; he would have accepted gleefully a challenge from the one-time fire-eating Mr Fitzgibbon; he would have defended himself intrepidly if arraigned before Lord Fitzgibbon on the Bench. But uncertainty as to what Fitzgibbon knew, as to what Fitzgibbon might propose to do, was terrifying—it imparted a curious creepy, crawly feeling. For this is what had happened.

It is an old reproach that when three Irish conspirators are gathered together, there are at least two informers in the company. The statement may have been more or less true in Tone's day, but it may have been less discreditable to Irishmen than it may at first appear. The man who for gain betrays his comrades is a villain; the Secret Service agent who ferrets out a plot but does his duty. And the Secret Service of those days seems to have been efficient.

There came to Ireland in mission from France one Mr Jackson. Mr Jackson apparently had been at one period of his life a Protestant clergyman; he had slid aside into the republicanism, atheism and other 'isms' in vogue in late eighteenth-century France; and his particular mission was to ascertain how the general publics of England and Ireland would view an attempt by France, high priestess of liberty, to liberate Ireland. Mr Jackson, one fears, *au fond* was no more percipient in this matter than Tone himself ; he did not understand that while Ireland was for France a convenient stick wherewith to beat England, the liberty of Ireland in the abstract was of less concern to France than the value of a five-franc paper *assignat*. Mr Jackson, according to Tone, in the end behaved " incomparably well " ; at the beginning he seems to have behaved like an incomparable fool. He probably was too unsuspicious for any world ; certainly he was too unsuspicious for the political world of the Ireland of his day.

Mr Jackson had no difficulty in finding a sympathetic English ear into which to pour his purposes. Conversely, Mr Pitt found no difficulty in placing the ear of a Government spy in juxtaposition to the mouth of Mr Jackson. The ear at once sympathetic and 'secret' was the ear of Mr Cockayne. Mr Cockayne shepherded Mr Jackson to Ireland. In Ireland Mr Cockayne introduced Mr Jackson to certain men of revolutionary principles, among them being Mr Wolfe Tone and Mr Arthur Hamilton Rowan : he also introduced him to Mr Leonard M'Nally, who might be described as confidential legal adviser to the United Irishmen. A meeting, two or three meetings, took place between Mr Jackson, Mr Tone, and Mr M'Nally, and certain projects were discussed.

Tone was no fool, he did not blunder headlong

into the first trap set across his pathway. Mr Jackson's sentiments were to his liking ; but at once the suspicion crossed his mind that Mr Jackson might be a Government *agent provocateur*. So with Mr Jackson Tone maintained an attitude of prudent reserve. He smelt something in the air, but he failed to locate the smell. There was a spy present ; but it never occurred to Tone that the spy might be M'Nally !

In truth, Leonard M'Nally is a puzzling figure. Wiser men than Wolfe Tone failed to understand him : it is a question whether M'Nally ever understood himself. Judged by what he actually did, M'Nally surely was one of the basest villains that ever drew the breath of life. Yet to the end of his days John Curran prided himself that he had won and retained the esteem of such a man as Leonard M'Nally. Together Curran and M'Nally defended, sometimes successfully, sometimes unsuccessfully, many of the United Irishmen charged with treason. At the close of the trial of one Finerty—he was acquitted— Curran in open Court addressed these words to M'Nally : " My old and excellent friend, I have long known and respected the honesty of your heart, but never till this occasion was I acquainted with the extent of your abilities. I am not in the habit of paying compliments where they are not deserved." Yet all the time M'Nally was betraying his clients to the Crown. Men were wont to wonder at the readiness and learning with which the Crown lawyers met obscure points of law raised by Curran and M'Nally : the explanation, which no one suspected, was

117

simple. Every point which the defence could raise was disclosed in advance by M'Nally to the prosecution. No man suspected him : he even suffered insult for his nationalist faith. He had a silver cup lettered Erin-go-Bragh : soldiers arrived at his house one day and took it away. M'Nally humbly petitioned the Courts for its return : Lord Kilwarden, most upright and humane of Irish judges, actually wept when he heard of this outrage on a man who had but faithfully discharged his duty to his clients. It does not appear that M'Nally was actually paid for his horrible treachery ; and the Government did not dare confer on him, nor did he dare accept, any office of profit. He was, and is, an enigma.

Perhaps some explanation may be found in the words which Verdi's Rigoletto addresses to the courtiers of the Duke of Mantua : " Hateful if I be, hateful yourselves have made me." M'Nally was in a way misfortune's child : Sir Jonah Barrington thus describes his outward appearance : " His figure was ludicrous ; he was very short, and nearly as broad as long. His legs were of unequal length, and he had a face which no washing would clean. He wanted one thumb ; and he took great pains to have no nails, as he regularly ate every morning the growth of the preceding day." The dirtiness of his person gave his Bar Mess excuse for refusing him admission ; and in a duelling age no gentleman would demean himself by ' going out ' with Leonard M'Nally. Brooding on the treatment which he received M'Nally may have developed within him a secret ' mad-doggery ' : it mattered not whom he bit, provided he could bite some-body.

Better days came for him—if Sir Jonah Barring-ton is to be believed—in an odd way. In Court one day, without any apparent reason, he grossly insulted Barrington. " You shall hear from me within an hour," said Barrington fiercely. " Half an hour," replied M'Nally exultantly. They met in the Phœnix Park ; they fired simultaneously ; Barrington felt a touch as of a red-hot iron across his thigh, and M'Nally staggered and fell. Then tragedy turned to farce. Barrington's bullet had struck M'Nally's suspender buckle : the blow had knocked the breath out of him, but no harm was done. And M'Nally with tears in his eyes thanked Sir Jonah. Now that he had exchanged shots with a leading K.C., no man could thence-forth insult him and refuse him satisfaction ; the Bar Mess without shame to itself could not refuse him entrance. It proved to be so ; but by that time M'Nally had gone so far on the path of dishonour that he could not retrace his steps.

There is another little point of interest about this strange creature. M'Nally was a poet, or at least a versifier of considerable skill. To the woman whom he married he wrote a once famous song, " The Lass of Richmond Hill." " The lady," says Barrington, " was absolutely beautiful, but quite a slattern in her person ! "

Mr Jackson had set down on paper his im-pressions of the political situation in England. He had concluded, very correctly, that while there was a considerable number of Englishmen who favoured in the abstract the republicanism of France and the claim of Ireland to independence, any attempt by France at intervention between England and Ireland would have the immediate effect of uniting all Englishmen against France. What were Mr Tone's views as regards the general feeling in Ireland ? There, too, would French intervention but result in a union of all Irishmen against the intruder ?

Mr Tone did not think so. He drew up a paper setting forth his reasons for believing that Irishmen, or the majority of Irishmen, would rally to the side of a French force invading Ireland. He handed his paper to Mr Jackson, and at once felt an uneasy suspicion that he had acted like a fool. He asked for the return of his paper ; and Mr Jackson without a word returned the paper apparently unread. Tone carelessly handed the paper to M'Nally : it might interest him, he might make a copy of it if he liked, but he was to be sure to burn the original. A copy, not in Tone's writing, could do no harm to Tone ; M'Nally was old enough and clever enough to know what he was doing, if he chose to keep about him dangerous papers in his own hand-writing. M'Nally duly burned the paper : Tone was conscious of some slight feeling of annoyance when he learned that M'Nally had made two or three copies. There may be safety in a multitude of men, but there is none in a multiplication of compromising documents.

M'Nally now arranged a meeting between Tone, Rowan, and Cockayne. Rowan at the moment was actually in prison. Rowan copied the copy, or embodied the substance of it in a letter : it was proposed that Tone should cross to France and deliver the paper to the French Directory. But Tone for the first time in his life hung back : was it prudence—he mentioned that he had a wife and children dependent on him— or did some sixth sense warn him that there was some strange danger in the air ? Cockayne undertook the transmission of the letter ; he left Rowan's prison with it in his pocket. By some strange chance (!) he walked straight into the arms of two police agents. The letter was found on him ; Jackson was arrested ; Rowan by bribing his jailor escaped from prison and made his way to France. Tone walked the streets of Dublin a free man. But he could not shake off the uncomfortable feeling that the eyes of John Fitzgibbon were following him.

It was a neatly contrived plot, a smart piece of Secret Service work by the Government of Ireland. And for most practical purposes the expression Government of Ireland at the time meant John Fitzgibbon. The question arises, what exactly were the Government and Fitzgibbon aiming at ?

It has been suggested that the intention was to trap Jackson, frighten him into turning King's evidence, and by his evidence hang Rowan and Tone. This intention was frustrated by the firmness of Jackson and by the flight of Rowan. It may have been so. But there are some straggling ends which spoil the neatness of the explanation.

The easy access of Jackson and Tone to Rowan in his prison for the purpose of concocting treason and armed rebellion is curious. Froude suggests airily that prison rules were lightly construed in favour of gentlemen of fortune ; and Rowan was a wealthy man. An ordinary criminal with money in his purse might easily enough have procured certain relaxations of discipline in his own favour. But mere bribery of a subordinate would scarcely have enabled a political prisoner under the special notice of the all-powerful Lord Chancellor to invite to his cell a more or less declared revolutionary such as Tone, and a gentleman from France, such as Jackson, whose every movement was watched by the secret agents of the law. It seems more probable that the interview in jail was but part of a carefully prepared comedy.

Again, Rowan escaped from jail by bribing the jailor, and from Ireland by an appeal to the chivalry of two poor Irish fishermen. The second part of the story is more credible than the first. Doubtless the jailor got his bribe ; but quite possibly he also got a hint that the escape of Mr Rowan would be a dereliction not very heavily to be visited on his head. Rowan certainly was ' papered,' that is, a reward was offered for his apprehension ; he was condemned *in absentia* for treason. The condemnation automatically entailed forfeiture of his estates ; but Fitzgibbon intervened to save the estates for Mrs Rowan. And later Fitzgibbon, by Rowan's own admission unsolicited, busied himself with Rowan's affairs, and offered sagacious counsel as to how Rowan might extricate himself from his embarrassments. It does not seem as though the Government of

Ireland or its directing force cherished any very implacable animosity against Mr Arthur Hamilton Rowan.

The evidence against Tone was about as strong as the evidence against Jackson. And the evidence against Jackson was strong enough to hang him : as a matter of fact Jackson only escaped the gallows by swallowing a dose of poison in the dock at the moment that sentence was being pronounced. Tone declares, no doubt quite truly, that he would never have given any testimony which might have inculpated Jackson. As a matter of fact he was never asked to do anything of the kind. Jackson may have gallantly refused to utter a word inculpating Tone. But he may never have been offered the chance of so doing.

Fitzgibbon was hard enough ; but he may have been a good deal less hard, less vindictive than his detractors allege ; more sympathetic with, more understanding of, the enthusiasms of young Irishmen. It may have been in his mind that Irishmen could find some peaceful solution of their difficulties if unprovoked to violence by agitators from outside. Foreign spreaders of ' French principles ' in Ireland could expect little mercy from him ; and assuredly the wretched Jackson received none. Tone was left unmolested : an intimation was conveyed to him that the matter would be overlooked would he but leave Ireland for America. Tone agreed : he is in no way to be blamed for so doing. He could not save Jackson : there was no point in his sacrificing himself.

He went forth with all the honours of war. He visited his revolutionary friends in the North ; and at M'Art's Fort he, Russell, Neilson, Simms, and M'Cracken took an oath " never to desist in our efforts until we had subverted the authority of England over our country, and asserted our independence." Tone has described an earlier oath-taking : " Gog and Mr Hutton worship one another ; they sign a document in blood and flourish their hands." There was nothing of the ' playboy ' in the taking of this last oath : at least three of those who took it died to keep it.

Tone is no longer preoccupied with such details as Catholic emancipation, he has ceased to bless everybody generally and to get to bed God knows how and when. Henceforth he is the far-sighted, toilsome planner of revolution, the man who pays unflinchingly with his life for the failure of his plans.

CHAPTER III.

WOLFE TONE was a man of his word : he gave his life to keep the promise which he made to others—and to himself—at M'Art's Fort. No man was ever less wont in the ordinary course of life to stand on quibbles. Yet he determined his own fate by the quibbling interpretation of an undertaking. It might have been a peaceful, industrious, unnoticed old age : it was a tragically early death and a posthumous immortality.

It had been intimated to Tone that the past would be overlooked did he but consent to leave Ireland for America. He accepted these terms ; but at once it occurred to him that the words of his undertaking would be satisfied by a voyage across the Atlantic. He had promised to go to America : nothing had been said about his return. Technically he was right : in plain common sense he was evading ' a gentleman's agreement.' He did not reflect that a quibble in fact and in morality can be a double-edged weapon, that the man who quibbles cannot complain of the quibbling of his adversary. One, Father Nicholas Sheehy, a fugitive from justice, was accused by the Government of Ireland of inciting to riot and rebellion. He offered to surrender and stand his trial, provided that the trial were not held at Clonmel. The Government accepted his offer : Father Sheehy was tried in Dublin on the specified charge and was acquitted. As he left the dock he was arrested on a quite different charge, sent to Clonmel for trial, convicted and hanged. By a strictly literal interpretation of words no promise had been broken ; but nevertheless the action of the Government of Ireland was an infamy. As this affair took place in Tone's own lifetime it is likely that he found in it material for scathing comment on the conduct of others. If he did, he should have remembered in 1795 that a possible charge of ungentlemanly trickery might lie against himself.

It is an unavoidable reflection that what Tone needed then and throughout his life was a sensible friend, older than himself and more experienced in the ways and thoughts of the world. Poor old Mr Tone no doubt meant well, but he was singularly unfitted to be the counsellor of such a son. In ' P. P.' (Russell) there was no counsel to be found. Mrs Tone was a girl of flawless courage, but a fellow enthusiast rather than a calm adviser. Keogh (' Gog ') of the Catholic Committee seems to have been a man of rather uncommon sagacity. There is, however, no evidence that Tone's personal acquaintance with Keogh was intimate ; and it is probable that Tone's barely disguised aversion from the Roman Catholic Church would have rendered intimacy between the two impossible. A self-devoted martyr certainly is not an easy person to advise ; but up to the last few months of despair Tone's eyes were fixed on the Crown rather than on the

Cross. He was confident of success ; and in his diary he does not conceal his belief that his country would not be unmindful of her liberator. It is a pretty touch that he valued most his prospective reward because it would enable him to end for his wife the long years of anxiety and penury which she had endured so uncomplainingly. " I hope (but I am not sure) that my country is my first object ; at least she is my second. If there be any before her, as I rather believe there is, it is my dearest life and love, the light of my eyes and spirit of my existence. I wish more than for anything on earth to place her in a splendid station." There is a demented aptness in the metaphor of the Cross and of the Crown. For the French authorities, apparently in good faith, later suggested to Tone that should a liberated Ireland unaccountably prefer a Monarchy to a Republic, the choice might conceivably fall on himself ! To the French, who had unmade a King and were in no long time to make an Emperor, the suggestion may have seemed less crazy than it did to Tone.

But a prudent friend might earlier have suggested to Tone a thought which later might have suggested itself with increasing frequency. No one could doubt Tone's sincerity ; but was it quite certain that his methods for securing the greater freedom, wealth, happiness of Ireland were the right methods ? Would it really be so great a thing to unrivet a collar from Ireland's neck but at once to rivet on another ? Was there nothing to be said for the policy of ' saving society,' of clearing away, perhaps, a superstructure which might be rotten, but of utilising foundations which might be sound? Was the Englishman *au fond* so much more selfish than the Frenchman? Almost at the very outset of his negotiations with France Tone notes, " I for one will never be accessory to subjecting my country to the control of France merely to get rid of that of England." He finds it necessary to warn the French General Clarke that " if he meant to admit a representative of the Republic into any part of our Government, it was what France ought not to expect or we to permit." Later, returned from the unsuccessful expedition of Hoche, he speaks his mind freely of the civil Commissaries who accompanied the army : they " would sell the liberty of Ireland, the interests of the Republic, for half a crown." A friend better versed in world politics might have warned Tone that one nation seldom does much for another from purely unselfish motives, might have bidden him ponder over his early suspicion that " France has nothing in view but to distress England for the moment."

At first Tone's quibbling may have been specu- lative rather than practical ; it does not appear that he definitely purposed to return ; he merely noted that he could return, if he so desired, without a formal forswearing of himself. He sailed for America on June 13, 1795, aboard the good ship *Cincinnatus* of Wilmington, and the circum- stances of the voyage may evoke a shuddering interest in travellers of to-day. The *Cincinnatus* was of 230 tons burthen ; she carried three hundred passengers ; and the voyage lasted forty-seven days! Food and drink for such a number and for such a time must have required some considerable stowage space : the space allotted to human beings may be estimated from Tone's description of his ' state-room.' This measured 8 feet by 6, and in it Tone, his wife, his sister and three children were accommodated. On shore, Tone observes, under such conditions two hundred out of the three hundred passengers assuredly would have expired : at sea they lost but one woman. It is not difficult to guess that in this floating misery there was a helpful Mark Tapley, and that his name was Theobald Wolfe Tone.

From Wilmington, the home port of the *Cincinnatus*, Tone moved to Philadelphia. He opened negotiations for the purchase of a farm, and in fact did purchase a farm near Princeton. Literally he had set his hand to the plough : unfortunately he looked back. On his arrival in America he had waited on Adet, the French Minister; he had fallen in with Hamilton Rowan and Napper Tandy; he had received letters from his friends in Ireland. The upshot was that on January 1, 1796, he sailed from America, and on February 1 landed at Havre. His wife, ardent little revolutionary, sped him on his way : she even concealed from him the fact that she was with child lest the coming tie should keep him by her side. But of another party to the adventure it is possible to speak with some asperity : this is Hamilton Rowan. If he so passionately desired the support of France for Ireland, why did he not solicit that support himself ? To all seeming he was the better suited for the enterprise : he was a wealthy man with influential social connections, surely a weightier ambassador of Ireland than the penniless adventurer Tone. But Rowan stayed in America, in due time sued out his pardon, returned to Ireland and to his estates, and lived to see his eightieth birthday behind him. Tone went forth alone to glory—and to the gallows.

By February 12 Tone had reached Paris, and by February 17 he had opened negotiations with the French Government. His sole introduction was a letter in cipher from Adet ; and it was not until a week after his first interview that the Directory inquired his *name !* His real name, that is ; Tone had introduced himself as ' Mr Smith '—of America ! He seems to have had some curious affection for this undistinguished patronymic, for writing from his Irish prison to the French Directory he signs himself " Adjutant General Theobald Wolfe Tone (called Smith)." The extremely ready access to the French Government may have been due in part to Tone's undeniable adroitness and charm, in part to the ' fluidity ' of French authority at the moment. Tone was at times to be perplexed as to *who* was directing *what*. The need of personal success was before the eyes of every would-be politician and army leader ; and a chance visitor who could indicate an avenue, no matter how dangerous, at the end of which success might be found, was a not unwelcome caller. This explanation certainly is not conclusive ; but it may in some degree account for the otherwise inexplicable fact that a young man, unknown in France and of no great status in his own country, scarcely able to make himself understood in French, did arrive in Paris and did in the course of a few days get sufficiently close to the Government of the country, or to those for the moment exercising authority, to be asked to submit in writing proposals for the risking of a considerable French army and a considerable French navy.

But business for a moment may wait its turn. Tone was in France from the spring of 1795 to the autumn of 1798, and throughout this period he was ' based on ' Paris. There were, of course, intermissions : he once got to the coast of Ireland ; he was in Holland ; he crossed the German frontier ; as an officer in French service he held occasionally and for short periods various appointments in various parts of the country. He was attached, for example, to the army of the Meuse and Sambre, and found himself responsible for the equipment of some 80,000 men : " I know no more than my boot what I shall have to do," he observes ingenuously. But it is, in the main, of Paris that he writes ; and his observations, reflections, thoughts concerning the city and its people are not the least interesting portion of his diary. And in what is written the reader can trace the development of Tone's own character. The frankness is the same ; but the subjects of the frankness are more pleasing. The days of ' mugging porter,' which so horrified Mr Froude, are past : gentlemen do not bawl on Burgundy. " At night sent for a bottle of Burgundy intending to drink just one glass. Began to read (having opened my bottle) 'Memoirs of the Reign of Louis XIV.' After reading some time found my passion at a particular circumstance kindled rather more than necessary as I fling the book from me with indignation. Turned to my bottle to take a glass to cool me . . . found to my great astonishment that it was empty! Oh ho! got up and put everything in its place exactly . . . examined all my locks . . . saw that my door was fast, as there may be rogues in the hotel . . . peeped under my bed lest the enemy should surprise me there." How different from " to bed generally drunk."

We are apt to picture to ourselves the France, and especially the Paris, of early republican days, as enthusiastic, disorderly, poverty-stricken, insecure. Tone's picture is different. He notes at once that enthusiasm for revolution has abated; the people are more anxious to test the practical working of the new dispensation than to prate about its theoretic excellences. He marks the close, keen cultivation, and wonders why the same methods cannot be applied elsewhere with the same admirable results. Does he allow for the difference between the French and the Irish temperament? The Irishman eternally proclaims that, would the sky but fall, he would catch larks in plenty: until the sky falls, he, of course, can do nothing. The Frenchman, if he cannot catch all the larks that there are in the world, is satisfied to catch the few that he personally needs: accordingly he makes use of the first practical expedient that suggests itself. Living in France Tone found very good, and at

first incredibly cheap : ironically he wishes that
his daily bill of fare could be posted up in England
for the edification of John Bull. The reason for
the cheapness later becomes plain to him : a
man with English money in his pocket was in a
position very different from that of the man
whose income is from France and is paid in French
money. It was a shock to find that his pay as
Colonel in the French army was just £3. 2s. 6d.
per mensem ! Particularly interesting is an
account of a visit to a French Court of Justice.
Tone admits that, like most other people, he had
founded his ideas of French justice on the Revolutionary Tribunal, " that consummation of all
iniquity and horror." In reality he found scrupulous fairness and moderation : no doubt he lets
slip an unintended compliment when he says that
the judge charged his jury " with great moderation
and exactly in the language of the English
law ! "

For the French people, as distinct from the
liberators-to-be of Ireland, Tone seems to have
conceived little affection. At first the language
may have been a difficulty ; but in no long time
Tone was practically bilingual ; he spoke French,
he says, " like a Nabob." He was bitterly
conscious of his loneliness in the great city;
" There is not at this moment a man, woman
or child in Paris that cares one farthing if I
were hanged " ; perhaps he never consciously
grasped the fact that the superficially affable
French are of all peoples in the world the most
difficult to know. It is remarkable that in the
diary there is no trace of a *French* friend. Hoche

Tone liked ; but Hoche, he notes, rather kept him at a distance. In fact he seems to have had no real friend of any nationality in these last years. Of just one man we catch a glimpse sufficient to make us wish for " more love and knowledge of him." This is Colonel Shee, an Irishman who had spent his life in the service of France. Colonel Shee was an old man, and wellnigh crippled with gout ; but he hobbled aboard the *Fraternité* when Hoche set out for Ireland, and he lay down in a hammock in the hope that by the time his native land was in sight he would have recovered sufficiently to crack the head of at least one Saxon. A glorious old man !

Tone's one relaxation was the theatre, and especially the Opera. He notes how far the French are in advance of the English in that they dress their actors in costume appropriate to the time of the play. Tone had been accustomed to Shakespearian characters in red plush coats and full-buttomed wigs : what would he now think of Hamlet in ' plus fours.' And his frequenting of the theatre leads him to contemplate distastefully one pronounced feature of the French character. In the matter of women Tone, like many Irishmen, was a good deal of a prude : " It is a scandalous fact that many deputies have availed themselves of their position to secure the possession of beautiful women. *I do not like to see the Republic pimp for Legendre.*" He adds a thought which has occurred to others : " Give me my own fellow countrywomen : they are the material to make wives and mothers."

134

Hoche's ' gallantry,' much admired by his fellow
officers, did not the more endear him to Tone.

But he had the distraction of his work. Within
a few days of his arrival in Paris he had been
directed to set down his facts and proposals. He
composed two papers : they survive and may be
read. They are written in sober, business-like
language, and they show at once the accuracy
and inaccuracy of Tone's estimate of the character-
istics of the Irish people. From and for the
Protestant ' oligarchs ' he sees no hope : they
have settled their fate in an independent Ireland
by " disdaining the station they might have held
among the people and which the people would
have been glad to see them fill." These words
might have been written with truth a hundred
years later. He pins his faith mainly to the
Dissenters of the North : of these he says
shrewdly: "They see that while they thought
they were the masters of the Catholics, they were
in fact but their jailors, and that instead of
enjoying liberty in their own country they served
but as a garrison to keep her in subjection to
England." But as respects the Catholics of the
South, the vast majority of the Irish population,
Tone showed himself wholly mistaken. He
represented them to France as ready to rise, as
certain to flock to the standards of the French
invader. In fact it proved to be the other way :
when Hoche's formidable flotilla lay off the Kerry
coast, an English General found the disposition
of the people to be from his point of view ' admirable ' : they co-operated heartily in his
preparations for defence. Tone, though an Irish-

man, was a Dubliner, a ' towney ' ; he had really never mixed with the ' country people ' ; he did not understand them, and it is questionable whether anyone outside their own class has ever understood them. He thought that with fifteen, or, better still, with twenty thousand French troops success might be anticipated : five thousand would represent but a gambler's throw. He was ready to go himself with a corporal's guard.

The end and outcome of the business was strange : the facts certainly are known, but it is not so certain that they have been correctly interpreted. On December 15, 1796, Hoche sailed from Brest for Ireland at the head of a large and well-equipped force. On the first night at sea the *Fraternité* was separated from the main fleet : she carried the General and Colonel Shee, the latter no doubt hoping, if not against hope, at least against the gout. She never rejoined the fleet. The rest reached Ireland without seeing a single English vessel ; they hung for days about the Irish coast, so close to it that Tone declares that he could have tossed a biscuit ashore ; no attempt was made to land the army ; a wind sprang up ; and the expedition sailed back to France again without seeing an English ship. It is perhaps the most amazing instance of pusillanimity and military incompetence in history. Yet no one suggests that the French of those days were either cowardly or incapable !

One would have expected, especially in view of the strict account to which revolutionary France held her officers, some questioning of the returning warriors : it could scarcely have been a matter for surprise had the General commanding the troops, or the Admiral commanding the ships, or both, been shot. Apparently some questions were addressed to Grouchy, on whom, in the absence of Hoche, the military command had devolved. Grouchy asked Tone to write a testimonial, and there the matter ended.

At the very outset Tone noticed a decided lack of co-operation between naval and military chiefs : Hoche, in fact, got rid of his first Admiral and replaced him by another. The professional competence of the French naval officers was not impressive : " Captain Bedout is a seaman, which, I fancy, is more than can be said of nine-tenths of his *confrères.*" Of the disappearance of the *Fraternité* Tone remarks, " I believe it is the first instance of an Admiral in a clean frigate with moderate weather parting company with his fleet." But surely there is a limit to incapacity : the commander of the *Fraternité* can scarcely have been such an utter fool as to get lost *sans phrase* on a calm sea. He had the Commander-in-Chief on board : what more simple than to inquire the destination of the fleet—if he did not know it already—and proceed there ? That he could not find Kerry seems inconceivable.

Now the following facts and dates are significant. In October 1796 Lord Malmesbury came to Paris to propose peace on behalf of England to France. The position of England at the time is suggested by a contemporary who remarked that Malmesbury walked all the way to Paris on his knees. He was contemptuously rebuffed. In the summer of 1797 he came again to France, and met the plenipotentiaries of France at Lille. The terms offered by France were such as would have meant the effective end of England as a first-class Power. But at no time was any mention made of the liberty of Ireland, or of any Irish interest. Had France wished to renew the attempt at invasion, she let slip the priceless opportunity, pressed on her notice by Tone, of the mutiny in the English Fleet. It is perfectly clear that the interests of Ireland, real or supposed, troubled France and the French Directory no whit. And so a more tragic element is added to the already tragic comedy of Tone's life. In him there was no shadow of turning ; he was brave and capable ; his heart and soul were in the cause to which he had devoted himself. But for the French he was just a pawn in a game, an actor to keep the audience amused while the carpenters behind the front cloth are setting the stage for another and more important act.

What was really in the mind of the Directory at the time is very hard to say : possibly the Directors did not themselves know definitely. Ireland was a useful stick wherewith to threaten England ; but while some probably envisaged with enthusiasm the possibility of throwing a large army into Ireland, others may have reflected with less enthusiasm on the very probable im- possibility of getting the army out again. Hoche at the time seems to have been in earnest ; but then Hoche was an army chief, young, capable and ambitious. On such the Directory looked with no very kindly eye. Dumouriez had turned against the Republic; Pichegru was suspect, and later to turn; Hoche might be a useful servant; a not too disastrous failure might suggest to him that he was not yet master. And a spectre may have been rising to plague the dreams of civil authority : in a note of April 1796 recording the victory of Montenotte, Tone mentions that " the French General is Buonaparte, a Corsican ! "

" February 1 . . . 8, 1797. 1 think I am growing sprightly once more . . . but God knows the heart ! " A month later he writes that he leads the life of a dog ; he has not a soul to speak to ; there are half a dozen Irishmen in Paris, but they are " sad, vulgar wretches." Tone battled on bravely to the end, but the fire of hope had been quenched within him. The diary is still interesting, but the personal note is silent ; it is now the reflections of a detached observer, and of an observer much older than a man in the early thirties.

For a moment the fire flares up again ; in December 1796 he learns that Mrs Tone and the children have reached Hamburg ; he is all agog to meet his " Dearest Life "; it is strange and sad how the fire seems to flicker and die into grey ashes. Tone still holds rank in the French army ; he is attached to the army of the Meuse and Sambre ; he is for a moment pleased at the good report of his superior officers, *l'activité et la grande utilité de cet officier ont été attestées par le bureau des officiers généraux.* He leaves for his new army appointment ; seemingly he is in no great hurry for domestic reunion ; it is mid-

April ere he obtains leave and sets out for a meeting-place appointed in Holland. There is something of the old fun in his description of his journeyings in Dutch post waggons, something of the old eye for country in the reflections on Dutch farming. But soon he is sunk again in melancholy. In the ' Leyden Gazette ' he reads, *" quelques ménaçantes que soient souvent les dispositions des Irlandais, rarement on les a vu produire de bien terribles effets."* He shakes his head : " The devil of it is the observation is too well founded." On May 8 he met his wife ; and the tale of the meeting suggests how old and weary Tone had grown. He meets his wife ; he arranges that she and the children shall go to Paris ; he returns to Germany and to the army. That is all.

There is now an intermission in the diary : when it is resumed we find Tone aboard the Dutch ship *Vryheid* preparing for yet another attempt on Ireland. There is a touch of comic opera about the inception of this affair.

The French had conquered the Dutch : quite magnanimously they left it to the Dutch to decide on the form of their future Government. But the devil of it is, Tone notes, that no two Dutchmen can agree an any form of Government : it would be well were the French to come in and govern people who show themselves abjectly incapable of governing themselves. Savagely he adds that he would be quite willing to apply the prescription to his own country. He has changed in spirit from the days when he proudly informed General Clarke that French influence in the new Government of Ireland was what France could not expect and what Ireland could not allow.

But General Daendels and Admiral de Winter, the strong men of Holland, had a brilliant idea : they would do *something* to prove that the Dutch Republic was a power, that Holland was still entitled to an honoured place among the nations. Why not invade Ireland ? Why not indeed ?

The French offered no particular objection. Tone's friend Hoche was now at the Ministry of War : he showed Tone a letter from the Directory which bade him be confident that France " would make no peace with England wherein the interests of Ireland should not be fully discussed agreeably to the wishes of the people of that country." And Hoche in his position must have been aware of the Malmesbury negotiations in which the name of Ireland was not so much as mentioned ! Tone brought another matter to the notice of General Hoche, a " grossly improper and indecent " proclamation of General Buonaparte to the Government of Genoa : such minatory language addressed to freeborn Irishmen could not but have a disastrous effect. General Hoche quite agreed : Buonaparte, he assured Tone, " was his scholar and certainly never would be his master." But about stiffening the Dutch invaders with French troops General Hoche was not quite so sure. The discipline aboard Dutch ships was said to be very strict ; it was not quite certain that the fraternal and equal soldiers of the Republic would endure it willingly or endure it at all ; if the Dutch Admiral could not apply discipline to one portion of his force, how could he apply it to another ? Tone recognised the force of the objection, and withdrew : did the thought ever cross his mind that Hoche was growing weary of him ? But it was not Tone's way to think ill of any man who had been, who still professed to be, his friend : he only noted with compassion that Hoche was a dying man. Hoche died of rapid consumption a few months later.

So Tone found himself at the Texel busied with preparations for the start. There was no Burgundy to drink (though Burgundy is never mentioned now), no Opera to visit, no friends to talk to. But there was a soul in one respect akin to his own : Admiral de Winter played the flute, and he and Tone chased monotony with melodious tootlings.

The end of the great Dutch expedition was even more comically ineffective than that of the French. The stores piled up, the troops were got aboard. But steadily the wind blew into the river preventing the Dutch from getting out ; and as steadily, with the favouring wind behind them, the English ships came sailing up. " Hell, hell," Tone raves hysterically in his diary. The English Admiral sends in an officer with a flag of truce, nominally to inquire about some petty regulation affecting neutral commerce, really to see how things are getting on. The Dutch Admiral, not to be outdone, sends out *his* messenger with a flag of truce : the messenger returning can only report that the English are in fine fettle, and daily growing stronger. A few months earlier the discipline of the English seamen had cracked ominously : the opportunity had been lost, and was never to come again. The provisions had been eaten up; the troops cannot be kept indefinitely aboard ship and inactive; there was nothing to do save disembark, and wait for something to turn up. Wearily Tone wanders away: he learns later that in defiance of common sense, with everything to lose and nothing to gain, the Dutch fleet had sallied forth, attacked the English, and had been sent to the bottom of the sea. Treachery somewhere, Tone observes.

He made his way back to Paris, and there in December 1797 he meets the Man of Destiny. " He is about five feet six inches in height, slender and well made; but stoops considerably; he looks at least ten years older than he is owing to the fatigues he underwent in his immortal campaign of Italy. His face is that of a profound thinker, but bears no mark of that great enthusiasm and unceasing activity by which he has been so much distinguished. It is rather to my mind the countenance of a mathematician than of a General." But from Buonaparte no help was to be had : his manner was cold, and he was curt when Ireland was mentioned; his eyes already were fixed on the East, and the Directory was only too anxious to speed him on an eastward voyage.

Henceforth, until its last tragic moments, Tone's life was to be a dreary one. There is nothing now about his wife and family : had Mrs Tone, one wonders, come to realise that the cause was hopeless, was she growing weary of her husband's obsession ? In May Tone offers to go to India :

143

France, he supposes, will make some provision
for his family. "My blood is cooling fast : my
May of life is falling to the sear, the yellow leaf."
Still in French military service he gets his baptism
of fire at Havre, and notes his sensations with a
curious detached amusement. He falls to sombre
musings over the past : he recalls the names

> Of all the lost adventurers, my peers . . .
> How such a one was strong, and such was bold,
> And such was fortunate, yet each of old
> Lost, lost.

Lord Edward, Arthur O'Connor, Hamilton Rowan,
Reynolds, Neilson : dead, exiled, imprisoned.
All gone. Just once a spark flashed as flint
strikes steel. He reads contemptuously Lord
Moira's pleadings for the United Irishmen. They
were but constitutional reformers, patriots, perhaps a little over-enthusiastic, but rebels—oh
dear no. There rises up a little man with piercing
grey eyes : the United Irishmen *are* rebels, they
would by force overturn the Government of
Ireland : they have asked for war—they can
have it. And Tone smiles grimly : John Fitzgibbon at any rate is a man ; he asks for no
quarter, and he will give none. Tone was soon
to learn how true his thought was.

He calls on General Kilmaine : he is coldly
received. The General has no good account of
the Irishmen in Paris : they are "mainly rascals."
Poor Tone : he did not realise that he had become
a bore.

"June 20. My birthday. I had hopes two

years ago. I have neglected no step. I will persevere to the last."

In August 1798 General Humbert, a rough French soldier of fortune, apparently without any very definite orders or purpose made a dash for the Irish coast. He had about a thousand men under his command, and with him sailed Barclay Teeling and Matthew Tone, he whom "we called the Spectator from his short face and his silence." He landed at Killala; unlike Grouchy, he found no difficulty in the operation; at Castlebar he defeated General Lake, whose forces fled with such enthusiasm that their battle has gained immortal fame as "The Race of Castlebar"; he even won another small success. But the issue never was, never could be, in doubt: poor as the troops under Lake's command might be, if they but turned and pelted stones their numbers must tell. Seventeen days after his landing Humbert surrendered. He and his Frenchmen of course were treated as prisoners of war. Matthew Tone and Teeling were hurried away, and summarily hanged. In September Napper Tandy and a few of his kidney sailed for Ireland in a fast boat. They certainly landed; they distributed (*more suo*) a few high-falutin' proclamations to all whom such proclamations might concern, and—they sailed away. Tandy is said to have been drunk when he came ashore, and still drunker when he re-embarked. Yet at Paris poor Tone had said of Tandy all that he could find of good to say. Tandy's claim to be an *ancien militaire* Tone found it hard to swallow or defend; but at least Tandy had held a commission in the Irish Volunteers. *Grand propriétaire* was a self-description scarcely less controvertible ; but Tandy had some means of living else he would scarcely be alive. Tone was charitable to all men—except perhaps to the Pope! In his darkest days of depression the defender of the Irish Catholics whooped with joy when he heard of the dethronement of the Holy Father.

At the tail of the tragic procession came the tragic victim. After Humbert came Hardy with a few thousand men : Heaven knows what purpose these senseless pinpricks at the English in Ireland were supposed to serve. They sighted an English fleet : quite rightly Hardy ordered his few ships to scatter and fly. But Bompart, who commanded the *Hoche* (a queer coincidence of name), was of different and tougher fibre. He had come for a fight, and he intended to have one. Tone was aboard Bompart's ship : on him, at least, the Frenchman urged the prudence, the justifiability of flight. Tone, to be sure, held a French commission ; but that, his fellow officers suspected, would scarcely avail at the end. And there was little doubt what the end would be. Tone would have none of it. He had declared again and again that he would come to Ireland were it with but a corporal's guard : well, he had kept his promise, and now he was in no mind for quibbling. It may be that he had lost the desire to live. The tragi-comedy was nearing its end : he had no mind that the curtain should go down on a note of ignoble farce.

Bompart fought the *Hoche* like an infuriated

devil, fought till his yards were shot away, his hull splintered, and his decks awash with blood. And at a gun Tone fought unflaggingly. *Selig der den er im siegesglanze findet ;* that good fortune was not Tone's ; he was not to die in battle's splendour. When nothing more could be done, the *Hoche* in some way signified surrender. It can hardly have been by the conventional hauling down of the flag : Bompart before he went into action had nailed his flag to the mast.

The survivors were taken ashore ; for two days Tone with the other French officers was hospitably entreated. No one recognised him : it is possible that no one *wanted* to recognise him. The soldiers and sailors probably knew that his position was a delicate one, and they would have no mind to embarrass an adversary who had fought a clean and open fight. But recognised he was in the end : some say that imprudently he inquired after a mutual acquaintance, others that he was tired of the comedy, perhaps had not the nerve to play it out and see what might befall.

He was fettered and carried to Dublin. There he was tried by court-martial as a rebel in arms against his sovereign : he was found guilty, and he was sentenced to death. The trial appears to have been scrupulously fair ; the officers who formed the Court treated Tone with courtesy. Tone, for his part, attempted no defence ; he accepted facts which were undeniable ; " The Court," he said, " will do its duty ; I shall not be found wanting to mine." But whatever the facts, the form of the trial was none the less a judicial murder.

Tone, in a word, was either a French officer, or he was not. If his French commission was in order—as apparently it was—he had committed no offence for which he could be tried by any Court. If it were held that he had never acquired French nationality—and it seems to have been so—then he was triable indeed, but triable only before the regularly constituted Courts of the kingdom. That the verdict, the sentence, would inevitably have been the same does not affect the argument.

One request Tone did make : he asked that he might be shot like a soldier, not hanged like a felon. The request was refused.

Sentence was passed on the evening of November 10 : on the morning of November 12 Tone was to die. On that morning John Curran moved in the King's Bench for a writ of *Habeas Corpus*. The presiding judge, Lord Kilwarden, at once agreed : at Curran's suggestion he despatched an officer to the jail with a message that a writ was being prepared, and with an order that the execution be deferred pending its issue. The messenger returned to say that the superintendent of the jail refused to obey the order of the Court : Kilwarden promptly despatched another officer with orders to take both Tone and the superintendent into custody. It was then announced that Tone the night before had cut his own throat, and was in the article of death.

The suggestion has been made that the case was one of murder, not of suicide. There seems to be no foundation for the suggestion : to put the matter at its lowest, the Government, had it decided on this crime, would not have bungled it so hopelessly. Tone lingered in agony for three or four days.

From his prison he commended his wife and family generally to the French Republic, and in particular to a friend named Wilson. To his wife he wrote a touching letter of farewell: he bade her be of good cheer; he had fought the good fight, and kept the faith. It does not appear that he saw his father: he wrote that a last meeting could only give pain to both.

He was buried in an unmarked grave in Bodenstown churchyard. Many years afterwards his widow married Mr Wilson. Two of his children died at an early age; a son became an officer in the armies of Napoleon.

LORD EDWARD FITZGERALD

1763-1798

"Woe, he went galloping into the war."
—BROWNING.

CHAPTER I.

THE CADET.

THE Irish have always had a peculiar fondness
for ' the ginthry ' ; this may be a reason why the
name of Lord Edward Fitzgerald awakened and
still awakens a thrill in hearts which the names of
greater men leave irresponsive. Of an ingenious
attorney in '98 it is related that, bound for
Dublin on business, he found himself stranded
in a village twenty miles outside the capital with
little hope of getting farther. Not a chaise, not
a horse was procurable, the posting-master informed him : all were bespoken. Dramatically
the attorney struck his hand to his forehead :
" My God, Lord Edward, shall I then be too late
to serve you," he moaned audibly. " Michael,"
roared the posting-master to one of his myrmidons,
" the best carriage and pair for the gentleman in
five minutes." The attorney sped on his way :
it is to be presumed that he selected another
road for his homeward journey. This is not
mere snobbery : no people are slower than the
Irish to worship a lord as such, none are quicker
to distinguish gilding from true gold. But a long
heritage of gentle blood usually does confer
some peculiar gentleness in the inheritor ; and
to be so universally beloved Lord Edward must

have been lovable. John Fitzgibbon was on the unpopular side in politics ; but would the people have detested him so heartily had not his speech and demeanour in moments of unguarded anger suggested that somewhere in him there was some ' common dhrop.' Wolfe Tone was the son of a Dublin tradesman : in '98 Lord Edward's name had ranked for six hundred years among the greatest in the land.

The Fitzgeralds, though long domiciled in Ireland, were not Irish by origin. They were Norman - Welsh or Welsh - Norman, and they came to Ireland prowlers in the train of Dermot MacMurrough and precursors of Strongbow. One of their tribe, though not by name a Fitzgerald, has won a curious immortality. The background of the centuries rolls by, but against it Gerald Barry, or du Barri, stands immovably planted on his head. He is the theologian *Cambrensis eversus :* there may be few living persons who have ever read a line that he wrote, but probably there are still fewer who have not heard his name. The Fitzgeralds throve in Ireland ; they founded the dynasties of Kildare and Desmond ; and for a considerable period the Earls of Kildare practically ruled a large portion of Southern Ireland under a somewhat nominal overlordship of the English King. Turbulent people, even for those days, they seem to have been. Earl Garrett, charged with burning the church of Cashel, thus answered his accusers, " By God I burned it because I thought the Archbishop was inside it." To the complaints of his Ministers in Ireland that all Ireland could not rule the Earl of Kildare, English

Henry answered, "Then in God's name let the Earl of Kildare rule all Ireland."

There are some curious coincidences—they are nothing more—in the history of the Fitzgeralds. The first parliamentary attainder on the Irish Statute Book is that of a Fitzgerald : the crime charged against him was treason, to wit, the besieging of Dublin Castle with one O'Connor. Almost the last, if not actually the last, attainder must be that of Lord Edward Fitzgerald. His plan for the overthrowing of the Irish Government of his day must have included the seizing of Dublin Castle, and an early colleague of his conspiracy was Arthur O'Connor. Garrett Fitzgerald, known as the Great Earl, had distinguished himself by an uncomplimentary reference to an Archbishop : Lord Edward's father, the last Earl of Kildare, is known to history by the remonstrance which he addressed to King George II. against the Protestant Primate of Ireland. Archbishop Stone the Earl described as "a greedy churchman, investing himself with temporal power, and affecting to be a second Wolsey in the State." The Earl was not far wrong in his estimate of the Archbishop : "This man," says Froude, "was for many years the virtual dictator of Ireland." Abominable charges were made against his private character : of these Froude acquits him, but adds sardonically, "of his virtues (for some virtues it is to be supposed he possessed) history has preserved no record." Earl James, father of Lord Edward and twentieth of his line, was the last Earl of Kildare in the sense that he became the first Duke of Leinster.

There is a portrait of him by Reynolds : His Grace stands in an attitude of expostulation (possibly he is confronting Stone), and the expression on his face is suggestive of a startled oyster.

The Duke embarked, perhaps unwittingly, on an adventure more strenuous than that of bearding Primates. In 1747, when he was twenty-five years of age, he married Lady Emily Lennox, daughter of the Duke of Richmond. She was a remarkable woman in the married state, and the marriages of her sisters were equally remarkable. One married Lord Holland, and thus brought Charles James Fox within the circle of Fitzgerald cousinship. Lady Sarah Lennox married Colonel Napier. But, unless popular report is very much mistaken, she might have been, had she so chosen, the wife of George III., and Queen (probably Parliament and people would have accepted her) of England. Lady Sarah (" Sal ") and her Colonel were as poor as Church rats, but another sister, Lady Louisa, married Tom Conolly, reputed to be the richest commoner in Ireland. Duchess Emily enjoyed or was afflicted by a devouring passion for maternity. She married at fifteen, she lived with her Duke for twenty-six years, and in that period of time she presented him with eighteen children. After his death she married again at the age of forty-two or forty-three, and added two more daughters to the tale of her progeny. Her labours in the cause of humanity do not seem to have affected her health, for she lived to the age of eighty-two. She was a singularly beautiful woman.

To be born of such a mother and into such a family must have had its effect on Lord Edward. He was quite distinctively his mother's darling, but the jostling of the tribe—it was a tribe rather than a family—must have saved him from any danger of mollycoddling. And the size of the family must have taught him, without his knowing it, the value of money. The Duke, no doubt, was a well-to-do man, but in such a household there can have been little money to burn. From his earliest years of manhood Lord Edward shows in his letters a prudent care about his income. There was nothing of meanness or closefistedness about the man ; but debt, in which the sprigs of nobility in his day wallowed, he frankly abhorred. And the abiding influence of his mother is seen in the fact that Lord Edward, though nothing of a prig or squaretoes, was a most attractively 'good' young man. The solemn apologies of his biographers for the fact that he was once known to have been decidedly drunk are quite unnecessary ; indeed the episode, as narrated by his sprightly aunt, Lady Sal Napier, is amusing rather than deplorable. There came to Lady Sal's house, just as she was about to go to bed, a party : it comprised Eddy's uncle (" drunk as an owl "), two colonels (" whom I had never seen ") and Eddy himself (" as drunk as his uncle "). Lady Sal was a strategist ; instead of vainly remonstrating, she plied the party with strong beer " to make them drunker " ; we may assume that her general idea was that they would either depart on a frolic or slide silently under the table, and in either case leave her to her repose. Eddy, she relates, ate voraciously and " drank like four " ; but he must have carried his liquor well, for his aunt describes him as her " only comfort " on the occasion.

And though Eddy was incurably sentimental, there was never anything of vulgarity or promiscuity in his love affairs. To his first love he was fickle, in his second he was disappointed, the third he married, and good-naturedly loved to his life's end. But his mother was the dominating female influence on his life. And it was not just a sweetly sentimental influence : the matriarch was formidably competent to make herself feared. One of her daughters, Lady Sophia, kept a diary : she named this diary oddly her " Bub," an allusion to Bubb Doddington, a wit of the day. From this we learn that Lady Sophia was bidden to a ball at the house of Lady Bective, and that the etiquette of the day demanded that, before setting out, she should present herself to her mother in her ball-dress. But her chaperone and sister-in-law, the young Duchess of Leinster, was in a hurry, and whisked the girl into her coach and away. Poor Lady Sophia, with premonitions of disaster in her soul, did not enjoy her ball ; in fact she could only muster up sufficient spirit to dance " one set." Next day, the diary informs us, the Dowager received her daughter " very coolly," and " told me how very much displeased she was with my behaviour to her." The end of it all was that poor Lady Sophia " cried most part of the night," although she calls Heaven to witness that she was entirely innocent of any intention to offend.

Indirectly the influence of mother and family may have been not entirely for practical good. Such a prodigious family, and especially one of such exalted social station, is apt to become ' a clan,' to lose touch with the world outside itself, to regard itself as governed by its own laws. The Fitzgeralds were a loving family, but a self-centred one : " the good family " one of the clan prettily names them in her letters. Lord Edward was adventurous, but it is doubtful whether he ever got quite clear of the Fitzgerald pool and into the open sea. He certainly was *in* the United Irishmen, but it is not so certain that he was quite *of* them : in fact it is not certain that he ever took the United Irishman's oath. His rank was an undoubted asset to the cause, and his military capacity was recognised as likely to be of great value in the almost inevitable event of conflict with the armed forces of the Crown. But somehow Lord Edward does not seem to have been able to gain and utilise the full confidence of those with whom he conspired. It was not that they doubted him—no sane man could have suspected Lord Edward of wavering or treachery—but between him and them a gulf was fixed. In his last days he seems to have had little grip of actual facts, little awareness of how matters actually stood. He was a General ready to lead, but a General very badly informed of the temper, equipment, preparedness of those who were to follow. And another point is to be noted. In letters exchanged between his relatives after his arrest there is perhaps some hint of surprise that the law should touch Lord Edward Fitzgerald, some expectation that against him the law will not be enforced so rigorously as it justifiably might be against a mere member of the common herd. What was surprise in Lord Edward's relations may have been suspicion in Lord Edward's adherents. Men embarked together on a desperate enterprise, but who suspect that their leader risks less than they do themselves, are likely to prove lukewarm followers.

Lord Edward's life was too short to admit of much change in his appearance after he reached man's estate. He was inclined to plumpness ; at one time, when for a short period he lived in a Kildare cottage domestically and cultivated his garden, his aunt, Lady Sal Napier, remarks that he was growing " as fat as a pig." This is how he appeared to the man at whose house in Thomas Street, Dublin, he was at last taken by the officers of the law : " He was about five feet seven inches in height, with a very interesting countenance ; beautiful arched eyebrows, fine grey eyes, a beautiful nose and high forehead, thick dark-coloured hair, brown or inclining to black. He was altogether a very nice and elegant formed man."

When Lord Edward was but eleven years old an event occurred in the household which certainly had an after influence on him, but which really seems to have fluttered Irish society in general rather more than it did " the good family." The Duchess, scarcely twelve months a widow, remarried ; and she, reputed to be the proudest woman in Ireland, chose for her second husband the tutor or servant of her children. The judgment of the uninstructed world probably was that an amorous fool, oblivious of self-respect, had married a handsome underling ; that a rascal had swallowed general contempt and eighteen step-children for the licking of a rich platter. In fact the matter was far otherwise. Mr William Ogilvy—this was the gentleman's name—was neither servile nor physically prepossessing : Lady Sarah Napier describes him as " very ugly and with a disagreeable manner." This may be family prejudice, but there is independent testimony.

The ducal children—or some of them—were not thriving at Leinster House : it is just possible that the Duchess herself began to find the eighteen pledges of her departed Duke's affection somewhat a trial of her patience and a tax on her strength. Although indeed she says, and doubtless with perfect truthfulness, that on each of the eighteen " my heart spent itself in maternal passion." She conceived the very sensible idea of sending an assorted half-dozen—in what spacious figures the Duchess could afford to think—to her country house at Blackrock, and she informed her friend, Lady Leitrim, that for their care " I have discovered a very worthy person, a Scotsman who has kept a school in Dublin, and was recommended to me by Dean Marley." Lady Leitrim was paying a call at Leinster House when the " very worthy person " first presented himself. An upper servant announced that the usher had arrived (probably he had been admitted by the servants' entrance) and was in the hall awaiting Her Grace's orders. Her Grace's orders were that the person be shown to a room, and supplied with tallow, *not* wax, candles. But the giving of those orders was interrupted by the sudden irruption of the person himself : " Your lackeys have left me standing in the hall," he said, " so I have made my way to your presence." A man who did not suffer willingly the careless insolence of menials. Lady Leitrim draws this picture of him : " Careless in his attire, unshaven, his shoes bearing the mud of the street, his hair unpowdered, he walked up the long room dragging with him a bag which doubtless contained his whole luggage." And Lady Leitrim, doubtless with a certain feeling of pleasurable anticipation, waited to see the intruder struck dead or dumb by the voice or eye of the proudest woman in Ireland. But the lightnings did not flash, the vials of Her Grace's wrath were not outpoured. The Duchess again directed that the visitor be shown to his room : " and *wax* candles," she murmured to her flunkey. It must have been a strange moment : perhaps for the first time in her life the daughter of one Duke and the widow of another was confronted by a man of the people composedly courteous but composedly conscious of his own dignity.

Mr Ogilvy took a squad of the Leinster children to Blackrock. He taught them their letters, he went a-riding with them, he interested them in gardening, he saw that their hair was brushed and their faces clean. And he saved the life of little Lady Mabel Fitzgerald. She was struck down by that scourge of the age, the small-pox : when the Duchess arrived at the sick-bed (she was no fearer of infection from her children) she found Mr Ogilvy nursing the child practically alone. But his greatest service had been " saying in his short way ' blethers ' " to the doctor who protested that fresh air was poison to the sufferer, and throwing the windows open. Thus the marriage came about.

It was, after all, the private affair of the Duchess and of Mr Ogilvy. They were old enough to know their own minds, to follow their own inclinations. Society was horrified ; and the Duke of Richmond's offer of a house at Aubigny in France may have been dictated by a desire to get his sister and her uncouth husband for a season at least out of his sight and thoughts. The " good family " seem to have accepted their step-father without demur ; it is possible that without their knowing it the strength of his character imposed acceptance on them. Twenty years later the Duchess writing to one of her Fitzgerald children (by this time Mimi and Cissy Ogilvy had their recognised place in " the good family ") speaks of Mr Ogilvy as " your dear papa," and rejoices that some little misunderstanding between step-daughter and step-father had been happily ended. On Lord Edward the influence of Mr Ogilvy seems to have been altogether good. Mr Ogilvy was an extremely efficient pedagogue—Lord Edward, by no means badly educated, admits that he never learned half so much from anyone else—and an admirable trainer of character. Lord Edward, when he joined the army, wrote to his step-father a cordial letter of thanks for " your affection for me in forming my principles and helping my understanding." And quite clearly Mr Ogilvy was no more a mere sentimentalist than was his wife. The Duchess with half rueful comicality writes to a daughter under Mr Ogilvy's displeasure for the moment, that with no one has " dear papa " been half so angry at times as with " dearest Eddy." And dearest Eddy himself recalls Mr Ogilvy's warning to his mother that by over-indulgence she might yet be " the ruin of the boy."

A lordling in eighteenth-century Ireland who did not elect to eat the bread of idleness had no very wide choice of occupation open to him. The mere suggestion of trade or commerce would have chilled the marrow in ducal bones. Of the learned professions, medicine as yet was held in no high esteem. Law and Divinity were more respectable ; but if it is difficult to picture Lord Edward Fitzgerald as a barrister, it is beyond the wildest flight of imagination to endow him with the gown and bands of a clerk in Holy Orders. There remained but the army ; and in young Edward's case the choice had much more than its inevitability to recommend it. The boy was a born soldier : his cousin, Charles James Fox, was not guilty of over-statement when he declared in the English House of Commons that " the service did not possess a more zealous, meritorious, and promising member." There was, of course, no scheme of systematic education for the would-be officer of those days ; but when young Edward Fitzgerald joined his regiment (the 96th) in 1781 he probably was a cadet singularly well instructed for his time, and quite well instructed for any time. His sagacious step-father, William Ogilvy, had observed the boy's taste for soldiering and especially for military engineering, and had encouraged both. As a ' schoolboy ' of sixteen Edward on a visit to his uncle, Duke of Richmond and Master of Ordnance, writes to his mother that there had been some considerable trouble about pitching the camp of a regiment, but that the section entrusted to him by his uncle had been found correct to an inch. In his earliest years of service the fortifications of the Island of St Lucia—or rather the want of them—excite his interest, and he bewails that his General is hampered by three engineers who seem stolidly incapable of *doing* anything. The observant eye which he cast on the defences of Cadiz during a Continental tour led to his being offered by Pitt the command of an expedition against Cadiz. The rejection of this offer, hereafter to be described, was the disastrous turning-point of his life.

And in a general way Edward came forth from the tutorial wing of Mr Ogilvy a well-educated lad. No one can read his early letters and fail to notice not only their perfect spelling and grammar — accomplishments probably by no means common among the gilded youth of the time—but also their admirable literary style. The relations that existed, the friendly sparring that took place between step-son and step-father, between pedagogue and pupil, may be inferred from this passage in a letter : " I am not affronted by your remark on ' a paucity of ideas ' and ' an empty skull,' and agree with you that they are great blessings ! Notwithstanding you declare you did not mean me, yet I do plead a little guilty to a paucity of ideas."

And above all, Edward had the true spirit of a soldier. Family influence could then do a good deal, and the boy quite frankly hopes that " Mr Ogilvy and you [his mother] won't forget to remind my brother [the Duke] about a company." A company at eighteen ! But on one point he is quite clear. If a company or any other form of advancement should stand in the way of his getting to the front and into active service, he will have none of such things.

The front, the active service, of the time was the last phase of England's struggle against her American colonies. A great deal of sentimental nonsense has been written about this first military service of Lord Edward Fitzgerald. " Ah ! I was wounded then in a very different cause : that was fighting against liberty, this is fighting for it," he is reported to have said to a visitor when he lay dying in a Dublin prison. If his own brother was denied admittance, is it likely that a casual visitor was allowed to enter ? It is unlikely that the subaltern of eighteen thought at all about ' the cause '—his only concern was with the fighting—if he thought then or later, his thoughts may have been those of that sad ironist, George Warrington, hero of ' The Virginians ' : " Braddock's expedition failed in consequence of the remissness, the selfishness, the rapacity of many of the very people for whose defence against the French arms had been taken up. The colonists

were for having all done for them, and for doing
nothing."

But, whatever his thoughts, to the front Lord
Edward Fitzgerald went. His earlier keenness
can be judged from his letters to his mother while
he was serving the first days of his apprenticeship
in Ireland. He is marching twenty miles a day
over rugged mountains ; he has struck up a
friendship with Captain Giles, "who is most
anxious to improve me as an officer." Such a
boy, if he escaped the mischances of battle,
should go far. But in America there was little
glory to be won. The struggle was wellnigh
at its end, and the energy of a lieutenant could
do little against the slackness and incompetence
of a number of Generals. Nevertheless Edward
managed to earn a severe reprimand, which was
really a very high commendation, for his reckless
bravery ; and he fell severely wounded at Eutaw
Springs, the last engagement of the war. This
had a curious sequel. Edward was picked up,
carried into safety, and tended by a casual
negro ; and the pair were never again parted.
'Tony' was his faithful servant for the rest of
his life : indeed Tony's devotion later proved
to be a source of danger to his master. For
Tony's black face was a conspicuous object in
the streets of Dublin ; and, however securely
Lord Edward Fitzgerald might be hidden, the
officers of the law could feel fairly well assured
that from where Tony was Lord Edward could
not be very far distant.

Recovered from his wounds Lord Edward

visited the West Indies on the staff of General
O'Hara. About 1783 he reaches home once more,
and for a year or two his life is outwardly un-
eventful. A young officer, brave, intelligent, keen
on his profession, and with immensely powerful
family connections, might seem to be floating
safely on the tide that flows into the haven of
fame. But beneath the surface of the tide
cross currents were tugging at him. These
currents were love and politics.

Lord Edward Fitzgerald was always, and
always quite honourably, in love. If letters can
be taken to represent trees, he certainly—

> carved on every tree
> The fair, the chaste, the inexpressive she.

To be sure it was not always the same ' she.'

The first was ' Kate,' or Lady Katherine Mead,
daughter of the Earl of Clanwilliam. Young
Eddy hopes that his mother will be kind to
" dear, pretty Kate " : " My dearest mother, I
want you to love her as much as I do." Mr
Ogilvy has been calling on Lord Edward, and
Lord Edward " makes him talk of Kate whether
he will or not." If Shakespeare was one of
Mr Ogilvy's studies, that hard-headed gentleman,
when he read or heard his wife read one of Eddy's
later letters, may have recalled Friar Laurence's
sardonic merriment at the expense of young
Romeo :—

> Jesu Maria, what a deal of brine
> Hath wash'd thy sallow cheeks for Rosaline !

For thus it was written : " I am glad sweetest

Kate is grown fat. I love her more than anything yet, though I have seen a great deal of Georgina."

Yet. Oh, Eddy, Eddy!

It is fair to say that the fickle swain did not leave a broken-hearted maiden to sigh her soul out for her lover's faithlessness. Lady Katherine thought little more about Lord Edward, if indeed she had ever thought about him at all. She married the Earl of Powerscourt.

Georgina was his first cousin, Georgina Lennox, daughter of Lord George Lennox, the brother of the Duke of Richmond and of the Duchess of Leinster. And Edward loved Georgina probably as deeply as he ever loved any woman other than his own mother. To her he was constant through years of discouragement. For the course of true love did not run smoothly. Young Edward gallantly proposed marriage : Georgina with eighteenth-century coyness referred him to papa. Alas, papa did not welcome the suitor cordially. Perhaps Lord George had a eugenic prejudice against first cousin marriages, perhaps he considered young Fitzgerald to be from a worldly point of view an extremely ineligible husband for his daughter. The Duke of Richmond championed Eddy's cause, but it skilled not. Lord George took up his pen. He addressed himself to " my dear lord," and he subscribed himself, " with great truth, my dear lord, your affectionate uncle." But this is a chilling passage : " With respect, therefore, to the manner of your proposal, it was not so material to me from the perfect security I always feel in my daughter's conduct ; and as to the propriety of yours, which you are so good as to say you hope I approve of, it is now needless to enter, since you did not think it necessary to consult me on it before."

Chiefs have lived before and after Agamemnon, and young men have been crossed in love before and after Lord Edward Fitzgerald. But rebuffed at home he may perhaps have been a little too ready to accept what Fortune offered abroad. For the moment Edward departed to Canada— Africa and big game had not yet disclosed themselves to disconsolate lovers—and when he reached home once more it was to find Georgina wedded to Lord Apsley.

He went to Canada on military service. There was no fighting to be done, but the true soldierly spirit peeps out of letters which suggest his constant care for the welfare of his men. To his work at this time a remarkable man paid later a remarkable compliment, and in so doing reflected grimly on the average British officer of the period. " He was," said an ex-sergeant-major, " the only really honest officer I have ever known." The sergeant-major was William Cobbett, and he was speaking to William Pitt.

Sledging, skating, moose hunting, exploring helped to pass the monotony of peace-time soldiering. Young Edward blazed a new trail from Frederickstown to Quebec : when he and his companions reached Quebec, " we had not shaved or washed during the journey ; our blankets, coats and trousers all worn out and pieced ; in short we went to two or three houses and they would not let us in." He was adopted into the Bear Tribe under the name of Eghnidal; and he wrote charming letters to his mother. The matriarch must have felt that she would have been assured of a warm welcome in this new land when she read that " in the backwoods the more children a man has the better : his wife being brought to bed is as joyful news as his cow calving." And she may have smiled at a picture of herself as a mother in squawdom smoking her pipe, while Mimi and Cissy Ogilvy fetch wood and water, and Ladies Sophy and Lucy Fitzgerald clean and cook the fish. He made a long journey through the American States on his homeward way ; and reached his mother's house in London to find that Georgina and her newly-wedded husband were dining there. And now the tide of politics began to sweep him towards the rocks.

Lord Edward Fitzgerald had been returned to, appointed to, or at any rate brought into the Irish Parliament by his brother, the Duke of Leinster, as Member for Athy. One may marvel at a parliamentary system which tolerated bestowal by dukes of seats at their sweet will and pleasure ; but was it really so different in practical effect from a system which permitted bestowal of seats by a so-called National Directory more than a hundred years later ? The free and independent elector of Ireland has never had much voice in the choosing of his representatives ! For a year or two his parliamentary duties seem to have weighed lightly on Lord Edward : his first significant allusion to politics is found in one of

his letters from Canada: " After the part dear
Leinster has acted, I should have been ashamed
to show my face in Ireland." And this is the
story of " dear Leinster " and of his part : the
story is typical and illustrative of eighteenth-
century Irish politics.

Robert, second Duke of Leinster, in his way,
was not a bad sort of man. He is said to have
been a good landlord : at any rate he lived in
Ireland, and spent in Ireland the revenues which
he drew from the country. He was also in some
measure a man of liberal opinions. He took the
chair at meetings of the Irish Volunteers; he put
his signature to a non-importation agreement
directed against England; to the British administration of England conducted by the Duke of
Rutland (with the aid of Mr John Fitzgibbon !)
he stood in an attitude of aloofness and opposition.
But with the coming of the Marquess of Buckingham the Duke modified his views. He drew
nearer to the Government, and it was this which
so provoked the indignation of his younger
brother. Really there was nothing in the least
reprehensible in the action. The Government of
Ireland being constituted as it was, opposition
to that Government was little more than a
perpetual and futile sterility. Mere sentiment
apart, a great Irish nobleman might have
served his country honestly and well by lending
his support to the Government, and by imperceptibly influencing that Government from
within.

But while it may have been possible to do
honest actions in Irish politics, it apparently was

quite impossible to do them honestly. "Dear Leinster's" affability was at once recognised by the Marquess of Buckingham by the gift of the great legal office of Master of the Rolls! Does the juxtaposition of the names Leinster and Buckingham recall an earlier juxtaposition of the names Buckinghamshire and Leinster? For in 1779 "dear Leinster" had waited on the then Viceroy, the Earl of Buckinghamshire: "The Duke," wrote Lord Buckinghamshire to England, "has been with me this morning, and presents his compliments. His brother, the seaman, being promoted is a point insisted on!"

Lord Edward, however, would have none of a brother who could obtemper to the British oppressor. And—very much to his honour—he informs Mr Ogilvy that he will accept no military promotion or other favour offered to him through his brother's influence. But he writes: "Though I think Leinster wrong, and told him so beforehand, yet, as he *has* taken that part, it would be wrong not to support him, we being certainly his members, and brought in by him with the idea that he might depend on our always acting with him." *Plus ça change, plus c'est la même chose.* The ducal brother in the eighteenth century, the democratic caucus in the twentieth!

But "dear Leinster" redeemed himself: says a historian of those days, "He returned to his natural allegiance." In the matter of the Regency he upheld the independence of the Irish Parliament: he was one of the deputation chosen to proceed to England and to invite George, Prince

of Wales, to assume the regency of Ireland untrammelled by any restrictions which the English
Parliament might seek to impose. And for his
gallant defence of the rights of Ireland the Duke
suffered: when George III. came (more or less)
to his wits, the Duke was deprived of his Master-
ship of the Rolls. But he was restored to his
younger brother's esteem: did poor, gallant,
straightforward Edward ever read, one wonders,
a letter addressed by Mr Charles James Fox to
another brother, Lord Henry Fitzgerald? With
George, Prince of Wales, as Regent, Mr Fox is
confident that he himself will return to his old
office of Foreign Affairs; and "one of the first
acts of the Regency will be to make Edward
lieutenant-colonel; and, if a scheme which is in
agitation takes place, I think I shall have an
opportunity of getting for you a lift in your
profession, which, I take it, is your principal
object. My love to the D.L." Much might be
said, but it is, perhaps, a futile task to gild
refined gold!

All this was bad enough, but political—or
family—ties were now to have their final and
fatal effect on Lord Edward Fitzgerald. His
military aptitude had not passed unnoticed,
especially his eye for the strength and weakness
of fortifications. An expedition against Cadiz
was mooted; Lord Edward on a peaceful Continental tour had shrewdly marked the defences;
Pitt offered him promotion and the command.
It was the chance of his life: he accepted, and
then drew back. No one dreamed of imputing
cowardice to him; but without his knowing it

the Duke of Leinster had returned him as Member
for Kildare, and he conceived it to be his duty
to stay at home and stand by the Duke. As
the Duke of Richmond not unjustifiably said,
Lord Edward broke his word to his Sovereign.
And to what useful end ?

Is Ireland then some Upas tree ; is there no
hope for the young Irishman but to escape from
the shade of its branches ? In 1787 a young
Irishman, fifth son of an Irish peer, was gazetted
to a lieutenancy and appointed aide-de-camp to
the Viceroy of Ireland. In 1790 he was returned
to Parliament as Member for Trim. In 1793 he
made a sober speech in which he " reprobated in
severe terms the conduct of the French to their
King, and their invasion of the territory of
foreign Princes." Quietly and indefatigably he
studied the science of soldiering ; he did a short
spell of active service in Belgium ; he returned to
Ireland to study still more deeply, and to defend
in measured words the British soldier against
the insults of Irish patriots. And then Arthur
Wellesley left Ireland—left her to become Gen-
eralissimo of the British forces that conquered
Napoleon, Field - Marshal of every European
army, Duke of Wellington, and Prime Minister of
England.

Lord Edward must have known that with his
refusal of the Cadiz command his hopes of
military distinction were ended. For a time he
played a humdrum, ineffective part in Irish
politics ; then he paid a visit to France. It was
a return to his early days at Aubigny ; and
possibly the knowledge of the French, of their

ways and of their language which he had then
acquired, was in the end a disservice to him.
He was always, though probably he never knew
it, slightly *dépaysé* : it would have been better
for him had he first gone to the Continent ten
years later than he did, or had he stayed steadily
in Ireland for ten years after he first returned.
Against the too strict insularity of young John
Fitzgibbon may be set the too easy cosmopolitan-
ism of young Edward Fitzgerald. The countries
of Lord Edward's earliest experiences—France,
America, Canada—were seething with new ideas ;
he acquired too soon a taste for new political
wine, and he was as yet too young to reflect
that the pouring of this wine into the old political
bottles of Ireland might be an operation attended
by hazard. Anyhow, the autumn of 1792 found
him in Paris. There, it is interesting to note,
he met Tom Paine, and found in him " a simplicity of manner, a goodness of heart, and a
strength of mind that I never knew a man before
possess." Wolfe Tone, Lord Edward's contemporary, but hardened by years of battling
with the world, judged the philosopher somewhat
less favourably : " I like him very well, but he
is vain beyond belief, and I find him wittier in
discourse than in his writings, where his humour
is clumsy enough."

On November 18 Lord Edward attended in
Paris a banquet of which the purpose was to
celebrate the victories of the French armies.
Democratic toasts were drunk. General Dillon
proposed, " May Government [presumably the
British Government] profit by the example of

France, and Reform prevent Revolution." And Lord Edward Fitzgerald renounced his title : is it ungenerous to remark that he renounced that which he never possessed ? The ' Lord ' prefixed to the name of the younger brother of a Duke is a mere empty courtesy.

Prudence may have come with the light : in a letter Lord—or should it be citizen—Edward Fitzgerald expresses a fear that the result of all this democratic fervour may be that " I shall be scratched out of the Army." His fears were not ill-founded : he was ' scratched out,' cashiered. It was on the occasion of the cashiering of Lord Edward that Charles Fox declared quite truly that the Service did not possess a more zealous and promising officer.

Cashiered, his employment gone, no present hope of a career before him, Lord Edward returned to Ireland. But he did not return alone. For in December 1792 Lord Edward Fitzgerald, son of the Duke of Leinster, was married to Pamela, daughter of . . . Well, whose daughter was Pamela ?

CHAPTER II.

THE LOVER.

THERE are ordinarily two parts to a marriage on the Latin Continent. The first is the civil contract which is obligatory, the second the religious ceremony which is at the option of the parties. The civil contract of Lord Edward Fitzgerald was drawn up by one Mr Dorez, a notary of Tournay : it states that Lord Edward and Pamela appeared before Mr Dorez, but, oddly enough, it does not state their purpose in so appearing. The record of the religious ceremony, discovered by Dr Madden, is drawn up by the Reverend Father Taffin, also of Tournay : the reverend gentleman's wits seem to have been wandering quite as far afield as those of his legal colleague. For he misdates the marriage by eight years : he gives the date as 1784, whereas quite indubitably Edward Fitzgerald married Pamela in 1792. There are some other points in these documents which deserve consideration.

In both, the bridegroom is quite correctly described. But in the first document the bride is described as " citizeness Anne Caroline Stéphanie Sims, aged about 19 years, living at Paris, known in France by the name of Pamela, a native of Fogo in Newfoundland, daughter of William de Brixey and of Mary Sims." In the

second document she is described as " Anne
Stéphanie Caroline Sims, native of London, aged
19 years, daughter of William Berkeley and Mary
Sims." So, unless the bride's mother is described
by her maiden name instead of by her married
name, Pamela was an illegitimate child. " de
Brixey " may possibly be a Frenchman's effort
at " Berkeley," but it is strange that the dis-
crepancy should have passed unnoticed by the
parties and by their witnesses. To make confusion worse confounded, Lady Sophy Fitzgerald
in a letter mentions that her brother Edward has
married " Miss Pamela Seymour."

Seymour or Sims—it is not a matter of great
importance. But among the witnesses signing
the first record are Stéphanie Félicité Ducrest
Brulart Silléry and Philippe Égalité. Philippe
Égalité also signs the second record.

Now Madame Silléry (to shorten the string of
her names) is better known to the world as
Madame, or the Countess de Genlis : Philippe
Égalité is the Duke of Orleans, and brother of
the King of France. Madame de Genlis was
governess in the household of the Duke ; and there
is, or was, a fairly widespread belief that Pamela
was the illegitimate offspring of the pair. She
is supposed to have been born in 1776, when
Madame de Genlis was inexplicably absent from
her duties with the Duke's family. This, of course,
would be impossible if Pamela at the date of her
marriage were, as stated in the civil and religious
records, nineteen years of age. But a perfectly
innocent remark in a letter of Lord Edward
suggests that Pamela's age may have been con-

siderably overstated in her marriage lines. Lord
Edward writes to his mother that " Pamela has
taken a fit of growing : she grows broad and long."
If Pamela were nineteen years old at her marriage,
she certainly might have ' developed ' or grown
in some small measure, but it is scarcely likely
that she would have grown so noticeably as to
attract the attention of her husband who saw
her at every hour of the day. Were she but
sixteen when married, she might quite naturally
have been expected to grow, especially when
removed from the feverish city life of Paris to
the quiet and pure air of the Irish countryside.
Again, the ' Masonic Magazine ' formally announced that Lord Edward Fitzgerald had married
" Madame Pamela Capet, daughter of H.R.H.
the *ci-devant* Duke of Orleans." The Fitzgerald
family took no notice of this statement : it may
be that if there must be a bar sinister on the
birth of their new relative, they preferred that
the bar should be royal.

In favour of a less exalted parentage the following arguments have been adduced. Pamela's
daughter (who married Sir Guy Campbell) records
a ' tiff ' between her mother and Madame de
Genlis. Said Madame de Genlis, " If you boast
that you are my daughter, I can assure you that
you certainly are *not*." To which tartly replied
Lady Edward Fitzgerald, " If I were your
daughter, it would be nothing much to boast
about." Miaou !

Pamela's presence in the Orleans household is
thus accounted for. The Duke desired to find an
English girl who would share the lessons of his

children, and, incidentally, accustom his children to speaking English. The Duke is said to have commissioned a friend to find him such a child ; and someone is said to have seen a letter from this friend in which occurs the remark : " I am sending you the prettiest little girl and the handsomest mare in England." This is very indefinite, and on the face of it improbable. Philip of Orleans was interested in the Turf, and presumably interested in the education of his children. But it seems unlikely that he would have entrusted commissions in respect of his stud and of his children to the same person. It seems still more unlikely that the Duke of Orleans would have been satisfied with the first casual guttersnipe as a companion for his children. Égalité's equalitarian sentiments probably did not carry him so far. And it is curious that Pamela, if an English girl, should never have been very much at home in the English language. To her husband's family she usually wrote in French : when she uses English she uses it incorrectly. In one of her letters there is a passage in perfect English ; but the passage, from its meaning, is suspicious or interesting. Its purport is to clear Pamela of complicity in her husband's revolutionary designs : it is possible that the passage was dictated by her husband with this end in view.

There is a story, a very improbable one, of how the marriage came about. In 1785 Pamela had been to England with Madame de Genlis. There she met the cynical Horace Walpole, who in a letter ungallantly speaks of Madame as " Rousseau's hen," and says that she has with her a little girl whom she is teaching to resemble her in face ! The innuendo is surely a hint at Pamela's parentage on one side. In 1791 the pair again visited England, and at Bath made the acquaintance of the amiably dissipated Richard Sheridan. The tale is told that Sheridan's wife (once the lovely Miss Linley), who then lay a-dying, was so struck by Pamela's beauty that she urged her husband to ask the girl, after her own demise, to be his second wife. A curious anticipation of the tale of Dora Copperfield and Agnes Wickham. Sheridan, it seems, did propose or was unmistakably about to propose himself as a candidate for Pamela's hand, when Madame de Genlis, quite understandably averse from the idea of a middle-aged bankrupt as husband for her ward or daughter, whisked away the girl to France. It is also said that Lord Edward Fitzgerald quite honourably admired Mrs Sheridan, and that a fancied resemblance of Pamela to that lady led him to ask Pamela to be his wife. All this seems wildly fanciful : there may be a more prosaic and probable explanation.

When Lord Edward went to Paris in 1792 he must have been in a very disgruntled mood. From a mistaken conception of the loyalty which he owed to his brother (" dear Leinster ") he had ruined his career in the Army, and he must have been perfectly well aware of the fact. The harmless and far too severely punished extravagance of his participation in a revolutionary banquet may have been due to this knowledge. And possibly his unfortunate affair with Georgina Lennox was still rankling in his heart. He had

loved honourably in his own class, among his own
relatives, and he had been rejected ; he was
incurably sentimental ; he was too clean-minded
to entangle himself with women of a lower class ;
he was an easy prey to the first charming girl
whose mother (or guardian) saw in the handsome
young brother of the great Irish peer an exceedingly eligible *parti*. The difference of nationality was no embarrassment : his boyhood at
Aubigny probably had made Lord Edward perfectly at home in the tongue and with the manners
of the French people. He saw pretty Pamela in
a box at the Opera ; a young man of his rank
would find no difficulty in obtaining an introduction. Some days later he writes to his mother
that he is dining with the Sillérys.

It is impossible to avoid the rather cynical
reflection that Madame de Genlis, a typical
Frenchwoman, played her noble fish with ex-
ceeding skill. She and Pamela were setting out
for Tournay, very probably in search of greater
security than Paris then afforded. Lord Edward
volunteered his escort, and his offer was accepted.
Almost inevitably a proposal followed. Madame
showed no imprudent eagerness ; she had a light
hand on the line. She received the suitor
graciously, but she reminded him that the wishes
of his family, of his dear mother, must be con-
sulted ; until their consent was obtained, she
could make no definite promise. So young
Edward set out for England. On the way a
courier overtook him : he came from Madame
de Genlis with a message. Her motherly (or
guardianly) heart had been touched by the pretty

picture of young love : did Madame la Duchesse but assent, she for her part would place no obstacle in the way of the happy pair.

What the formidable Duchess thought of the business it is difficult to conjecture. Dear Eddy was certainly making a hasty, perhaps an imprudent marriage. But she knew her son's temperament, she knew that he would never be happy unmarried, and that the odds were very much in favour of any suitable marriage turning out to be a happy one for such a sweet-tempered, thoroughly decent young man. Edward had found a pretty girl who was also a lady ; he was, or imagined himself to be, very much in love. His nerves were rather frayed : maternal sternness at such a juncture might alienate from the Duchess the affections of her best-loved child. And if the marriage *was* an imprudent one, well, the marriage of the Duchess of Leinster to the dour tutor of her children had seemed to most people a positive flying in the face of Providence and of sanity. And yet that crazy marriage had brought happiness to all immediately affected by it. The Duchess gave her consent.

The " good family " received their new sister with seeming affection : they speak prettily in their letters of pretty Pamela. But did Edward's marriage tend imperceptibly to edge him out of the charmed lagoon of the Fitzgeralds and into the stormier waters that lay without the reef ? With none of her sisters-in-law save Lady Lucy Fitzgerald does Pamela seem to have been particularly intimate. Lady Lucy stayed frequently with Edward and Pamela at their country cottage ; she was one of the party which Pamela prettily but unorthographically named the " beloved quoituor." But Lady Lucy's affection may not have been wholly disinterested. There were four, not three in the party ; the fourth was Arthur O'Connor ; and with Arthur O'Connor Lady Lucy was quite certainly " pullin' a sthring." Young Lady Edward was an officially adequate, but probably an extremely indulgent, chaperone.

The dowager Duchess of Leinster appropriated the first child of the marriage, a boy named Edward. It may be that the old lady had a provident eye for the future of her grandson, or it possibly may be that the fire of maternal passion was still burning in her breast. Pamela in a prettily sad letter, written like all her letters in French, resigned the child. But the Duchess, whatever her motives, cannot have given in the matter much thought to the feelings of her daughter-in-law. Two daughters—daughter-in-law seems to have been wellnigh as industrious as mother-in-law in the business of maternity— Pamela kept with her. At a later date she writes to the Fitzgerald family that in her straitened circumstances she is finding it difficult to bring up " Miss Fitzgerald " in the manner which befits her rank. A curious way for a mother to speak of her child to the members of her husband's family, unless the relations between herself and them are distant. And when Lord Edward's life came to its tragic end, the Fitzgeralds really seem to have hustled poor Pamela out of Ireland and out of the United Kingdom. They did little or nothing subsequently for her : for a time she lived at Goodwood, presumably at the charges of her husband's uncle, the Duke of Richmond. Thereafter she passed out of the ken of the Fitzgerald family. The greater part of her life she spent on the Continent. She married again; she became Mrs Pitcairn, wife of an American citizen. But the marriage proved to be an unhappy one; husband and wife were soon parted. She died in Paris: it is said that the Vicomtesse de Chabot, daughter of the second Duke of Leinster and therefore niece of Lord Edward Fitzgerald, visited her on her deathbed. Is it an unfair surmise that Pamela was never wholly accepted by " the good family," and that the non-acceptance of the wife within the charmed circle may have brought about in some measure the withdrawal of the husband from it ?

Pamela was a coquette to the last day of her life, but no whisper of scandal ever touched her during her married life with Lord Edward. But perhaps she was found to be by the society to which she was now presented a foreign body, somewhat difficult of digestion. Lord Edward in one of his letters speaks of everyone being against the war with France, but unconsciously he may have attributed his own feelings to his friends, and his attitude towards France and the French may have differed widely from that of the majority of his own class. The French people had practically declared war on aristocrats of every sort and kind, and the Anglo-Irish aristocrats of Ireland were held in no particular favour by the Irish people. Pamela was a reminder, though a very pretty one, of what had happened in France :

it was not altogether unthinkable that scenes enacted in Paris might yet be re-enacted in Dublin. Pamela's father—if he was her father—Philippe Égalité had voted for the death *sans phrase* of his own brother, the King of France ; and utterly fantastic tales actually were current that Pamela herself had joined in the street dancings of blood-drunk ' patriots ' in Paris.

' The best people ' of Dublin may have thought no small beer of themselves ; but Pamela as a child had been brought up in a Royal household in the most brilliant capital of Europe. In her secret heart she may have considered Dublin society provincial, ill mannered, stupid. She loved dancing, but once returning from a dance she told her husband that she would go to no more balls where she met such ill-bred people. The modesty then demanded of young Irish ladies may have awakened the sprite of ridicule in the little French bride. Mamma-in-law writing *à propos* of a ball-gown to one of her daughters thus observes, " I am glad your nakedness extended no farther than your pretty white Pole, as it might have given you cold to have bared your dear bosom. The idea of the indecency of showing the back of one's neck is beyond me." There is a picture of Lady Edward Fitzgerald as Diana gone a-hunting with bow and hound : she shows not only " the back of her neck " but also (*horrescimus referentes*) a liberal allowance of leg well above the knee. Possibly the society in which the young Fitzgeralds at first naturally took their place looked slightly down its nose at her little ladyship newly arrived from across the

English Channel. Lord Edward writes, "My differing so much in opinion with (*sic*) the people that one is unavoidably obliged to live with here, does not add much to the agreeableness of Dublin society." No doubt political opinion was mainly in his mind, but political opinion is made up of many elements.

Again, it is possible that Lord Edward Fitzgerald, best of sons and husbands, just as he inclined a little to plumpness, so may have inclined just a little to over-domesticity and—dulness. He draws a pretty picture of his happy life to be for his mother : "I think when I am down there [in his country cottage] with Pam and the child, of a blustering evening, with a good turf fire and a pleasant book, coming in after seeing my poultry put up, my garden settled—flower beds and plants covered for fear of frost—the place looking comfortable and taken care of, I shall be as happy as possible." A pretty prospect, but one which may have seemed just a little tame, a little lacking in excitement to the girl fresh from her own gay land. All through her short life Pamela had been playing fairly near to the political fire of France. Perhaps she found it interesting ; perhaps, almost without knowing it, she pushed her husband nearer to the political fire of Ireland.

Had Edward Fitzgerald married Katherine Mead or Georgina Lennox, quite possibly nothing more would ever have been heard of him. He might have subsided into a worthy country squire, and have left no immortally tragic memory to Ireland. Or an orthodoxly ambitious wife might have pushed him on to distinction in the Army, to a peerage in his own right, to a portrait of General Lord—Something-or-other— looking majestically down on succeeding generations of Fitzgeralds from the walls of Carton.

Lord Edward by the grace of God and the favour of " dear Leinster " was a Member of the Irish Parliament, and in the year immediately following his marriage he made his first notable contribution to Parliamentary debate. He produced the effect of the bull in the china-shop, of the cat let loose among the pigeons. The matter concerned " that singular body " (Mr Froude's phrase) the Irish Volunteers.

The Volunteers had somewhat subsided after their encounter some years before with Mr John Fitzgibbon ; but happenings on the Continent of Europe put new heart into them. They proposed to hold an armed parade, nominally to celebrate the victory of French democracy over reaction typified by the Duke of Brunswick, really to assist the Irish Parliament in coming to some democratic decision on the questions of Catholic emancipation and Parliamentary reform. The Viceroy, Lord Westmoreland, "proclaimed," that is, forbade the parade. No doubt he was quite right in so doing. The Government of Ireland was bad enough, but a Government which allows armed citizens to assemble with the scarcely disavowed purpose of intimidating itself has reached a stage of badness that is as inconceivable as contemptible. The feeling of Parliament was with the Viceroy, and in the formal vote of thanks for his address pointed allusion was made to the proclamation. Whereupon Lord Edward Fitzgerald arising in his place pleasantly observed, " I give my most hearty disapprobation of the address of thanks, for I think that the Lord Lieutenant and the majority of this House are the worst subjects the King has."

Bedlam broke loose. There were yells of " take down his words " and " to the Bar." Lord Edward called upon to withdraw was more explicit if less dramatic than a Member of the English House at a much later date. He did not strike an attitude and declare that he " never withdrew " ; he simply said, " I said it, 'tis true, and I'm sorry for it." His sorrow presumably being for the truth of his statement, not for his making of it. The House found this withdrawal insufficient ; next day he was summoned to the Bar ; he explained himself further, and the House by a majority accepted his explanation. The explanation was probably frankly blunt rather than grudging—it was not in Lord Edward's nature to do anything grudgingly— for more than fifty Members of the House voted it unsatisfactory.

It was a trivial incident, and one to which more importance has been attached than it deserved. Yet in a way it is characteristic, explanatory of Lord Edward's career and fate. It was easy, and probably justifiable, to condemn the Viceroy, his Ministers, and the Irish House of Commons in one short ejaculatory sentence ; it would have become the speaker better had he been able to understand and to expound the reasons for his condemnation. Lord Edward might have

reflected that he himself embodied a principle
entirely vicious in any House of Representatives.
He was the fettered nominee of his brother,
"dear Leinster," not the free representative of
the free choice of the Irish people. "Dear
Leinster," with his tergiversations and jobberies,
was an incarnate symptom of the disease which
poisoned the Irish body politic. It was, on the
whole, true to say that the Government ruled by
corruption ; but were the Irish politicians, the
great family satrapies, amenable to rule by any
other means ?

For a time after this rather theatrical escapade
Lord Edward seems to have concerned himself
little enough about politics. In one of his letters,
indeed, he anticipates a modern Irish heresy.
He cannot understand Mr Grattan's "worst
doctrine ever laid down" that Ireland must
support England right or wrong, in any war
that England may undertake. Mr Grattan did
not enunciate this extremity or absurdity of
doctrine : he held that the fate of Ireland is
inextricably interwoven with that of England.
So long as England continues to exist, Ireland
can only achieve complete independence of England by coming under the domination of some
other power. It is a homely and probably true
proverb that, generally, the devil I do know is
better than the devil I don't. In the mind of
Wolfe Tone, as he watched the French preparations for the liberation of Ireland, there was some
dim perception of a truth stated by an American
humourist, "It's easier to get a fish-hook in than
it is to get it out."

We find Lord Edward busy with domesticity, with the setting up of a home for himself, his young wife, and his expected family. There is no word of the chagrin that he must have felt at the ending of his professional hopes as a soldier ; of the fundamental political issues of the day, Catholic emancipation and Parliamentary reform, he shows no comprehension. For the moment he is living with Pamela at Frescati, the Blackrock villa of the Duchess of Leinster ; and the arranging for an independent home of his own gives him enough to think about. The old prudent, honourable care about money matters is in evidence : just as in his first Army days he had written to his mother that he has £25 or £30 in hand and is keeping well within his income, so now he weighs for her inevitable outgoings against possible incomings. At first he fixes his eyes on a property between Wicklow and Arklow. It is charming ; but the rent is £90 a year, a matter for consideration. There follows an unconscious and honourable testimony to Lord Edward's independence, to his aversion from sponging on well-to-do relations. Tom Conolly, husband of his Aunt Louisa, has offered to *give* him a little house near Kildare. Lord Edward is delighted ; the little house seems to be just what he is looking for, and its nearness to his own scrap of property will give him an opportunity for trying his " prentice hand at farming on a prudently small scale." But such a *gift* he cannot accept from anyone : he will gladly make trial of the house for a time, and, if it suits his purposes, he will *buy* it, lock, stock and barrel, from Mr Conolly.

The estimated value was £300 ; and Tom Conolly's income was said to be £25,000 a year !

So to Kildare Lord Edward and Pamela came, and for their country life Lady Lucy Fitzgerald, a young lady of sentiment and humour, is the authority. Incidentally, Lady Lucy's notes and her correspondence with her mother throw a quaint light on the domestic habits of ' the quality ' in that age. " I was not well, took a bath," she writes. Was she unwell because she took a bath, or was the taking of a bath a thing so out of the common as to need sickness for its justification ? And when the old Duchess learns that her daughter is leaving Kildare for Leinster House she issues strict injunctions that the housekeeper is to sleep in Lady Lucy's bed for a week beforehand, and that, to make sure, " Betty Hall " is to make trial of the bed on the night before Lady Lucy's arrival. That the sheets thus treated would be dry may be assumed : it is a twentieth-century suggestion that they might be dirty.

However clannish the ' good family ' might be, there was nothing of snobbery or exclusiveness about Lord Edward. He was a gentleman to his finger-tips, and he could be easily at home in the society of his social inferiors without forfeiting their respect or his own. He has ' the apothecary ' to dine, and after dinner there is a little dance. Seven couples take the floor, the servants and the maids being called in to share in and make up the fun. The apothecary dines again, and to the dance which follows the butcher's daughters have been invited. Lord

Edward proves himself to be a capital hand at a jig. All this is charming. But Lady Lucy's notes are somewhere in the period '96-'97, and such a picture at such a time, charming though it may be, is scarcely the picture of a great national leader in the making. Is it a disappointing thought that in all probability Lord Edward would never have meddled with revolutionary politics had he not been pushed or beguiled into them ; or a saddening thought that, however he did enter into such politics, he entered guilelessly and only to his own undoing ? To the last day of his life he was an incompetent conspirator : he had no grip on the realities of the life in which he found himself, no proper acquaintance with or understanding of the men whose cause he made his own. " I knew Fitzgerald very little," writes Wolfe Tone, protagonist of the Irish revolution, " but I honour and venerate his character." His character, we may surmise, rather than his intelligence !

Lord Edward, as we have seen, was no snob, but the revolutionaries of Ireland he was not likely to meet, to be acquainted with, to understand. All of them came from a class not his own, and from a ' middle ' class which he probably would have found more ' difficult ' than he did the apothecary and the butcher's daughters of Kildare. With just one, a somewhat sinister figure, he was on terms of intimate friendship. This was Arthur O'Connor, no eloquent tribune of the people, but a man of Lord Edward's own social rank. O'Connor was the nephew and the heir-presumptive of a peer. He had entered the Irish Parliament in 1790 as Member for Philipstown ; with him, and, like him, elected for the first time, two remarkable men took their seats. One was Robert Stewart, Member for Down, later to be known as Lord Castlereagh ; the other was Arthur Wesley, Member for Trim, Arthur Wellesley to be and Duke of Wellington. Was the friendship of Lord Edward for Arthur O'Connor the friendship of Faust for Mephistopheles ?

To Arthur O'Connor Lord Edward's sister, Lady Lucy, for a time quite undeniably lost her little heart. He is introduced in her diary as ' Mr O'Connor ' : almost imperceptibly he merges into ' Arthur.' He was a remarkably handsome man, and there was about him something of the gloom, later dubbed Byronic, which makes an unfailing appeal to the young and sentimental female. Mr O'Connor, it seems, proclaimed himself an atheist ; and little Lady Lucy listened round-eyed while he expounded his philosophy in the drawing - room. Lord Edward, sad to relate, had fallen asleep ; possibly he was snoring softly. Arthur was eloquent, and Lady Lucy was grieved to tears at such a mind supposing itself perishable ! In the end no harm was done : Arthur O'Connor passed out of Lady Lucy's life, and Lady Lucy lived to marry a British naval officer.

O'Connor was a clever man, a courageous man, an aristocrat ; but there seems to have been a touch of the gangster in him. He may have been trustworthy; but there were those in his day who distrusted him. In his admitted utterances, as well as in utterances but supposedly his, there is something which does not ring quite true. He addressed himself to the people of Ireland through a Belfast newspaper : Lady Lucy thought his address ' glorious,' the Government of Ireland thought it seditious, the reader of to-day will probably think it rather cheap fustian. "Abandoned Administration who have trampled on the liberties of my country "— and much more to the same effect. The upshot of it was that Mr O'Connor was arrested : Lady Lucy saw him at his dungeon window, and noted that he "looked very melancholy." He found opportunity of communicating with the Fitzgeralds : "I can bear my own sufferings without a sigh, but the sight of you, my dear, dear friends, brings torrents from my eyes." Considering that Mr O'Connor was not at the moment loaded with chains, but had merely been detained for a few days pending a charge, this eloquence seems slightly overstrained.

This is the rest of Arthur O'Connor's story. He was released from durance vile on the security of Thomas Emmett and Lord Edward Fitzgerald. He started a newspaper called ' The Press,' and in its columns appeared incitements to assassination signed "Satanides." In the early part of 1798 he was arrested at Margate in the company of a priest named Quigley and some admitted revolutionaries. The party—or some of them—were held for treason ; Quigley was hanged ; O'Connor, largely owing to the testimony of aristocratic friends to his general character, was acquitted. After sundry other adventures he reached France, entered French military service, rose to be a General, married the daughter of Condorcet, and died at a very advanced age. He meddled no more with Irish politics ; but the belief was current in Ireland in '98 that his escape to France had been facilitated by his betrayal of Lord Edward Fitzgerald. This belief had for its foundation the fact that O'Connor arrived in France possessed of considerable sums of money : for the credit of humanity one must believe this belief to be mistaken.

Probably it was Arthur O'Connor, by nature a conspirator, who first brought Lord Edward Fitzgerald into touch with the United Irishmen, a body which in a very short time had diverged widely from the principles of its first foundation. These principles are sufficiently set forth in the obligation taken by the first members of the Society : " To use all my abilities and influence in the attainment of an adequate and impartial representation of the Irish nation in Parliament . . . to form a brotherhood of affection, an identity of interest, a communion of rights, and a union of power among Irishmen of all religious persuasions." The original members of the Society were, in the main, Ulster Presbyterians, the most democratic and progressive element in the country ; and for them religious toleration was a means to an end rather than an end in itself. They saw that no country could thrive under a system which denied to the vast majority (the Catholics), and to the influential minority (the Dissenters), the elementary rights of citizenship. The wished-for end of religious toleration was a cleansing of these Augean stables, Dublin Castle and the Irish Houses of Parliament. Whether the means would have achieved the end is a question which is now impossible to answer.

But a change came over the ideals of the United Irishmen. The new recruit of a few years later certainly pledged himself to form "a brotherhood of affection among Irishmen of all religious persuasions," and to secure "an equal representation of all the people of Ireland." But there is now no mention of where that representation is to be : the word ' Parliament ' is significantly omitted. Possibly the thought was current that the Irish Parliament was past reformation : it might be destroyed, but it could not be amended. This Parliament was the child of Grattan's political genius, the child on which he bestowed the benediction, *esto perpetua*. There is always a curious irony in the management by Irishmen of their own affairs! And the new obligation concluded with these ominous words : " I do further declare that neither hopes, fears, rewards nor punishments shall ever induce me, directly or indirectly, to inform on or give evidence directly or indirectly against any member of this or similar societies for any act or expression of theirs, done or made collectively or individually in or out of this society in pursuance of the spirit of the obligation." Men who have no illegal or treasonable purpose to conceal do not need to take such an oath against revelation. The terms of the obligation are wide enough to cover wellnigh *anything* : " this or *similar* societies . . . *any*

act or expression . . . *in or out* of the society
. . . *in pursuance of the terms of the obligation.*"
And when men take an oath against treachery, it
is a fair surmise that they already suspect the
presence of traitors.

There may have been several reasons for
the change, but assuredly one reason for the
change was the fact that no Irishman, however
benevolent his bosom towards his brother, has
ever been willing to allow his brother to reach
Heaven—or another place—by the road that he
prefers. Wolfe Tone's " valorous entry into the
city of Rathfriland " was made with a view to
the reconciliation of two contending elements,
the Peep-o'-Day Boys and the Defenders, who
were only distinguishable in a common ruffianism
by the fact that the first were Protestants,
the second Catholics. Some measure of super-
ficial success Tone did attain ; but fundamentally
the disruptive strength of religion in Ireland
remained unabated. The Peep-o'-Day Boys became the nucleus of the Orangemen, the Defenders
coalesced with the United Irishmen. The democratic Societies of Orangemen and United Irishmen were soon sundered as widely as the Poles,
and as unassimilable as oil and water.

Even after the change there was for a long
time no distinctively Catholic note in the United
Irishmen. But the Catholic religion, or rather
the treatment accorded to those professing it,
was undoubtedly a factor in bringing about the
change. The partial Catholic emancipation of
1793, which permitted Catholics to vote at
Parliamentary elections but forbade them to

sit in Parliament, disgusted Conservative Catholics quite as much as Liberal Protestants. As Lawrance Parsons truly said, "This measure flatters the Catholic rabble and insults the Catholic gentry." The lamentable episode of Lord Fitzwilliam in 1795 convinced a great many men of all creeds that justice and fair play could never be expected of England, that England deliberately preferred the private interest of an Irish oligarchy to the general interest of the Irish people.

And quite possibly a seemingly ineradicable element of weakness in the Irish character began to assert itself. The Irishman has always loved conspiracy for itself, quite irrespective of any purpose that conspiracy may accomplish. It is a cynical but inevitable reflection that about the period '96-'98 there was in Ireland a great deal of cry for a very little wool, that conspiracies were great but the results of them singularly small.

It seems to be the general opinion of historians that Lord Edward Fitzgerald was never formally admitted by oath to the Society of United Irishmen. This is a significant circumstance. In a sense there was no need for an oath : no string of oaths could add to Lord Edward's honour, and no one in the thirty-five years of his life, or in the hundred and thirty-five that have rolled by since his death, ever suggested that he would or *could* betray a confidence. But treasonable conspiracy—for conspiracy by a subject against the established Government of his country, however bad that Government may be, *is* treason—does not admit of nice discrimination between conspirators. The risks, obligations, knowledge of all conspirators must be the same. Poor gallant Lord Edward might be described not unfairly as an ' honorary conspirator.' He had a general and generous perception that Ireland was unhappy, but he had little real understanding of the causes of her unhappiness. He was ready to lead in the field, to lay down his life for the cause that he had espoused. But a leader who must act in the field on plans which others have prepared and but half disclosed to him is unlikely to advance his cause very far.

In the early summer of 1796 Lord Edward, accompanied by his wife and by Arthur O'Connor, set out for the Continent. Undoubtedly the purpose of the journey was to negotiate with the French Directory for the invasion of Ireland. Even then political differences had not wholly made an end of social amenities—so late as 1797 the young Fitzgeralds met and chatted with the coldly relentless Earl of Clare, a guest in the Duke of Leinster's house party at Carton— and as Lord Edward passed through London a hint was conveyed to him from a high quarter that he was setting his feet on a very dangerous path. But he persisted.

Lord Edward, Pamela, and Arthur O'Connor went to Hamburg : there Pamela remained, while her husband and O'Connor journeyed to Basle, where conversations were opened with an agent of the Directory. Who this agent was is not quite certain : it may have been General Hoche, the one considerable man in France determined *à l'outrance* on the invasion of Ireland. Whether he was equally determined on the liberation of Ireland from the rule of England or France is another question. At least Hoche, if he was not actually present at Basle, was quite *au courant* of all that there took place; and a curious passage in Wolfe Tone's journal throws a light on the disingenuity—or was it, after all, but the indecision and stupidity—of the French in their dealings with the Irishmen.

Tone was, or imagined himself to be, in the fullest confidence of General Hoche in the matter of the expedition to Ireland. In the month of July he called on the General, who inquired whether the proposed invasion would have the support of solid men, of men of property in Ireland. Tone, with commendable candour, hastened to disabuse the General of any such idea : "He should rather reckon on all the opposition that class could give him. It was possible that when the business was once commenced, some of them might join on speculation, but it would be sorely against their real sentiments." There followed a seemingly careless question : Did Tone know anything of one Mr Arthur O'Connor? Why, of course : Tone entertained the highest opinion of Mr O'Connor's talents, principles and patriotism. "Well," inquired the General," will he join us?" "Undoubtedly," replied Tone. A pause, and then a question more studiously vague : "There is a Lord in your country ; he is son to a Duke ; is he not a patriot?"

Says Tone, "I immediately smoked my lover,

Lord Edward Fitzgerald, and gave Hoche a very good account of him." There is no need to suppose that Tone professed to have any intimate acquaintance with Lord Edward. This word 'lover' is one of his verbal idiosyncrasies: he applies it even to a bore who insisted on sharing his carriage during a journey. But Hoche to all outward seeming had given his fullest confidence to Tone; yet he did not disclose to Tone that he had been actually in conference with the two persons whose names he professed vaguely to recall. Nor does it appear that Hoche disclosed to Lord Edward and to O'Connor his negotiations with Tone. A conspiracy in which the right hand is kept ignorant of the doings of the left is unlikely to be crowned with success. There was, indeed, an element of blind man's buff in all this; and in the buff one fears that Lord Edward was the blind man. He, the possessor of a title (the French probably would not understand that the title was a mere courtesy) and brother of the great Irish Peer, was put forward by the Irishmen to impress the French with the weight of support to be expected in Ireland. The appearance of Lord Edward would convince Hoche and the French of the 'seriousness' (if the word be taken in its French sense) of the United Irishmen and of Tone. But possibly Tone was for Hoche a touchstone whereby to test the 'seriousness' of the United Irishmen and of Lord Edward: his questions were very much to the point for all their carelessness.

Was Hoche's next question ironical? He made an inquiry concerning—John Fitzgibbon!

"I endeavoured to do Fitzgibbon justice," says Tone, "and I believe I satisfied Hoche that we will not meet with prodigious assistance from His Majesty's Lord High Chancellor of Ireland!"

Directly, even the expedition of Hoche had no very great effect on the fortunes of Lord Edward Fitzgerald. Indirectly, the journey to Hamburg was for him the beginning of the end.

CHAPTER III.

THE CONSPIRATOR.

AT Hamburg occurred an event interesting directly to Lord and Lady Edward Fitzgerald, and interesting indirectly to the historian. There Pamela gave birth to her second child and eldest daughter. She may quite naturally have desired to be with her husband at such a time ; but her choice of Hamburg for her confinement perhaps suggests that she was drawing away from Anglo-Irish life and without the circle of ' the good family.' The old Duchess had adopted or seized the first-born of the marriage, the son of her own best-loved son : thereafter, one may surmise, she neither felt nor showed any very great interest in her son's wife. In fact, although Pamela again visited and resided in Ireland, her home for the rest of her life as Lady Edward Fitzgerald was in Hamburg. Her withdrawal from Ireland may have meant a loosening of the ties which bound her husband to his family, a drifting of his barque from the safe moorings of Parliamentary opposition. Although, indeed, one could scarcely deem ' dear Leinster ' a particulary secure anchorage or dependable anchor. Lord Edward henceforth was constantly in negotiation with Continental supporters of the cause of Ireland. '' All important negotiations between the Revolutionary Committee in Dublin and their Paris agents passed through Lady Edward's hands. The Paris letters were transmitted first to her at Hamburg. By her they were forwarded to Lady Lucy Fitzgerald in London. From London Lady Lucy was able to send them on unsuspected." This is the report of a spy hereafter to be mentioned.

A pretty woman who is ready to go to bed with a man on the chance of worming some information out of him is an asset to a Government in its dealings with a conspiracy. A pretty woman whose virtue is unassailable is a liability to a conspiracy in its dealings with a Government. For such a woman expects, perhaps unconsciously, that her sex, her beauty, her character, her social grace will win for her some relaxation of the rigour of the rules of the game. It is not so when the stakes of the game are life and death, when one of the opposing players may be a man "who had long rioted on the spoils of his country, bartered domestic peace for national dissension, smiled at the torture which his sanguinary hand had inflicted, and, like a second Nero, exulted in the flame which menaced his country with ruin." It is doubtful whether such a being ever existed on earth ; but such is an Irish patriot's description of John Fitzgibbon. Opposed to such a man, supported as he was by a formidable efficient subordinate intelligence service, poor Ladies Pamela and Lucy were as earthenware pots jostling in the stream against a hammered vessel of iron.

As a matter of sober fact the patriot's description of Fitzgibbon may in its turn be described as melodramatic nonsense. Fitzgibbon and others who espoused the cause of 'the Government' in the troublous last decade of the eighteenth century in Ireland may have been no less sincere than the most ardent United Irishman, and unquestionably they were much more efficient. It is the rankest folly to imagine that vituperation can atone for underestimation of an opponent's ability. Fitzgibbon indeed dealt with detected conspirators rather than with the details of detecting them : a far more effective agent in this particular business was Robert Stewart, better known to the later world as Lord Castlereagh. It is worth while turning aside for a moment to view another of the men against whom Lord Edward and his associates had to contend.

Robert Stewart had entered the Irish Parliament "supported not only by the suffrages but by the pecuniary contributions of the friends of civil and religious liberty " (Teeling). He went another way : what way may be seen from the narrative of Mr Teeling, who is the artist of the somewhat unflattering word-portrait of John Fitzgibbon.

Mr Teeling was riding with his father, when " we were met by Lord Castlereagh, who accosted us with his accustomed politeness. We had proceeded up the street together, when having reached the house of his noble relative, the Marquess of Hertford, we were about to take leave of his Lordship. ' I regret,' said he, addressing my father, ' that your son cannot accompany you,' conducting me at the same moment through the outer gate, which to my inexpressible astonishment was immediately closed, and I found myself surrounded by a military guard." Poor Mr Teeling "expostulated in no very measured language " : he inquired the reason for his arrest. " Treason," was the laconic answer. Lord Castlereagh's bite was very much worse than his bark, wherein he differed from a good many Irishmen. And Teeling's artless story brings into prominence an aspect of Castlereagh's character still more dangerous to those who played the great game against him. The man's personal charm was irresistible ; by evening the captive was chatting amiably, and in all probability much too freely, with his captor over ' a slight repast ' and excellent wine. Castlereagh was no crude practitioner of the Third Degree ; but there is a meaning in a suggestion sent later from England that he should have a talk with Mr Arthur O'Connor, when O'Connor lay in Margate jail after his arrest in the company of Quigley and Binns. Quigley was hanged.

But to resume the story. Lord Edward returned to Ireland after his negotiations with the French, and at the close of the year a liberating, or, at least, an invading force sailed from France for the Irish coast. It was made up of 15,000 picked French troops admirably equipped ; and seemingly no fault could be found with the competence of the men selected to command. In Ireland, if Mr Teeling is to be believed, the numbers of the United Irishmen " had hourly increased until nearly the whole active population was committed in this universal Association." Against the gallant French and the patriotic Irish the Government of Ireland had " no talent to direct the disposable force with which they were ill prepared to encounter a bold and adventurous foe. Hurry, confusion, and disorder marked the advance of the army ; all was terror, doubt, and dismay ; troops disaffected, horses wanting, the munitions of war badly supplied, and even the bullet unfitted to the calibre of the cannon. The troops had to contend with the severity of the winter's storm, the mountain's torrent, roads broken up by floods and rendered impassable by the depth of the drifted snow ; peril and dismay in the front, hunger and privation in the rear. And thus prepared the unwieldy Dalrymple faced to the south to meet the invincible Hoche, the victor of La Vendée followed by the bravest troops the republic of France could boast." And yet French and Irish between them accomplished nothing : the French never landed, the Irish never rose. The whole affair proved to be the most pitiable fiasco known to history.

Private Smith probably ' goes over the top ' because it never occurs to him to doubt that his next man, Private Brown, is going on the word of command. But if there be no word of command, and if each man is awaiting a lead from the other, it is unlikely that either Private Smith or Private Brown will ever lift his head above the trench parapet. The " unwieldy Dalrymple " had to face the victor of La Vendée and the bravest troops of France ; but had he nothing to fear, had Grouchy (who commanded in the somewhat inexplicable absence of Hoche) nothing to expect from the Irish ? As Grouchy did not land, the Irish did not rise ; as the Irish did not rise, Grouchy returned to France. Dr Madden has described the organisation of the United Irishmen. No one has ever called the Irish cowards : it is impossible to avoid the conclusion that the United Irishmen were excellently organised for conspiring, but much less well organised for *doing* anything.

Dr Madden's description is too long to quote, and without meticulous reading rather difficult to understand. But on paper it was a well thought out scheme to mobilise at once a political association into a combatant army. The floggings, pitch-cappings, half-hangings of Lake, Judkin Fitzgerald, and others at a later date brought to light a vast quantity of weapons by no means ineffective according to the standards of the day. Yet nothing was *done*. In fact, the eighteenth century United Irishmen suggest to-day an admirably designed motor-car amply equipped with petrol, oil, water, but lacking a driver. They had no definite leader ; they only found one, when it was far too late, in Father John Murphy of Boolavogue in the County of Wexford. Opportunity ordinarily knocks at the door but once : if she is not welcomed, she does not knock again.

On the appearance of the French, Arthur O'Connor, according to his own statement, "dissuaded his countrymen from arming to oppose an invasion which the crimes of the Administration had provoked." He did nothing more.

Lord Edward was at Kildare with his wife and sister. He did nothing at all. He was not the man to hang back in the hour for action ; but obviously the French, with whom he had negotiated, had given him no precise information of their intentions; the United Irishmen, on whose behalf he had negotiated, had given him no precise information of their preparations. He was the tragic element in this comedy, a General genuinely anxious for battle but looking for his supporting troops to stage supers disguised as soldiers.

Even after the fiasco the leaders of the National movement—or conspiracy—in Ireland did not abate their efforts. They sent to France as their accredited agent one Mr E. J. Lewines, and among the tasks allotted to him was the raising of a loan of approximately half a million sterling from either France or Spain. And as France made some inquiries concerning the military preparedness of the Irishmen, Lord Edward proceeded to London to confer with an agent of the Directory. In June '97 Dr MacNevin went to Paris to urge strongly the need for French help : there is an entirely unconscious humour in Moore's account of the success which attended his efforts. " He found the French authorities fully disposed to second his most hostile views. It was, however, by the Batavian republic that the honour had now been claimed of taking the lead in an expedition for the invasion of Ireland." Englishmen and Irishmen alike cling pathetically to their ideal or delusion of the French as the brave, sentimental, carelessly reckless champions of forlorn hopes. Perhaps even at the present day relations between France and England would be improved would the Englishman but accept the Frenchman for what he is *au fond,* the hardest-headed, least sentimental, most coldly calculating business man in Europe. The French had enjoyed the experience of invading Ireland : they were quite prepared gracefully to cede the honour of further experiment to anyone who hankered after it. The end of the Dutch experiment—imbecility with possibly an admixture of treachery —has already been described.

But in Ireland the foundations of the National movement were cracking ominously. Or, to employ another metaphor, the ship was already sinking when Lord Edward Fitzgerald went aboard.

There may have been some military reason for the Frenchmen's choice of the south-west coast of Ireland as the jumping off point of their invasion. But the north-east would have been a far wiser choice. Had the Frenchmen been able to get there—and there does not seem to have been any very definite reason to the contrary—they would have found the grim, half Scottish republicans of Ulster more ready to act than to talk, more ready to fight than to conspire. The inertia of the South gave the Northerns pause for half angry, half contemptuous reflection and reconsideration. And beneath the main current of politics the separate currents of sectarian religion already were diverging widely. Oil and water will not unite anywhere ; Protestant and Catholic will not for very long unite in Ireland.

And as the Peep-o'-Day Boys (now Orangemen) steadily rose in the moral scale, so did the Defenders (now United Irishmen) steadily sink. Much has been said, and quite truly said, of the savagery of the Government of Ireland in dealing with the Nationalist insurgents ; but there is another side to the story. " Colonel St George dined at Mr Uniacke's house on the 9th of February. As Mr Uniacke and his wife were lighting him at night to his bedroom, fourteen men with blackened faces appeared on the landing place from the back stairs, while others showed themselves below. Mrs Uniacke threw herself before her husband. They flung her over the staircase on the pavement of the hall. They stabbed Uniacke through and through, then hurled him down beside her. They attacked Colonel St George next, killed him, and hacked at him till they were tired, and then, pitching his body on the bodies of his friends, they left them together in their blood." The methods then of practical patriotism in Ireland do not seem to have been widely different from what they were a hundred and twenty-five years later.

" The cowardice or prudence of the Dublin faction had disgusted him. He considered now that the conspiracy was likely to fail, or that, if it succeeded, *it would take a form which he disapproved.*" This is Froude's report of the words of the man who disclosed to Lord Downshire that Pamela in Hamburg and Lady Lucy Fitzgerald in London were the channels through which the conspirators in Ireland communicated with France. And probably Froude has reported the words, or, at least, represented the mind of the man, with absolute accuracy. A country in which such things as the murder of Colonel St George and the Uniackes could take place was not the Ulsterman's idea of a liberated Ireland.

This man was for a century and more one of the mysteries of Irish political history. His identity was entirely unknown : in the most secret State documents he figured simply as " Lord Downshire's friend." His comings and goings were those of a will-o'-the-wisp. The patient research of Mr W. J. Fitzpatrick has unveiled the secret : Lord Downshire's friend was " Samuel Turner, Esq., LL.D., barrister-at-law, of Turner's Glen, Newry, *one of the shrewdest heads of the Northern executive of the United Irishmen.*" Turner, no doubt, was a traitor to his friends ; but the words attributed to him by Froude, although they scarcely justify or render tolerable his treachery, explain very clearly the reason for it. The Northerns, the brain and sinew of the whole business, were daily growing more and more ' fed up.'

On the constitutional side of politics there was very little to encourage a thinking patriot. In the course of the year Henry Grattan and " the Opposition " formally seceded from, quitted the Irish Parliament. No doubt in the circumstances of the day opposition was a sterile and thankless task. But the Irish Parliament, after all, was in the main Grattan's creation : however threatening the weather, however unpromising the voyage, he should not have abandoned the ship which he had launched. " Dear Leinster " improved the shining hour by a characteristic piece of fatuity. About April 1797 he wrote to the Viceroy informing him that he proposed to petition His Majesty to dismiss his present Ministers. The Viceroy not unnaturally remarked that, in such case, the Duke would doubtless resign a civil office of profit held by him under the Crown. Whereupon the Duke dramatically declared that, as the Viceroy deemed him unworthy of civil office, he must likewise deem him unworthy of military trust. And the Duke of Leinster resigned command of—the Kildare militia. Yet in Ireland, where all things are possible, this admixture of childish imbecility and childish insolence found its admirer, its sacred bard. A youthful militia officer resigned his commission : " I received," said he, " this sword from your Grace. To your hand I return it untarnished. And may it rust in its scabbard ere it be drawn to support a faction that has insulted my country in the person of Leinster's Duke." Had Wolfe Tone been present, he probably would have noted in his Journal, " Huzza. God bless everyone generally. To bed drunk." It is not thus that revolutions are made or nations liberated.

Samuel Turner's information, important though it was, was not directly the cause of the arrest and death of Lord Edward Fitzgerald. For this the guilt or responsibility falls on meaner agents. And Turner cannot fairly be dubbed a mere receiver of blood money. He certainly does suggest in one of his letters that Mr Pitt might let him have " a cool five hundred " ; but he adds, and there seems to be no reason to suspect him of untruth, that he had spent three times that sum in obtaining the information which he placed at the disposal of Dublin Castle.

Dissatisfied though the Northerns might be with the indecision, vacillation, procrastination of the South, there were still amongst them many who urged a bold attempt, a desperate throw of the dice, an effort by Irishmen to do something for themselves without the help of outsiders. They urged an attempt to seize Dublin Castle : they were confident, or had been led to believe, that many of the Irish militia regiments were disaffected and would come over to their side. With this bolder policy Lord Edward, as might have been expected, was in fullest sympathy : he was never the man to let ' I would ' wait upon ' I dare not.' There is something pathetic about the figures on which he based his hopes of success, or rather in the reliance which he placed in mere figures. Lord Edward calculated that he would have at his disposal some 280,000 Irishmen. Certainly he ' spoke by the book,' but a revolutionary army on paper is a vastly different thing from a revolutionary army in being. And one consideration might have given Lord Edward pause. Nothing can be done in this world without money ; and the United Irishmen proposed to borrow half a million from France and Spain. But the total sum raised from Irishmen for the freeing of their country from the yoke of England was less than fifteen hundred pounds ! Still, Lord Edward was all for action : his pleadings, as recorded by Dr Madden, with a doubting Thomas among his followers have been aptly likened by

Miss Taylor to the pleadings of Abraham with the Lord in the matter of the cities of the plain. If fifteen thousand supporting French troops could not be obtained, might not the attempt be made with ten, even with five thousand ? But were five thousand Frenchmen a more likely prospect than fifteen ? And doubting Thomas uttered some words which, sensible enough in themselves, would have been still more sensible if, in a sense, ' inverted.' " My Lord," he said, " you delegate your authority *to those whom you think to be like yourself.*" This was but a partial truth. Lord Edward did not hand down authority to subordinates : rather he accepted authority handed up to him without due inquiry as to the capacity, courage, honesty of those who professed themselves ready to accept his orders. And while Lord Edward manœuvred his paper armies, while the Executive Committee of the United Irishmen busied itself with paper conspiracies, very practical hands were preparing to drop the curtain on the childish tragi-comedy.

The Nationalists of Ireland have complained, and with justice, that at every step the men of '98, or, more accurately, the forerunners of the actual rising of '98, were betrayed by their associates. In the immortal metaphor of a later-day politician those who are rowing in the same boat should not throw stones at each other's glass. No treachery can be imagined baser than that of Leonard M'Nally who betrayed to the Crown the defence which his clients proposed to set up ; but, says Teeling in a mood of complacent self-congratulation : " The Crown lawyers have often viewed with amazement the powerful exertions of our inimitable Curran when defending the life of a client ; and it seemed to them a matter of the most unaccountable surprise how this popular advocate could anticipate the most important disclosures. In fact the United Irishmen had friends in many departments of whom Lord Camden and his advisers little dreamed." Lord Camden and his advisers also had their ' friends.' *À bon chat, bon rat.*

Mr Thomas Reynolds was a duly sworn United Irishman : he was also husband of Miss Witherington, the sister of Mrs Wolfe Tone. His marriage may have seemed to the unthinking a guarantee of his fidelity. Yet he proved to be a traitor, a betrayer of the men who placed implicit trust in him. There has been much and unfruitful discussion of his motives : discussions, apologies, excuses, explanations will not alter facts. The basest villain seldom acts at first with a clear apprehension of the measure of his villainy. There is not much more to be said.

The closer connection of Lord Edward with Reynolds seems to have been accidental, the result of a chance meeting in Dublin. The fact in itself suggests how very little Lord Edward knew of the inner workings of the conspiracy to which he committed himself. This much at least may be said in Reynolds' exculpation : he did not seek the acquaintance and confidence of Lord Edward with the express intention of betraying him. Lord Edward, indeed, seems rather to have thrust his confidence on Reynolds ; it is said that he proposed to appoint him a Colonel in the armed forces of the insurrection. It is not at all improbable that Reynolds was one of these conspirators who much prefer conspiring to fighting : so long as the proceedings of the United Irishmen showed no sign of advancing beyond the stage of mysterious meetings, returns of rather mythical troops, secret correspondence with the agents of foreign powers, Reynolds would have remained dumb and faithful. But the sudden introduction of a realist element or realising agent alarmed him. To protest one's readiness to die in chains for Ireland's sake was one thing ; to face a bayonet thrust or death at the end of a rope was quite another thing. To hang back in the hour of action might have meant for the coward something much more unpleasant than the mere imputation of cowardice : were the call to arms never to come, Mr Thomas Reynolds could never be blamed for his reluctance to answer it. Reynolds at once betrayed the conspiracy and provided for his own safety.

A meeting of the Executive Committee had been arranged for the morning of March 12th at the house of Oliver Bond. Reynolds was to have been present : he sent a note begging to be excused on the score of a sudden and serious illness of his wife. In his place there came the Town Major with an adequate force of armed men. It is said that they obtained admission by means of the password disclosed by Reynolds : this may or may not be true, but truth or falsity is here of little importance. Officers of the law on the tracks of treason are not held back by a childish playing with words and signs. Wellnigh all the fish were found in the net; and a profusion of documents elucidatory of the conspiracy and damnatory of the conspirators was available for the inspection of Dublin Castle.

Lord Edward Fitzgerald was not among those taken : it is quite possible that, kept as he was in practical ignorance of the United Irishmen's proceedings in council, he had received no summons or invitation to attend the meeting. And indeed at the moment there was very little which the Government could charge against him. That he was ready to lead the United Irishmen in the field probably was a matter of fairly common knowledge ; but mere willingness to play an active part in a rising which has not taken place, and which may never take place, is not an offence against the Law. He had prepared a plan of Dublin, noting some strategic points, and he had drawn up an informing but somewhat academic pamphlet on street fighting. Such documents adduced after overt action might be proof of intention : when neither preceded nor followed by action they, in a Court of Justice, were not worth more than the paper on which they were written. And whether he himself desired to make use of it or not, there was still cast over Lord Edward as a protective cloak the vast influence of the Fitzgerald family. It is a significant fact that warrants were issued for the arrest of four persons not present at the meeting in Oliver Bond's house. Three of these persons were apprehended without difficulty : the fourth, Lord Edward Fitzgerald, apparently was indiscoverable. The truth of the matter is

contained in a remark half good-humoured, half
contemptuous, of John Fitzgibbon to one of Lord
Edward's family : " For God's sake get that
young man out of the country. Every port is
open to you."

But Lord Edward would not accept the
opportunity offered to him. No doubt flight and
safety, while others faced the music and paid
the price, were abhorrent to him. Yet it is
difficult to see in his courage much more than
romantic silliness. He had done all that in him
lay, or that he had been allowed to do : the cause
of the United Irishmen had fallen on irretrievable
ruin through no fault of his. His position henceforth was undignified for himself, inconvenient
for his friends, and in the end disastrous for one
of his humble protectors. Here was no wily fox
baffling the hounds by trick and stratagem. Of
the underworld of conspiracy Lord Edward knew
nothing : he had not the faintest idea of how to
' go to ground.' He was utterly incapable of
concealing himself : he was passed from hand to
hand like a bale of goods among people on whom
the duty of concealing him was thrust. On one
occasion his hosts, apprehensive of a domiciliary
visit, put him to bed dressed in a woman's night-
gown and nightcap with a bottle of medicine on
the table by his bedside.

Pitched from pillar to post Lord Edward
arrived for the first time at the house where in
the end he was taken. This was the house of one
Nicholas Murphy, a feather merchant of Thomas
Street. Thomas Street lies south of the Liffey :
it is part of a continuous street line that runs

due west from the gate of Trinity College. Murphy was not a United Irishman; there is nothing to suggest that he had the slightest knowledge of, or sympathy with, the plans of the United Irishmen. But when he threw himself, or was thrown by others, on the protection of Nicholas Murphy, Lord Edward struck a note in the Irish character which has never rung false. Conspiracy in Ireland was then, and always has been, riddled with treachery : it is a common Irish saying that in a meeting of three Irish conspirators there are always two informers. But the man who, without the slightest claim on his host's generosity, throws himself on the generosity of his host, is never betrayed. Hamilton Rowan, when a reward of £1000 was offered for his arrest, boldly revealed himself to two poor fishermen of Howth. Wealth incalculable for them was within their grasp : " Divil a fear, your honour, but we'll put you safe in France," was their answer. Nicholas Murphy, perhaps with a shrug of his shoulders, accepted his guest and set about his concealment. It was not an easy task : Lord Edward himself could give no help, and his immediate friends offered little but hindrance. Tony with his black face was questing round in search of his master ; a United Irishman named Samuel Neilson, of gigantic stature and singularly small intellect, patrolled the street with sly nods and winks and adjurations to caution. Finally some demented sympathiser conveyed to Mr Murphy's house a set of garments which, in his opinion, Lord Edward might suitably don and walk abroad. These were a coat, jacket and trousers of green and red, with a cap of weirdly original design. Poor Mr Murphy bestowed these things beneath his feathers, and at one moment of alarm hid Lord Edward in an angle of the roof of his warehouse.

From Mr Murphy's house Lord Edward was removed to the houses of Messrs Cormick and Moore, also of Thomas Street ; thence he was shifted to the house of Mrs Dillon at Portobello ; and from Portobello he returned once more to Thomas Street and Mr Nicholas Murphy. Murphy may well have sighed when he saw him. For by this time the arrest was a matter of police craft rather than of state craft ; and unimaginative policemen set to the task of an arrest set about the task with matter-of-fact competence, and without afterthought or ' underthought ' of the hunted man's personality. To make the arrest was their duty : what might follow thereupon was none of their affair.

But ere Lord Edward was actually taken, an attempt was made to take him in which we hear the soft sibilance of the kiss of Judas. Thomas Street, as said already, lies south of the Liffey. From Thomas Street Watling Street leads due north to the river bank : intersecting Watling Street and parallel to Thomas Street runs Island Street. On Island Street was the back entrance to the house of a barrister, one Francis Magan. Magan was a friend of Moore, at whose house Lord Edward for the moment lay : he offered his own house as a refuge, and he suggested with seeming prudence that Lord Edward might enter by night through the garden door opening on

Island Street. He had disclosed this invitation to Edward Cooke, a secretary at Dublin Castle, and he had been promised ample blood money for his disclosure. The trap was set, and the mouse walked into it : that he walked out again was due to one of those accidents which now and then intervene in the affairs of mice and men.

The officers to whom the business of Lord Edward's arrest had been entrusted were named Sirr, Swan, and Ryan. To their names the title ' Major ' is usually prefixed—" Said Major Swan to Major Sirr " is the beginning of a well-known Irish street ballad—but it seems likely that all three were ' officers of the watch ' rather than commissioned officers of the regular army. Lord Edward was to repair to Magan's house on the night of May 18 : unobtrusively every street was beset. In Watling Street Lord Edward actually bumped into Major Sirr : the business was as good as done. But on that night Lord Edward had as his companion one Gallagher, a man of prodigious strength and probably somewhat of a desperado, to act as bodyguard. Gallagher was armed with some kind of sword or dagger : he attacked Sirr and his men with such fury that in the *mêlée* Lord Edward made his escape. Gallagher gave Sirr seven ferocious thrusts. But beneath his clothes Sirr wore a chain mail shirt : this saved his life, but the mere force of Gallagher's blows for the moment incapacitated him. Lord Edward returned to his hiding place at Nicholas Murphy's house.

But evidently the end was in sight. Lord Edward *must* be somewhere in the small quadrilateral formed by Thomas Street on the north, Island Street on the south, Watling Street on the west, and Dirty Lane on the east. The faithful but foolish Neilson on guard in the street was proof that Lord Edward was somewhere near : the step from an indefinite somewhere to a definite where could not now be a long one.

Lord Edward had dined on the afternoon of May 19, and had retired to his bedroom. Some hours later Nicholas Murphy went up to his room to call him down to tea. He heard a noise behind him ; he looked round ; Major Swan was in the room. What followed is not quite easy to make out in detail.

Apparently Lord Edward, armed with a dagger, sprang at Swan. Swan raising his pistol fired at him : either the pistol missed fire or Swan missed his aim. Swan then struck Murphy—who does not seem to have done anything on either side of the fight—in the face with his pistol butt, and directed a soldier who entered at the moment to take Murphy away. Ryan was next on the scene : Lord Edward fell on him, and stabbed him in the stomach. What Swan was doing at this moment is not very clear : it is suggested that, as Ryan entered the room, he left it and ran downstairs to summon further aid. He returned with Sirr : Ryan was lying mortally wounded on the floor. Swan closed with Lord Edward ; they struggled, and, it may be supposed, for a moment fell apart. Sirr, drawing his pistol, fired point blank at Lord Edward and hit him in the right shoulder. Now came more soldiers : Lord Edward was overpowered and

bound.   He was taken in a sedan chair to Dublin
Castle.

There was something chivalrous in Wolfe
Tone's refusal of Bompart's advice, of the entreaties of his French comrades to leave the
Hoche ere she went into action against hopeless
odds.   If Bompart and his crew could fight, so
could Tone.   In fair fight upon the open sea
Death might come to Irishman as easily as to
Frenchman : that Death, should the inevitable
end of the battle find the Irishman still living,
might come again with a hangman's rope in his
hand was a contingency too remote to be worth
the worry of thinking about it.   Gallagher's
wild onset in Watling Street—he was not fighting
for himself—was the almost automatic act of a
brave, simple man.   But this murderous rough
and tumble in a bedroom was another matter.
There was no hope of escape : resistance could
effect nothing.   And the manner of Lord Edward's
resistance suggests some sudden throwback to
twelfth-century savagery, the awakening of some
savage spirit long dormant but not dead in the
Fitzgerald blood.   The ferocity with which he
stabbed the luckless Ryan may be judged from
the horrible and yet half comic condolence in a
letter written by Sirr to Ryan's son, " I viewed
his intestines with grief and sorrow."

Moreover, so far Lord Edward had not really
so much to fear.   All pious assurances to the
contrary, the Law is still somewhat a regarder of
persons, and in eighteenth-century Ireland the
Law made small pretence of being anything else.
The influence, the testimony of aristocratic friends

had extricated Arthur O'Connor, nephew of Lord Longueville, from the very tight corner into which the company of Messrs Quigley and Binns had led him : it would be strange if the prodigious influence of the Duke of Leinster, the Duke of Richmond, Lord Holland, Charles James Fox, and others could not do as much for Lord Edward Fitzgerald. But treason, something abstract and intangible, is one thing ; the killing of an officer of the Law is quite another thing. Treason is mainly a matter of opinion ; murder is altogether a matter of fact. And whatever may be the appropriate penalty for treason, the inevitable penalty for murder is meted out on the gallows.

Nevertheless " the good family," or some members of it, did their best. It is interesting that the chief to whom the clan first turned for the handling of the affair was the dour William Ogilvie, once Lord Edward's tutor and now husband of his mother. It is suggested to him that the Duchess of Leinster might throw herself at the King's feet, plead for exile, for anything rather than that which " the good family " shudderingly foresaw. Evidently William Ogilvie bestirred himself : the position which he had now won may be judged from the people with whom he corresponded. The Duke of Richmond rather quibbles ; the Duke of Portland is courteous, but his letter contains the ominous warning that little hope is entertained of Mr Ryan's recovery. Even " George P." writes to Mr Ogilvie from Carlton House : evidently Ogilvie had approached him. The Prince would be willing to write to the Earl of Clare—Royalty would appeal to the clemency of John Fitzgibbon —but he fears that such action might be misconstrued, might do more harm than good. Charles Fox is of opinion—probably he is right— that his going to Dublin would, if anything, prejudice the cause of Lord Edward. In Ireland some of "the good family" desired to visit Lord Edward in prison. Permission was refused to them, and, in the circumstances, not unreasonably refused.

But as the days passed by it became plain that Lord Edward Fitzgerald would never appear for trial by an earthly Court. And now Lady Louisa Conolly, sister of the Duchess, on her knees before the Viceroy made her plea for just one moment, one word of farewell to the boy whom she had loved. There could be no question now of earthly advantage or indulgence to the prisoner : surely Lord Camden might have granted a woman's prayer. He refused coldly ; and in her extremity Lady Louisa turned to the strange man to whom everybody, everything in Ireland turned at last—to John Fitzgibbon, Earl of Clare and Lord High Chancellor of Ireland.

The Lord Chancellor was entertaining friends at his house in Ely Place : he left his guests to receive Lady Louisa. " I cannot set aside the order of the Lord Lieutenant," he said, " but I can myself take you to the prison." There was small likelihood that any subordinate would plead orders from above did the Earl of Clare demand admittance.

So they drove away together. What may have been Lady Louisa's thoughts ? Lord Edward Fitzgerald had six hundred years of well-nigh royal blood running in his veins ; she was daughter of a Duke and sister to a Duchess. The man by her side was grandson of a peasant : his talents, his iron will, had made him virtual Dictator of a people that still looked upon him as an upstart. Lord Edward had fought against him, and had been beaten to the earth ; she had begged for his mercy, and she had not been denied.

Fitzgibbon broke the silence : " Would Lord Henry Fitzgerald wish to see his brother ? "

" Yes."

" We shall call for him at Leinster House."

Lady Louisa and Lord Henry were with the dying man for an hour or so : Fitzgibbon waited apart. He, says Teeling, " was a monster whose delight was the misery of man, and the harmony of whose soul was the shriek of despair." When aunt and brother came from the death-bed, they found the cold, stern Earl of Clare weeping.

In the early hours of the morning of June 4 Lord Edward Fitzgerald died. The tragic comedy was played out, the curtain had fallen for the last time. Somehow the passionate apostrophe that ends Whyte-Melville's ' Good for Nothing ' recurs to the mind : " The blinding tears did my old eyes good. The bright, the brave, the beautiful, and was it all to end like this. Oh, my boy, my boy."

Lord Henry Fitzgerald had taken the packet for Holyhead : he did not pay to his brother the poor compliment of accompanying the corpse to its burial place at St Werburg's Church.

Nicholas Murphy, who had sheltered Lord Edward, spent a year and more in prison. He came out to find his stock looted, his house a shell—it had been used as a barracks—his furniture destroyed or stolen. Friends advised him to approach the Duke of Leinster. " His Grace," he writes, " allowed me the honour of an interview, and on seeing me he seemed to feel very much, and I thought I saw a troubled melancholy in his countenance. However, in our conversation I clearly understood that His Grace was not inclined in any way to offer me the smallest pecuniary assistance. My friends as well as myself were disappointed."

Dear Leinster !

ROBERT EMMET

1778-1803

" When he who adores thee has left but the name
  Of his faults and his sorrows behind,
Oh, say wilt thou weep, when they darken the fame
  Of a life that for thee was resigned."

—MOORE.

CHAPTER I.

THE DREAM.

IN the bitterest sarcasm there is often something cathartic, something wholesome for its recipient. This is a picture of the eighteenth century Volunteers freeing Ireland from her chains : "The half Americanised artisans of Belfast and Newry, officered by attorneys and shopkeepers, glittered glorious in their new uniforms. Ireland was free ; Ireland was a nation. The strings long silent of the Irish harp were sounding in the breeze ; the green flag was blowing out with the emblem blazoned on its folds, *Hibernia tandem libera*, Ireland at length the free ; free with the help of arms which had been begged at the gate of Dublin Castle ; free from the fell authority which, notwithstanding its stupid tyranny and still more stupid negligence, had given Ireland its laws and its language, had prevented its inhabitants from destroying one another like howling wolves, and at least enabled them to exist ; free from this, but not free from sloth and ignorance, from wild imaginations, from political dishonesty which had saturated the tissues of her being." Certainly it is a wonderful picture of a tawdry theatricality. Probably it is a truer picture of Irish patriotism than most Irishmen are willing to admit.

In graver mood and in another connection Froude writes again : " There is no word in human language which so charms the ear as liberty. There is no word which so little pains have been taken to define, or which is used to express ideas more opposite. There is a liberty which is the liberty of a child or savage, the liberty of animals, the vagrant liberty which obeys no restraint for it is conscious of no limitation. There is a liberty which arises from the subjugation of self and the control of circumstances, which consists in the knowledge of what ought to be done, and in a power to do it obtained by patient labour and discipline."

Has Ireland ever understood or sought that liberty which is based on man's just appreciation of circumstances and unsparing judgment of his own weaknesses ? Or has liberty been for the Irish some indefinite toy to be handed to them ready-made by some Fairy Godmother, to be enjoyed to-day and thrown aside as unsuited to the whims of to-morrow ? " Free Trade," cried the Irish in 1779, and trailed about King William's statue before the Irish Parliament House two pieces of cannon with " Free Trade Or This " emblazoned on them. " Free Trade," wrote an Irish patriot a hundred years later, " another familiar demon of Government—Free Trade that carries off our harvests of the year before—comes in, freights another ship, and carries off from Cork to Liverpool a cargo against the American cargo."

Ireland would be ' free ' of England. Such freedom may be in a measure possible and advantageous ; but no device of politics will win for a nation freedom from the facts of geography and economics. Switzerland is politically independent of France and Italy ; but she cannot continue to exist in economic independence of both, or in open hostility to either. Ireland can perhaps with advantage to herself make her own laws, control her own commerce ; but she cannot isolate herself, a little stagnant pool, from the great trade currents of Europe. She can exist in freedom as England's friend : she can exist as England's enemy only as the subject of some other Power. In the eighteenth century she was for France, in the twentieth for Germany, a potentially useful stick wherewith to beat England : about few things did France or Germany care less than what might happen to the stick in the process of beating. Freedom will not endow an individual, a nation, with capacities, potentialities which are not in him or them. " The artisan or the artist learns in an apprenticeship under the guidance of others to conquer the difficulties of his profession. When the conquest is complete, he is free." True : but only so far as in him lies to conquer. No striving, no guidance of others will endow the average pupil in a drawing school with the freedom of Turner's hand. The completest freedom to dig will not enable the Englishman to find gold, the Italian coal, beneath his native soil. Incessantly the Irish have sought a freedom that shall lift them above all human necessities and restraints : they have not found it, because no such thing exists, or ever can exist in this world. For a brief moment the leader of the fantastic hunt for the crock of gold at the rainbow's foot is a hero in the eyes of those who follow him. Next moment he falls, and is forgotten. Robert Emmet sought to win ' this freedom ' for his fellow countrymen at the price of his life : seemingly no one of them troubled to mark with certainty where his body, mangled by the public executioner, was laid to rest.

The circumstances of his birth are a tragedy, or a satire on the morals of his father's day. In the year 1760 Robert Emmet, a successful physician, married Elizabeth Mason ; and in the succeeding seventeen years the unfortunate bride bore to her husband sixteen children. Dr Emmet had a habit of quoting Latin tags ; and a line frequently on his lips was the Vergilian *tantum religio potuit suadere malorum*. He was, no doubt, a ' religious ' man according to the thought of his day, one who would have recoiled in pious horror from sexual relationship outside the marriage tie. Did it never occur to him that licence can be intra-marital as well as extra-marital, that philoprogenitiveness is not a sufficient excuse for infanticide ? Of sixteen youthful Emmets twelve died in infancy : so wholly unregarded did their deaths pass that popular report ordinarily credits Dr Emmet with but three sons and one daughter. There is an added grimness in the doctor's bestowal of his own Christian name on the Irish patriot-to-be. It had already been bestowed on four preceding sons, no one of whom lived long enough to pronounce it. The family history of the Tones and of the Emmets should give pause to the celibate opponents of birth control to-day. This, say such, is an interference with an immortal soul. Is it lawful to create immortal souls only that the bodies which contain them may perish as perishes the spawn of the fish of the sea ?

Robert the fifth may have owed his survival to the fact that he was the last of his mother's children, and that a certain measure of maternal care could so be devoted to his upbringing. He was born in 1778 in Dublin, probably at a house in St Stephen's Green to which his father had recently removed from Molesworth Street. Grafton Street, Dawson Street and Kildare Street run parallel to one another, and from north to south. St Stephen's Green is the southern boundary of all three ; and Molesworth Street, north of St Stephen's Green and running west to east, connects Dawson Street with Kildare Street. Perhaps even in Dr Emmet's day the movement of society and wealth across the Liffey from north to south had started. By the end of the nineteenth century the splendid Georgian mansions of north Dublin had sunk to be slatternly ' tenement houses.'

For most people within and without Ireland Robert Emmet the younger lives in Moore's sugary sentimental lines addressed to Emmet's fiancée, Sarah Curran :

> She is far from the land where her young hero sleeps
> And lovers around her are sighing ;
> But coldly she turns from their gaze and weeps,
> For her heart in his grave is lying.

Some may be repelled by this public exhibition of a dead man's secret and sacred affections. Emmet himself on the brink of the grave asked that the world should extend to him " the charity of its silence." But Moore has offered a more seemly tribute to the friend of his College days : " Were I to number, indeed, the men among all I have ever known, who appeared to me to combine in the greatest degree pure moral worth with intellectual power, I should among the highest of the few place Robert Emmet. Wholly free from the faults and frailties of youth—though how capable he was of the most devoted passion events afterwards proved—the pursuit of science seemed at the time the only object that at all divided his thoughts with that enthusiasm for Irish freedom which in him was a hereditary as well as a national feeling." Alas, the word ' enthusiasm ' is too aptly descriptive of the Irish patriots of that day. Enthusiasm is a noble sentiment ; but it needs to be guided and controlled by reason and experience. These Irishmen sought with enthusiasm a vague ' liberty,' and sought it vaguely if enthusiastically. The story of the seeking would be comic, had it not so often a tragic ending. Save for the dreadful scene of September 23, 1803, the story of Robert Emmet would be somewhat of a farce.

Two of the elder Emmet children had no influence on the fate or fortunes of their youngest brother. These were Christopher and Mary. Mary Emmet grew up, married, died : there is nothing more to be said about her. Christopher Emmet, the eldest son, seems to have been an exceptionally brilliant young man. He was called to the Bar ; almost from the day of his call he attracted the attention of j ¹ges and solicitors ; a great career was opening before him ; when suddenly he died at the age of but twenty-nine. One of his little peculiarities has its interest. He was extremely short-sighted, but he refused, it is said from motives of vanity, to wear spectacles. The explanation of his refusal, perhaps plausible in the case of a young girl, seems utterly unbelievable in the case of a young professional man. But myopia and the neglect of it seem to have been common in the Emmet family ; for Robert, too, was short-sighted, and like his elder brother he neglected to wear glasses. When a prisoner in the Newgate of Dublin, awaiting a trial to which there could be but one ending, he formed a plan, futile as were most of the unfortunate young man's plans, of escape. He wrote to some friend outside—of course the letter was intercepted—explaining how he might possibly slip out unobserved, and asking that a change of dress for him be smuggled into the prison. Spectacles, he thinks, will help the disguise ; from which the inference may be drawn that he did not habitually wear them. And he adds casually the information, "No. 5 fits my sight." A man so far blind must be very blind indeed ; and, if Robert Emmet habitually refused or neglected to wear glasses, it is a not unreasonable supposition that while engaged in an extremely delicate and dangerous conspiracy he can scarcely have been able to identify or recognise his fellow conspirators. This seems, to say the least of it, an extremely stupid course of conduct ; but there is something more to be said. What is to be thought of a parent, a reputedly competent medical man, who allows his children to wander through life hampered by a physical defect at once so serious and so easily remediable? And another story of young Robert's boyhood occurs to the mind. He was fond of playing with chemicals, and he had the childish habit of biting his nails or sucking his fingers. On one occasion, having busied himself with chemical experiments and having neglected to wash his hands, he imbibed by way of his fingers some drug which made him extremely ill. He dosed himself with some primitive medicament, suffered tortures throughout the night, and appeared next morning with his face " pinched and yellow as an orange." It is strange that he did not consult his father, who presumably could have relieved him. The shoemaker's wife is proverbially the worst shod, and the doctor's child may be the child who suffers most from the lack of medical care. But there is a limit to the application of proverbs ; and these facts suggest that Dr Emmet, whatever may have been his other virtues, was a negligent, unobservant parent ; that the son had either little confidence in his father's ability, or else little expectation of his father's sympathy. Young Emmet grew up in a shiftless household : his mother, poor woman, exhausted by her dreadful succession of childbirths, can scarcely have been an effective influence in her children's lives.

Not indeed that old Dr Emmet was a spineless

nonentity. In his letters he affects somewhat
the tone of Hebrew patriarch or Roman father.
To one of his children he issued an extraordinary
order with which the child complied. When
Christopher Emmet died, his brother, Thomas
Addis, was a qualified medical man aged about
twenty-five years. His father directed young
Dr Thomas Emmet to abandon the career which
he had chosen, and to qualify himself to take his
brother's place at the Bar. Young Dr Emmet
meekly fell in with his father's wishes. It is
difficult to conjecture what motive can have
prompted the father. Possibly the early success
of Christopher Emmet suggested to him that the
Law was a much more lucrative profession than
Medicine. Possibly there was some element of
snobbery working in his mind ; for undoubtedly
in those days a ' gentleman of the long robe '
took social precedence of ' the apothecary.' But
Christopher Emmet's uncommon aptitude for
Law was scarcely a guarantee that his brother
would prove equally apt ; and in any case to
throw aside at once, and unused, hardly won
professional qualifications, and to start specu-
latively on a preparation for an entirely new
career, seems to be an extraordinarily feckless
course for a father to advise or for a son to
follow. Dr Thomas Emmet, however, was in
due course called to the Bar ; and, if he did not
disclose the marked ability of his brother, he
appears soon to have laid the foundations of a
fairly satisfactory practice. Yet, indirectly, the
change of profession may have been a disadvantage to him. A medical man is of necessity

compelled to take little but concrete, proven facts into his consideration : the derangements of the human frame may be set right, but the frame itself cannot be reconstituted, even in imagination, on some new and better plan. The facts of anatomy might have been for an enthusiastic young Irishman at the close of the eighteenth century a more stabilising study than legal and political speculation. And, in some small measure at least, it was Thomas Emmet's influence that dragged young Robert into the vortex of Irish political extremism : the influence may not have been very great, but, so far as it went, it was scarcely salutary.

Young Robert was educated at one or two Dublin schools, presumably day-schools, and in due course he entered Trinity College. The customary age of entrance to the University was then much lower than it is to-day : Robert Emmet entered in October 1793, before he had completed his sixteenth year. His College career was ended by a practical, if not formal, expulsion in February 1798 ; and this date at once provokes the question what was he then doing in Trinity. In the ordinary course he should have taken his degree in October 1797. He was not engaged in a post-graduate professional school, nor was he a candidate for Fellowship. It seems a natural if disagreeable inference that Robert had failed to take his degree at the appointed time, and that he failed from want of work rather than from want of wit. Mr Daly, who has edited some of Dr Madden's manuscripts, makes a strange muddle of this part of Emmet's life by stating that Emmet was born in 1782, entered Trinity in his sixteenth year (1798), and left Trinity in 1798. This is obviously absurd. Moore, the poet, who knew Emmet well, remarks that Emmet was about "a class" senior to himself. Moore entered in the spring term of 1794.

Of Emmet as a University student one of his biographers has said that he "was brilliant and took several prizes." This very vague statement may mean anything or nothing. Emmet's formal University record is extant, and it may instructively be placed in juxtaposition to that of his forerunner in Irish patriotism, Theobald Wolfe Tone. The records read as follows :—

"Tone, Theobald Wolfe, Pen. (Mr Craig), Feb. 19, 1781, aged 17 ; s of Peter, Mechanicus ; b Dublin. Sch. 1784. B.A. Vern. 1785. LL.B. Vern. 1789."

"Emmet, Robert, Pen. (Mr Lewis), Oct. 1793, aged 15 ; s of Robert, Medicus ; b Dublin."

For those unacquainted with the formal terminology of Dublin University some explanation of technical abbreviations may be needful. "Pen." denotes an ordinary undergraduate, or Pensioner. Neither Tone nor Emmet was a Sizar (Poor Scholar), nor was either a Fellow Commoner. A Fellow Commoner is a relic of snobbery now, it is to be hoped, buried and forgotten. Such undergraduate, in virtue of paying double fees, was entitled to prefix a 'Mr' to his name, to dine at the High Table in Hall, and to wear a velvet cap. The names in brackets (Craig and Lewis) denote the 'tutors' of Tone and Emmet respectively. A young man entering

Trinity College must enter under a 'tutor,' one
of the Fellows of the College, who throughout
the undergraduate's career acts as his guardian.
The word ' tutor ' thus used has not necessarily
a connotation of teaching.

The entry " Sch. 1784 " against Tone's name
is of some importance. ' Scholarship ' in Dublin
University had in Tone's day and for more than
a hundred years to follow a meaning somewhat
different from the same word as used in the
English Universities. There were a certain
number of scholarships on the Foundation of the
University; they were awarded only in classics
and mathematics, and they were tenable for five
years. Undergraduates ordinarily competed for
scholarships in their second or third academic
year, and the winning of a scholarship was regarded as proof that an undergraduate had
stepped forward from the rank and file. Degrees
and their dates explain themselves. Compared
with Tone's record that of Emmet is inglorious.
It would be absurd to judge a young man once
and for ever by academic successes achieved
within his first twenty-one years. But the test,
such as it was, was the same for Emmet as for
Tone, and the result of this early test is confirmed by the history, tragically short though
that history is, of their later lives. Tone, tried
by any test, was quite incomparably the abler of
the two.

Both young men were, in their day, members of
the College Historical Society, the youthful
Parliament of the University. Tone became its
Auditor, or Leader : here, as elsewhere, he

forges to the front. By the rules of the University current politics were excluded from the debates of the students ; but Moore truthfully remarks that in his day " though every care was taken to exclude from the subjects of debate all questions verging towards the politics of the day, it was always easy enough by a side-wind of digression or allusion to bring Ireland, and the prospects then opening upon her, within the scope of the orator's view." Similarly, a hundred years after the time of Tone and Emmet, the direct discussion of the then burning topic of ' Home Rule ' was forbidden. Nevertheless, for all practical purposes, discussion was easy. It was but necessary to move that " the House considers (or does not consider) Mr Pitt's Irish policy to have been justified."

If Moore is to be trusted, Robert Emmet's speeches, in which the speaker took full advantage of all " side-winds of digression and allusion," on such proposals as the superiority of Democracy to Aristocracy, at these College debates had a quite amazing, and, in the eyes of Authority, mischievous effect on the minds of his hearers. So much so, indeed, that the Board took the unusual step of sending to a meeting a speaker expressly charged to confute young Mr Emmet. And Moore, to his credit, relates with complete but rueful candour the result of the mission : the emissary of Authority (his name is said to have been Geraghty) in argument absolutely annihilated his opponent, " much to the mortification of us who gloried in Emmet as our leader." The completeness of Geraghty's victory may be judged by Moore's description of Emmet's defeat : " He began, in the full career of his eloquence, to hesitate and repeat his words ; and then, after an effort or two to recover himself, sat down."

If the story be true, it exhibits the old Dons of Trinity in a human rôle, and in a rôle extremely creditable to themselves as educators of youth. The subject of the debate is not known : it may have had no particular connection with current Irish politics. Mr Geraghty (if this was his name) apparently made no use of his official position (if he enjoyed any such position) to confute his undergraduate adversary : he relied entirely on his eloquence and on his technical skill as a debater. And he prevailed utterly. Really no better educational experiment could be devised than that of affording able, but because of their youth inexperienced speakers an opportunity to measure their strength fairly against a strong and wily opponent. Much may be learned from a defeat at the hands of a superior. It was possibly a humiliating, but assuredly a salutary experience for Mr Gigadibs, " the literary man " and annihilator of religious creeds, to cross blades with that courteously formidable ecclesiastical swordsman, Nicholas Blougram.

One more curious but characteristic anecdote Moore tells of Emmet. He was playing the piano in his rooms, and Emmet was listening. Suddenly at an Irish air Emmet started up : " Would that I were marching to that air," he exclaimed, " at the head of twenty thousand men." But marching why, where and whither ?

And it is easier to march with twenty thousand men than to march at their head!

Emmet's College career ended suddenly at the visitation of Trinity held in February 1798 by John Fitzgibbon, Vice-Chancellor of Dublin University, Earl of Clare and Lord High Chancellor of Ireland. About this whole business Moore makes this very sensible remark : " Imperious and harsh as then seemed the policy of setting up a sort of inquisitorial tribunal, armed with the power of examining witnesses on oath, and in a place devoted to the instruction of youth, I cannot but confess that the facts which came out in the course of the evidence went far to justify even this arbitrary proceeding." As regards Robert Emmet the facts were these.

The Vice-Chancellor directed his inquiry to the discovery of how far the teachers and pupils of Trinity were concerned in, cognisant of the plottings of the United Irishmen for the subversion of the established Government of Ireland. He summoned various persons before him, and to them he addressed his questions. Some of these summoned appeared and gave their answers, satisfactory or unsatisfactory as the case might be : some, although summoned, neither appeared nor answered. It is a fair presumption that they had no satisfactory answer to give. Says Moore : " There were a few—and among that number poor Robert Emmet—whose total absence from the whole scene, as well as the dead silence that day after day followed the calling out of their names, proclaimed how deep had been their share in the unlawful proceedings inquired into by this tribunal." In the end it was perfectly clear that the Vice-Chancellor was about to recommend the expulsion of a certain number of students (the number is said to have been eighteen), among them being Robert Emmet. Emmet saved himself from expulsion by voluntarily taking his name off the College books. It may be that permission to do so was accorded to him as a favour.

" Imperious and harsh " as may then and later have seemed the policy and orders of John Fitzgibbon, it scarcely can be denied that Fitzgibbon's proceedings were entirely justified, and that he himself did but his manifest duty. However bad a Government may be—and few will assert the surpassing excellence of the Government of Ireland in the year 1798—to plot the forcible subversion of such Government is treason. The success of a Revolution may justify—it is indeed the only thing that can justify—Revolution. But, success or failure apart, it is impossible to maintain the righteousness, even the expediency of boys engaging themselves in treason or taking part in Revolutions. A much heavier responsibility rests on those who knowingly permit boys entrusted to their care and instruction thus to incriminate themselves. On some such Fitzgibbon's hand fell heavily and deservedly.

In judging this particular affair, Englishmen—and there are many such—who extend their sympathy to the youthful idealism of the United Irishmen, and voice their condemnation of the Government of Ireland as it then was, would do well to remember that the eighteenth century in Ireland was not the twentieth century in England, and that there is a very marked difference between the English and Irish natures. The young Irishman, reputedly the playboy of Europe, takes himself and his engagements much more seriously than does his English counterpart.

In at least one of the great English Universities there flourishes a Communist Society. Its members on occasion promenade the streets bearing banners which proclaim their sympathy with the poor and toiling masses, their detestation of capitalistic wars ; on occasion they show themselves conspicuously ill-bred towards their own invited guests, and conspicuously contemptible before the memorial of those who died to keep their freedom for them. By appearance they are ordinarily well fed, well clothed, well shod ; it seems unlikely that any considerable number have ever worked for themselves, earned for themselves, known what it is to want. Seeing them the genuine working man not improbably spits ; the comfortable bourgeois smiles indulgently if a trifle contemptuously. And the indulgence of the bourgeois smile is justified.

For it is in the last degree unlikely that any one of these youthful advocates of Red Revolution in England will ever take any overt action towards carrying his theories to their logical conclusion in concrete fact. The English student revolutionary, usually well provided with this world's goods, is fairly certain in no long time to develop into a staunchly Conservative upholder of the British Constitution. That youthful impulses of generosity, however fantastic, should stir within his breast is in nowise to be regretted. The young Irish revolutionary of Emmet's day was painfully in earnest : he was ordinarily willing to sacrifice his own life, and invariably willing to sacrifice the lives of others, if thereby his ends might be attained. And while it may at times be expedient that one or more men should perish for the good of the community, impulsive, half-instructed boys are not best fitted to decide on the men, or to pronounce on the degree of expediency.

There are two word-portraits of Robert Emmet as he appeared about the time that he left Trinity. One is by Dr Madden : " In stature he was about five feet eight inches ; slight in his person, active, and capable of enduring great fatigue ; he walked fast, and was quick in his movements. His features were regular, his forehead high and finely formed ; his eyes were small, bright and full of expression ; his nose sharp, remarkably thin and straight ; the lower part of his face was slightly pock-pitted, and his complexion sallow. There was nothing remarkable in his appearance, except when excited in conversation." The other portrait Mr Postgate describes as " almost insulting " : certainly it is not complimentary. " Nearly twenty years of age, of an ugly, sour countenance, small eyes, but not near-sighted ; a dirty brownish complexion ; at a distance looks as if somewhat marked with smallpox ; about five feet six inches in height, rather thin than fat, but not of emaciated form ; walks briskly, but does not swing his arms."

This portrait was drawn by Dr Elrington of Trinity at the request of the police. Inasmuch as Elrington knew Emmet personally, and Dr Madden did not, the latter portrait is presumably more accurate than the former. Yet a few thoughts will suggest themselves to anyone acquainted with Trinity and its ways. Elrington at the time that he drew his picture had not seen Emmet for about five years, and may have had no very vivid personal recollection of him. Again, while Elrington, as a law-abiding subject, would comply with the demand of the police for information, it is quite possible that, as a Trinity man, he took no especial pains to make his information meticulously accurate and helpful. Save in some matter involving utter moral turpitude, it is difficult to imagine a Trinity don over anxious, or indeed over willing, to aid the Law in the apprehending of one of his former pupils.

Thus at the age of about twenty Robert Emmet found himself, in a sense, adrift on the world. He was in no danger of want : old Dr Emmet in one of his rather pompously philosophical letters describes himself as enjoying " a very competent share of wealth and health," and it does not seem that he grudged the means of subsistence to his youngest son. Indeed it would have been well for Robert Emmet, the younger, had Heaven made him the son of a father poorer, more intransigent, less tolerant of a boy's neglect to make practical use of opportunities hitherto afforded to him. Even if in the end it was Robert Emmet's destiny to be a seditious conspirator against the Government of his country, or a patriot seeking at the risk of his life to free his country from a foreign yoke unjustly imposed on her—his life and activities can be viewed from one angle or from the other—he would have been an incomparably more efficient conspirator or patriot had he served a preliminary apprenticeship in the training school of life. Tone, for all his wildness, strove with the everyday world, and prevailed against it to the extent of supporting himself, a wife and a child, until at the age of twenty-nine he became secretary to the Catholic Committee ; and thereafter he wrested a hardly and quite honestly earned livelihood from the profession of politics. " Peter, Mechanicus," may have helped him a little at the outset, but quite obviously he could not help him very much. Lord Edward Fitzgerald, born to a station in life very different from that of Tone or Emmet, did study to some purpose under his dour Scotch stepfather ; and, or ever he turned his thoughts to Irish politics, he had marched for miles with his regiment over the Irish mountains, faced death in American battlefields, blazed a trail through a Canadian wilderness, commanded men, and, *teste* William Cobbett, won those men's ungrudging respect. Like Tone he had married a wife, and like Tone had provided for her from a none too ample fortune. Tone and Fitzgerald had *lived* life ; poor Emmet up to the day of his tragic death had but looked on at life. It is an old proverb that the looker-on sees most of the game : the same thought is expressed with a dash of salutary sarcasm in the Irish saying that the best hurler is always on the ditch. No amount of looking on at a game, an exercise, a business, will fit a man for active participation therein : still less will mere looking on at the work of others fit a man to take the lead in any pursuit, sportive or serious, to which he may address himself. To hew coal at a coal face is a better preparation for the Prize Ring than the most critical study of ' Boxiana.' Especially the rough-and-tumble of practical life sets a man, almost without his knowing it, on guard against deception. Save the arch-scoundrel Leonard M'Nally no Irishman ever hookwinked Tone ; and M'Nally would have hoodwinked Satan himself. That Tone's eye did not follow the twisting threads of French policy can hardly be accounted to him for lack of intelligence : it is unlikely that these threads either started from or led up to one competent and purposeful French hand. Of the two men least fitted in the world to plan and conduct revolutions a contemporary specifies Emmet as one : " He had no knowledge of the world ; he placed trust in every man ; he was the most honest and single-minded of human beings."

It was not very clear what Emmet actually did, how he occupied himself from the time of leaving Trinity up to the time of his futile and fatal attempt to head a rising against the Government of Ireland. For a while he seems to have been nominally attached to the business of one Patten, a friend of his father. But unluckily he no more gave to business his undivided attention than he had given it to his College studies. He was everlastingly playing, as he had played in

Trinity, with political extremism. His rôle suggests a sixteenth member of a Rugby team, a ninth forward in mufti wandering aimlessly on the skirts of the scrummage. In the beginning of the new century he went abroad : when he returned to Ireland, he returned to his death.

He was a plastic figure moulded in the press of events rather than the controller of events that mould out men and measures. To understand Emmet it is necessary again to glance at, to summarise, the events of his time. A measure of repetition is unavoidable.

CHAPTER II.

AN English politician of the nineteenth century observed that it does not greatly matter what lie a political Party tells, provided that all individual members of the Party agree to tell the same lie simultaneously. The thought may be transferred in a measure to conspiracy. Whatever the intrinsic merits or demerits of the cause, the first essentials to success are that all the conspirators should have a common and clearly defined purpose, and that their efforts to attain their object should synchronise. The Irish conspirators or patriots of the 'nineties of the eighteenth century never seem to have visualised clearly the end at which they aimed, and they seem always to have been incapable of timing, co-ordinating their efforts. Furthermore, it has been alleged and generally has been admitted that they were the victims of treachery. It is the primary duty of conspirators to take reasonable precautions against betrayal ; but in this matter the Irishmen were criminally careless. Two stories will illustrate their carelessness.

The first story is told of John Keogh, the Chairman of the Catholic Committee in Dublin and the " Gog " of Wolfe Tone's Journal. The story may be apocryphal, for it is not certain that

Keogh was ever in sympathy with, or even cognisant of, the political doctrines grafted by Tone and others on the tree of religious toleration. But thus it is told. A meeting was held to consider proposals involving much more than the civic rights of Catholics. Keogh silently watched the company assemble ; then silently tapped Richard M'Cormick (Tone's " Magog ") on the shoulder, and beckoned him outside. Without, " Come away, Dick," he said, " no man's life is safe here." For this was what Keogh had noticed. A., undoubtedly trustworthy and in sympathy with the most extreme proposals, had brought with him his friends B. and C., who, he fancied, *might* be sympathetic and trustworthy. B. and C., in their turn, had brought with them D., E., F. and G. And so on. That traitors crept into conspiracies thus conducted is not surprising.

The second story is told by Sir Jonah Barrington of himself ; and Sir Jonah's peculiar position at the time that he committed his recollections and reflections to paper is some guarantee of his truthfulness. He was an old man when he wrote : he had no reward to hope for, no further punishment to fear. His career had been a strange one. After a successful career at the Bar he was raised to the Bench : thirty-two years later he was removed by the customary procedure of an Address from both Houses of Parliament praying for his removal. The charge against him was dishonesty : certain ' derelict ' monies, monies, that is, lying unclaimed and at the disposition of his Court, he had converted to his own use. He survived his disgrace by about two years, and he occupied his leisure and distracted his thoughts by the composition of his Memoirs. These Memoirs are extraordinarily well written. In them Sir Jonah essays no defence of himself : indeed he never alludes to his fall. He writes as an ' unmoral ' but rather kindly old worldling, surveying with a serene and impartial smile the scenes, friends, adversaries of his youth. And he tells this tale.

In the year 1798, before his elevation to the Bench, he was a barrister in very large practice, and as a politician he was in a general way sympathetic with the cause of Ireland. But he had never professed, nor had he ever given to anyone reason to suppose, that he either entertained a wish for the forcible subversion of the existing Government of Ireland, or that he would countenance any effort directed to that end. In the month of April he was invited to dinner at the house of Bagenal Harvey ; and at the dinner table his fellow guests discussed without reserve the forthcoming insurrection, and made no secret of the extent to which they themselves were committed. In fact, at least five of the guests at that table were hanged within a few months. Barrington, to quote his own words : "immediately wrote to Mr Secretary Cooke, without mentioning names, place or any particular source of knowledge, but simply to assure him that there was not a doubt that an insurrection would break out at a much earlier period than Government expected. I desired him to ask me no questions."

It would be wholly unjust to blame Barrington,

or to impute 'betrayal' to him. Barrington did not intrude himself, he was invited, into the company of Harvey and his friends, and he had never asked for their confidence. Persons who in the hearing of a citizen proclaim their intention of provoking insurrection and civil war have no cause for complaint should such citizen take the steps which seem to him best suited to preserve the peace. Harvey had but his own careless or boastful folly to blame.

In such a school of conspiracy young Robert Emmet received his early training. It was a singularly bad school.

Furthermore, the Irish conspirators seem to have been always incapable, metaphorically, of keeping step with one another, and, metaphorically, of getting off the mark at the sound of the pistol. Their cause never had such a chance of success as when in '96 Tone arrived off the Kerry coast. He had found means of informing his friends that a French invasion might be expected ; but not an Irish finger was stirred in support. It is unlikely that Grouchy, however irresolute, entirely failed or neglected to establish *some* communication with the shore : that seemingly no blame for his pusillanimous retreat was attached to him on his return to France may perhaps be explained by the supposition that he convinced the Directory that they had been utterly misled as to the intentions and preparedness of the Irish. And this dismal exhibition gave pause to the Northerns, the most determined republican element in Ireland. Samuel Turner, it will be remembered, was described as one of the shrewdest of the Northern Directory. His betrayal of Lord Edward Fitzgerald may not have been altogether an act of baseness. He may have been quite willing to risk his neck for Ireland, but entirely unwilling to offer it as a sacrifice to irresolution and incapacity.

Nevertheless, even after the failure of Tone, conspiracy was carried on in a straggling, desultory fashion. Seemingly the realisation of the conspiracies of '97 was to have been an armed rising in '98 under the command of Lord Edward Fitzgerald. But of the duties and details of his command Lord Edward, as has already been pointed out, seems to have been very badly informed. This conspiracy was baffled, in the main, by the treachery of Reynolds. Acting on Reynold's information Major Swan on March 17, 1798, entered a house in Bridge Street and arrested some eighteen persons, among them being MacNiven, Oliver Bond, and Thomas Addis Emmet, the doctor-lawyer brother of Robert Emmet. Arthur O'Connor had been arrested in company with the priest Quigley about a month earlier ; the discovery and death of Lord Edward followed a few months later. Lord Edward could have, and should have, escaped. And by all rules of ordinary prudence, after the wholesale arrest by Swan on March 17, conspiracy should for the time have gone to ground. Bond, Thomas Emmet, O'Connor and others were for the time being consigned to jail : unfortunately for himself Robert Emmet was allowed to remain in communication with them. He was at the time only twenty years of age, and he was smarting under the disgrace of his practical expulsion from Trinity. He was in no frame of mind to form a cool and considered judgment of men and matters.

On May 21 John and Henry Sheares were arrested at their home in Dublin. Their proclamation announcing complete success has already been described. And the discovery of the Sheares put the police on the track of yet another conspiracy. This was some scheme fathered by Neilson, the physically strong but extremely stupid Ulsterman, whose theatrical 'secrecy' had helped to disclose the hiding-place of Lord Edward. What exactly Neilson's scheme was it is impossible to say. But there exists a letter from John Sheares in which Sheares describes Neilson's scheme as vile and desperate, and threatens denunciation to the police should Neilson persist in his design. All that is definitely known is that Neilson contemplated an attack on Newgate prison. It appears that Neilson actually sallied forth with a band to make the attack ; then realised that without scaling ladders it would be impossible to effect an entrance. A few nights after the arrest of the Sheares brothers a sentry noticed a man prowling about the jail walls ; he challenged, then grappled with the prowler. It was Neilson.

Some days later the great Irish rebellion of '98 broke out, 'exploded.' It lasted a little over a month, and its events passed as a panorama before the eyes of young Robert Emmet. It must be remembered that he was a free man ;

he was in no way implicated in the charge against his elder brother.

The word 'exploded' is used of set purpose, for it is a common charge of Irish historians that Fitzgibbon and Castlereagh 'exploded' the rebellion, that is, fostered it, provoked it, brought it into being. The charge deserves some examination.

The gist of the allegation is this. Fitzgibbon and Castlereagh were determined to bring about a Legislative Union of England and Ireland : they therefore created the Irish rebellion in order to prove that the Government of Ireland by any means other than a Union had become impossible. But surely this is to impute to two very clever men the mentality of Charles Lamb's Chinaman, who burned down his house in order to roast a pig. There were a great many other and easier ways of bringing about a Union : in fact the Union *was* brought about by wholesale bribery.

If the charge is that Fitzgibbon and Castlereagh forced the hand of the conspirators, then there seems to be very little substance in it. For this charge implicitly admits that a conspiracy did exist. If men are to be at liberty to conspire against a Government, then assuredly that Government must be at liberty to deal with their conspiracy as it thinks best. Those who attack a tiger should remember that a very considerable element of danger attaches to the adventure. The Irish leaders were prepared to strike when the proper moment arrived : they should have reflected that the 'zero hours' of attack and defence do not necessarily synchronise. All questions of morality apart, they should have realised that there is a very large measure of brutal common sense in the lines—

> Thrice armed is he who hath his quarrel just,
> But four times he who gets his whack in fust.

The words of a Wild West newspaper describing a saloon scrap fit the situation : " They broke even for the guns, and Bill lost." The Irish conspirators played the part of " Bill."

The story of the Revolution of '98 is a story of atrocities committed by both parties. It would be utterly stupid to deny or justify the atrocities of the Government troops. There were hangings and floggings galore ; but there were also some horrors so curious and revolting as to deserve especial mention.

First was the ' pitch-cap.' This was a form of torture used to induce confessions, or discovery of concealed arms. A cap was made of stout brown paper ; the inside was thickly smeared with warm pitch. The cap was then forced on the victim's head : when the pitch cooled the cap adhered to the scalp, and removal of the cap meant wellnigh the removal of the scalp. There was then the ' walking gallows.' This was a fiendishness devised and executed by one man ; it was so unbelievably hideous that, without undue charity, one may assume that this man was mad, a sadistic maniac. His name was Hoppenstal. He was a tall man of amazing strength. His method was to put a noose about the neck of a rebel or suspected rebel ; then hoist the man on to his own shoulders by the rope's end, and walk, run, dance, until the wretched creature was strangled. As a pleasing variant of this procedure Hoppenstal at times let down his victim *half-strangled*, allowed him to recover, then hoisted him up again!

Accusations of outrages committed on women were freely made. Here is an extract from a speech of John Philpot Curran pleading the cause of a rebel in the dock: " The ruffian gang enters—the feast of plunder begins—the cup of madness kindles in its circulation—the wandering glances of the ravisher become concentrated on the shrinking and devoted victim." But it is significant that these charges have been laid only against the Government forces— not against the rebels. The Government troops thus attacked were for the most part Irish ' yeomanry '; and however bad Irishmen may be (and some can be very bad indeed), outrage on women is not a crime ordinarily chargeable to them. It would be very strange indeed if such badness were to be found only among Irishmen of one shade of political opinion. Such accusations are very easily made. Before the final secession of the American colonies a fracas between English troops and American citizens took place in a street of Boston. An American historian comments thus on the occurrence: " Although there is no recorded instance of a soldier having offered the slightest affront to any Boston girl, orators ranted about ' our beauteous virgins exposed to all the insolence of unbridled passion—our virtuous wives, endeared to us by every tender tie, falling a sacrifice to worse than brutal violence, and perhaps, like the famed Lucretia, distracted with anguish and despair, ending their wretched lives by their own fair hands.' " A historian, whose sympathies certainly are not with the Irish Government of the time, has considered this particular accusation coolly and dispassionately. He finds but two charges indubitably proven. An officer undeniably violated an Irish girl: he disappeared, and his fellow officers offered a considerable reward for his apprehension. An Irish woman visited her husband under arrest; changed clothes with him; and so enabled him to escape. The soldiers held a mock court-martial on her, and sentenced her to deprivation of all clothes not lawfully her own! All that the lady had retained of feminine attire was her chemise and stockings; to these the soldiers stripped her. Then they tossed her in a blanket and let her go. It was a brutal jest, but at the same time a not unsalutary warning that a woman may presume too far on the protection which her sex affords her.

It is a curious fact that much of this misbehaviour of the Government forces may have been provoked by the man on whom sympathisers with the Irish rebels rely for proof that such misbehaviour was common. This was General Abercrombie. Abercrombie took over the Irish command a month or two before the outbreak of the rebellion; and within a very short time of his assuming command he published a general order in which he declared that the troops were in a state of indiscipline and licentiousness which rendered them formidable to everyone save the enemy. His statement may have been correct ; but surely there can be no more glaring example of a man doing the right thing in the wrong way. A possible parallel may be Lord Fitzwilliam's attempt to introduce Catholic emancipation by the precipitate dismissal of John Beresford. Beresford deserved dismissal ; but there is a time for doing all things, and a proper method of doing them. Abercrombie should have taken order, quietly and determinedly, with his disorderly command ; but certainly he should not have held up his men to the contempt of their enemies. His order had a most unfortunate sequel. Lord Camden, the Viceroy, endeavoured to pass the matter over in silence, but the Government of England called for an explanation. Camden perforce transmitted the demand to Abercrombie ; Abercrombie shilly-shallied, and finally resigned. Nothing more calamitous, said Camden very truly, could be imagined than the manner of his resignation : " The army will suppose that they have gained a victory over Sir Ralph Abercrombie, and all that was amiss will grow worse." General Lake took over the command ; and to his severity in disarming the country the outbreak of the rebellion is frequently attributed. But dates do not support this view. Lake took over command on April 23 : that a rebellion was in preparation long before that date is proven and undeniable. Lake's methods may have made it clear to the people that they must choose between the alternatives of fighting and giving in ; but, at least, he offered them a choice.

And there is a good deal of truth in Froude's rather cynical comment : "Assassins and their accomplices will not always be delicately handled by those whose lives they have threatened." Against the floggings, hangings, pitch-cappings may be set Wexford Bridge and Scullabogue barn. The rebels shut up a hundred prisoners in a barn at Scullabogue, then burned them and the barn together.

The whole episode of this rebellion was a nightmare. But young Emmet seeing but one side of the suffering, hearing but the argument on one side of the case, can have been in no mood to apportion guilt fairly. For all his prejudices Froude has uttered the fairest judgment on this horror : "They were all to blame : the careless, tyrannical landlord, the scheming politician, the patriotic agitator, the uncertain, vacillating Government of England." But as against Froude there is weight in the reflection of Jonah Barrington : "No well-governed people will desire to exchange real and present blessings for the danger and uncertainty of remote and fantastic speculation : and if ever they are found to commit their lives and fortunes to such desperate experiments, it is the most conclusive proof that they are badly governed."

It seems almost an insult to human credulity to suggest that the Government and Administration of Ireland throughout the eighteenth century were other than bad, or other than very bad indeed towards the close of the century. Yet against Barrington two curious pieces of testimony may be quoted. This is the first :

" There is not a nation on the face of the habitable globe which has advanced in cultivation, in agriculture, in manufactures, with the same rapidity in the same period." The name of the speaker may with many discredit this witness to the virtue of his own day. The speaker was John Fitzgibbon. But Fitzgibbon's words are not so lightly to be passed over. These words are cited by another, Dr Thomas Emmet, a descendant of the Emmet of Fitzgibbon's day and an almost frenzied decrier of England. It is Dr Emmet's thesis that the Union contrived by Fitzgibbon ruined Ireland : if he relies on Fitzgibbon to prove that Ireland before the Union was prosperous, he must accept the same words even when they conflict with his own arguments.

The second testimony is that of Barrington himself : " The country had prospered beyond all possible anticipation, and was still further advancing in prosperity under the existing administration." How are these contradictions to be reconciled ? One may draw an odd analogy from the unlikely topic of fox-hunting.

There is a loud and increasing outcry against the cruelty of this sport. Certainly it is absurd to pretend that the fox can enjoy his own death at the teeth of the hounds ; but quite as certainly it is absurd to intensify the fox's sufferings by attributing to him the mentality of a human being. The mere thought of being pursued by a pack of hounds is terrifying to a man : mere pursuit, so long as it does not end in his death, is not at all discomposing to a fox. He must regard pursuit as natural : otherwise why does he quite naturally fly? The susceptibility of a fox to pain we do not know; but a horse which has undergone one of the cruellest operations known to surgery will the next moment crop the grass apparently unconcerned.

So it is a mistake to judge the events of the eighteenth century with the mentality of the twentieth. Ireland was then disfranchised; but were the people of Ireland at that day really more disfranchised than the people of England? There were Irish 'rotten boroughs' in Ireland at the disposition of patrons: there were also such in England. And 'rotten boroughs' were defended in England not altogether unplausibly by a speaker who remarked that they afforded the only means of entering Parliament to a man of ability *uncursed* with an aptitude for flattering the mob! The lot of the petty Irish agriculturist was miserable: Charles Kingsley's 'Yeast,' written half a century later, does not suggest that the lot of the petty English agriculturist in Kingsley's day was a happy one. The life of the Irish working man was hard: was it harder than the lot of the Manchester operative in 'the hungry forties'? The utterances of public men in Ireland then may to-day strike us as atrocious. For example, when George Ponsonby advocated in the Irish Parliament Catholic emancipation and equalisation of commercial legislation between the two kingdoms, the Solicitor-General of the day answered thus: "What is it come to in the Irish Parliament that we should listen to one of our own members degrading the character of an Irish gentleman by language which is fitted for the hallooing of a mob." And the Solicitor-General traced Ponsonby's proposal to " the execrable and infamous nest of traitors known by the name of United Irishmen, who sit brooding in Belfast." But while we certainly may hold the Solicitor-General was a mistaken man, is it fair to write him down at once as a deliberately wicked man ? Men were wont to express themselves strongly in those days.

Moreover, at least some of the hardships of Ireland were of her own making. By Irish law *one* witness was sufficient in a case of high treason ; by English law two were required. John Curran at the trial of the Sheares thus upbraided the jury : " You, to be sure, are too proud to listen to the wisdom of an English law. Illustrious independents. You may murder under the semblance of judicial forms, because you are proud of your blessed independence." But is not this utter fustian ? On nothing did Irishmen insist more determinedly than the right of the Irish Parliament to make the laws affecting Irishmen in their own country. The Irish Parliament had made a law : Curran could scarcely demand the benefit of an English law when it suited his need.

Again, miseries, measures, men, notwithstanding, the world does progress to a greater gentleness. The demagogue of to-day points to unemployment, proclaims the misery of the working classes. No one will claim that the working man's lot is what it should be ; but no thoughtful working man denies that, on the whole, the condition of his class has improved and is still improving.

Undoubtedly there was progress in Ireland, a small but constant striving towards gentleness. Two stories of Sir Jonah Barrington may be cited in illustration. The first is of his great-aunt, Elizabeth Fitzgerald, who ' flourished ' about the year 1690. She lived with her husband at Moret Castle, near Ballybrittas, and at a certain time the Fitzgeralds were somewhat at variance with the O'Cahills. The O'Cahills beset the castle, but were beaten off. Unluckily for himself Squire Fitzgerald, during a lull in hostilities, went a-walking in his garden and was captured by the enemy. The O'Cahills paraded him before the castle and informed his wife that, unless she would surrender her castle, they would hang her husband. Dame Elizabeth, reflecting prudently that a second husband is much more easily procurable than a second castle, bade them hang. They hanged.

Thus Elizabeth was left a widow, and a well-dowered widow to boot. She delayed unaccountably in her choice of a second mate, and the youth of the countryside resolved to help her to a decision. They drew lots for her husband-to-be ; the lot fell upon one Cromarty O'Moore ; and twenty-four young blades bound themselves to assist Cromarty in the carrying off of his bride. The strategy and tactics of Dame Elizabeth resembled quite startlingly those of Fitzgibbon and Castlereagh a hundred years later. With oaths and maledictions she publicly dismissed her faithful servant Jug Ogie ; and the gentle Jug (a female) sought refuge in the camp of the enemy. To these she disclosed the readiest way into Castle Moret, and they in turn disclosed to her their plan of attack. Jug, the Reynolds or Turner of her day, brought the information to her mistress. Elizabeth, Castlereagh-like, forthwith ' exploded ' the conspiracy. The ravishers had gathered together the night before that on which the rape was to be effected ; and that night Elizabeth struck. She gathered together twenty-five of her adherents, explained the situation, and gave them her benediction : thoughtfully she inquired whether they would like " a touch of the priest " before setting forth on the crusade. So the priest was summoned, and fortified by his ministrations the party stole out. In the gentle bickering which followed Elizabeth's champions lost six killed and six desperately wounded ; but they completely routed their opponents. So complete was the Fitzgerald victory that the twenty-four—or those of them who were left alive—sued for peace. This Elizabeth accorded ; but she stipulated that in token of submission Cromarty O'Moore should cut off and present to her the lock of hair which grew over his right ear. She found it impossible to enforce this article. For Cromarty was dead ; and one of the Fitzgerald party had practically carved his face off with a skene.

A hundred years later, when Sir Jonah Barrington was alive, the serving of a process in Connemara was a matter attended by difficulty, even by risk. It was the pleasing custom of the people, when they caught a process server, to make him eat his own process. There came to Connemara one Burke, bearer of a ' Chancellor's Bill.' He was captured, and his captors bade him eat. But the Bill was engrossed on parchment, and proved tough eating. The captors obligingly made the Bill 'tindher' with *poteen;* and for fourteen days Burke ate. During that time he, in his own words, had " kinder treatment and better liquor nor ever the villain of a sub-sheriff ever gave any poor man." His eating finished, Mr Burke was free to go ; but he pointed out to his hosts that the Chancellor would require an explanation. Together they made up a tale of how he had been left for dead by the roadside, and the Connemara men swore that they " would make his word good for him." So they made Burke drunk, drunk beyond his wildest dreams, hopes, prayers, and deposited him by the roadside. Thus the affair was ended with good will on both sides. The manners of Ireland in Barrington's day may not strike us now as over gentle, but certainly they were gentler than they had been in the brave days of his ancestor, Elizabeth Fitzgerald of Moret Castle !

But Robert Emmet at twenty years of age could scarcely take this broad, tolerant view of the progress of his country and of his countrymen. Still less would he have understood, appreciated one of Barrington's profoundest judgments : one cannot put the worldly sagacity of seventy years into the headpiece of twenty.

Invariably, says Sir Jonah, the common people of Ireland, the rank and file of insurrection, were let down by their leaders. A leader of insurrection, in his opinion, should possess " a commanding presence, an authoritative voice, and impetuous bravery." In many of the Irish leaders one or more of those qualities were lacking : from Bagenal Harvey, leader of the insurrection of '98, all were absent. " A more unprepossessing or unmartial-like person was never moulded by capricious Nature." Harvey had been bold enough when insurrection meant nothing more than boastful disclosures over the dinner table : when the hour for action struck he was found wanting. At the moment that the rebellion blazed out he was actually in jail : presumably he had been committed on suspicion, or else to keep him out of harm's way. The rebels stormed the jail and sought Harvey to proffer their allegiance to him. Mr Postgate tells the story thus.

A rebel deputation entered Harvey's room— and found it empty. While they gazed about them in wonderment, a voice from space, a disembodied voice, addressed them. " Angels and Ministers of Grace defend us," the deputation doubtless would have exclaimed, had their tastes leaned towards the study of the Elizabethan dramatists. The voice protested its dislike of fighting, its total unfitness for command. Suddenly there was a crash ; and Bagenal Harvey fell down the chimney ! Presumably against his will leadership was thrust on him ; at the first real check he lost control of his followers and of himself ; he fled, and his followers drank. Captured, Sir Jonah sadly notes, he did not even do the one decent thing left for him to do : he did not die as a brave man should die. Yet Barrington is charitable. Harvey, he suggests, may have been brave enough as an individual ; but a man brave against an individual opponent may lose his head and his courage in a *mêlée*. The Great War of the twentieth century afforded proof that this judgment of Sir Jonah may not have been a mistaken one.

One leader in the field the Irish rebellion of '98 did throw up. This was Father John Murphy of Boolavogue. Why he joined in the rebellion it is difficult to say. He had been educated in Spain ; he had come to Ireland as a priest ;' for many years he had attended quietly to the duties of his parish, seemingly taking no thought of politics ; in '98 he was no hot-headed youth, but a man approaching fifty years of age. Possibly there was a fire of fanaticism smouldering beneath his calm exterior. He is said by some to have shown himself cruel, relentless, murderous : he certainly proved himself to be dauntlessly brave in action and to possess the eye of a born general for a campaign. But of the end for which he was fighting he knew nothing : he had no conception of what would follow on success. After the final rout of the rebels he was taken prisoner, and was hanged summarily.

The fighting in the rebellion took place south of Dublin : as well as Father Murphy, Harvey, Colclough, Grogan, and other leaders implicated were hanged out of hand by process of martial law. It is time to return to Dublin, where Robert Emmet was a free man.

The Dublin jails were full of United Irish leaders. Arthur O'Connor had stood his trial with Quigley (who was hanged) at Maidstone and had been acquitted. But on another charge he had been returned to custody. Thomas Emmet, Oliver Bond, MacNiven and others had been captured through the treachery of Reynolds. The brothers John and Henry Sheares had been arrested on the information of Captain Armstrong. Armstrong, it may be remarked, did but his duty in disclosing knowledge of a conspiracy which had come to him unsolicited. Yet a prejudice persisted against him in Ireland : he avoided ingeniously the danger which then attached to prejudice. He was a man of considerable property ; and it was his practice to grant leases to his tenants for three lives, one life being his own ! Thus he created for himself a bodyguard of Irish agriculturists keenly interested in his survival. Samuel Neilson had been arrested while reconnoitring outside Newgate jail. There were many others ; and with these the ordinary law now began to take its course.

John and Henry Sheares were brought to trial on July 12. They were convicted, and sentenced : they were hanged on July 14. The next was John MacCann : he was hanged on July 19. William Byrne—" Billy Byrne of Ballymanus was a man of great renown " is a famous Irish street-song—was convicted on July 20 and hanged on July 25. Oliver Bond was convicted on July 23, and his execution was set for July 26.

Not unnaturally consternation reigned amongst the remaining prisoners : they had not expected anything like this. Many hard things were said in the eighteenth century, and were repeated in the nineteenth, of the readiness of the Crown to obtain a verdict of guilty by packing the jury. But in truth the blame always was imputable much more to the jurors who were packed than to the Crown officials who packed them. It was impossible in the eighteenth century and for long afterwards to get an honest verdict from an Irish jury under any circumstances : the Crown must either procure the empanelment of a jury which might convict on weak evidence, or else look on idly at the empanelment of a jury which would acquit in the face of all evidence. The somewhat academic conspirators of Dublin were disagreeably surprised : whether the Crown was packing juries with exceptional skill, or whether juries were finding evidence so glaringly sufficient as to necessitate a verdict of 'guilty,' were not questions of great practical interest. The result in either case was the same for those affected by the verdict.

The United Irish leaders sued for mercy : they offered to make a free and full confession provided that their lives were spared. Probably the Crown officials had artfully chosen for the first trials those possessed of least influence and therefore most likely to be convicted : they assisted Bond to come to a decision by hanging Billy Byrne outside his window the day before that appointed for his own execution. That the offer of confession was accepted seems to have been due in a considerable measure to Fitzgibbon. It is quite unnecessary to portray the Chancellor as moved at this conjuncture by any especial feelings of compassion : he certainly was doubtful whether on any evidence a conviction against

Arthur O'Connor could be secured. O'Connor's immense family influence had saved him once, and might save him again ; and he might drag the others into safety by his coat tails. By a full confession at least this much would be gained. There were then, as ever, many in England ready to place the worst possible construction on every action of the servants of the British Crown. The dissatisfaction of Ireland by such was imputed wholly to the shortcomings of the Irish Administration : the suggestion (founded on undeniable facts) that these particular Irishmen had conspired with France against England was scouted. "Good God, that disloyalty and the name of O'Connor should be mentioned in the same breath," exclaimed an indignant witness at the first trial of Arthur O'Connor. Confession that the Irish officials had been fully justified in their suspicions and charges would have silenced criticism, for the time at least, effectively. The offer was accepted.

While these hectic and rather horrible proceedings ran their course, Robert Emmet was in touch with his elder brother. Whatever the guilt or innocence of Thomas Emmet, the influence of the whole business on an emotional boy cannot have been other than evil. And the influence of what followed may have been, in the long run, even more evil.

Confident that their necks were safe, the United Irishmen made their confession. The confession was drafted by Arthur O'Connor, and proved to be a surprising document. It was, in fact, a flamboyant justification of righteousness, not a humble admission of guilt. O'Connor had placed the Government of Ireland in a quandary. The Government of England were furious : they recommended that the offer of pardon be withdrawn, and that the trials do proceed. This was plainly impossible. In the first place, it would be a violation of every canon of human decency to offer pardon to a man conditionally on his making a confession, and then revoke the offer when the confession was made. In the second place, it was not at all certain that, if the trials did proceed, the result would be what the Crown desired. If it be not indecent to jest on a matter involving the lives of men, it may be said that Fitzgibbon had bluffed on a rather weak hand. Arthur O'Connor had called the bluff, and had got away with it.

It was a fortunate happening for Thomas Emmet at the moment, but in the end a very unfortunate one for his younger brother. For it implanted the idea in young Robert's mind that one could generally ' get away with ' high treason against the Government. Up to the very last moment of his existence Robert Emmet cherished some hope of escape.

A certain compromise at last was reached, an arrangement was made. The Government of Ireland refused to accept or to publish the confession : in turn *they* bluffed and likewise ' got away with it.' A Committee of the Irish House of Lords was sitting to inquire into the causes of the rebellion : before this Committee the United Irishmen agreed to depose. Their depositions proved conclusively enough their conspiracy with France.

So much had been accomplished. But now arose the question, what was to be done with these Irishmen? To hang them was impossible: it was equally impossible to turn them loose in Ireland. It was proposed that they should emigrate to some country at peace with England; and, as in the case of Wolfe Tone, America at once suggested itself to England as their abiding place. But the Americans, who a few years before had shaken off the yoke of England, showed themselves by no means willing to welcome to their bosoms those Irishmen who desired that Ireland should follow America's example. Mr Rufus King, the American Minister at the Court of St James, wrote thus to the Duke of Portland: "The principles and opinions of these men are in my view so dangerous, so false, so utterly inconsistent with any practicable or stable form of Government, that I feel it to be a duty to my country to express to Your Grace my earnest wish that the United States may be excepted from the countries to which the Irish State prisoners shall be permitted to retire." This was plain speaking.

The Government of England decided the matter thus. They sent the United Irishmen to Fort St George in Scotland, and kept them there until the Peace of Amiens was signed with France in March 1802. Then they allowed the prisoners to go their ways. Thomas Emmet went first to Belgium, then to France, and finally to America. Arthur O'Connor went to France, and remained there in French military service. As an old man he paid one visit to Ireland ; but he interested himself no more in Irish affairs.

But this is to anticipate. Robert Emmet visited his brother in the Scottish Fort, and what he saw there can scarcely have tended to the use of edifying. For, as was almost inevitable, the moral tone of the prisoners deteriorated. Samuel Neilson, ' the physically strong,' took heavily to drink, and bickered with Oliver Bond. Thereby hangs a curious tale. Bond was found dead in his room one morning : there seems to be no doubt that he died in a fit of apoplexy. But the night before there had been a furious quarrel between him and Neilson ; and to the end of his days Neilson was haunted by a fear that he had killed Bond in his drunken fury.

Arthur O'Connor and Thomas Emmet fought like devils. Emmet asserted then, asserted later, and his descendants after him asserted that O'Connor was a Government spy. The two swore to settle their differences by arms at a convenient opportunity : somehow friends prevented their meeting. Certainly it was not lack of courage that kept them apart.

Towards the close of '98 Humbert invaded Ireland : his invasion cost Matthew Tone and Bartholomew Teeling their necks. Later in the year came Wolfe Tone : his story has been told. And in 1800 came about the Union between England and Ireland, that Union which, in the words of John Fitzgibbon, "would withdraw the highest orders of Irishmen from the narrow and corrupted sphere of Irish politics, and direct their attention to objects of national importance ; would teach them to improve their nation's energies and extend the resources of their country ; would encourage manufacturing skill and ingenuity, open useful channels for commercial enterprise ; and, above all, would seriously tame and civilise the lower orders of the people, inculcate in them the habits of religion, morality, industry, and due subordination ; relieve their wants and correct their excesses." John Fitzgibbon had failed to save Irish political society as he found it : it is doubtful whether he improved it greatly when he essayed to remake it ! Such were the events which young Emmet saw, on which he reflected, for the two years following his removal from Trinity College.

In the year 1800 Robert Emmet left Ireland for the Continent. His movements and actions are difficult to follow : it appears that he visited Switzerland, Holland, France and Spain. Probably it was to his advantage to leave Ireland for a season : what with his practical expulsion from Trinity, the arrest of his brother, the uncertainty as to his brother's fate, the association with his brother in prison and at Fort St George, he must have been on the verge of a nervous collapse. A highly strung boy cannot endure these experiences with the equanimity of a man. The difference between man and boy is well exemplified by the difference between Robert and Thomas Emmet. Thomas Emmet, as the Diary (later to be referred to) kept by him in Paris shows, had a remarkable vein of cool critical shrewdness in his composition. Robert to the end of his short life was an unpractical visionary.

But it would have been well for Robert had his father insisted that on this Continental trip he should cut himself altogether free from Ireland and Irish politicians, apply himself definitely to some study or training for practical life. This might not have altered his essential opinions, but it would have composed his mind, rendered his judgment clearer. A desultory holiday extending over years could not possibly be good for a young man. And unfortunately Robert Emmet either started on his journey with politically undesirable companions, or else fell in with such by the way.

CHAPTER III.

THE BUSINESS.

THERE is an obscure point in the sad history of Robert Emmet, one which in all probability can never now be made clear. When was the beginning of his ill-starred love affair with the lady immortalised in Moore's song? This was Sarah Curran, youngest daughter of the famous advocate John Philpot Curran. It may be helpful to recapitulate a few dates. Robert Emmet was expelled (practically) from Trinity College in February 1798. In 1800 he went to the Continent. In October 1802 he returned to Ireland. The 'Emmet rising,' such as it was, took place on July 23, 1803; and on September 19 of that year Robert Emmet was sentenced to death.

Only conjecture is possible : all that there is of evidence is but two letters written by Emmet just before his death. One to Richard Curran, Sarah's brother, was written an hour or two before the execution. It proves that, whatever his failings, Robert Emmet was no coward. He wrote a beautiful hand ; and every line of this letter is perfectly straight, each individual character is perfectly formed. The meticulously accurate punctuation of those days is scrupulously observed. The italics in the following passage

283

are not in the original : they have been introduced for the sake of greater clearness.

Robert Emmet to Richard Curran : " I have injured the happiness of a sister that you love, and who was formed to give happiness to every-one about her, instead of having her own mind a prey to affliction. I have no excuse to offer, but that I meant the reverse ; I intended as much happiness for Sarah as the most ardent love could have given her. *I never did tell you how much I adored her :* it was not a wild or unfounded passion, but it was an attachment increasing every hour, from an admiration of the purity of her mind, and respect for her talents. I did hope that success, while it afforded the opportunity of our union, might be the means of confirming an attachment, *which misfortune had called forth.*"

The first words italicised suggest that Richard Curran had been aware for some time of his friend's attachment to his sister, although Emmet had not declared to him that attachment in so many words. Young men do not ordinarily make these express declarations to one another. The last words italicised are curious : to what *misfortune* does Emmet allude ? Before his rising he was confident of success, he was not thinking of failure and misfortune. He can scarcely be speaking of the disastrous failure of July 23, 1803 ; although, as a matter of fact, it was his effort to communicate with Sarah Curran after the event that was a main cause of his capture. Is it possible that the allusion is to his expulsion from Trinity, a serious misfortune for a young man on the threshold of life, whatever his position, prospects, political opinions ?

If this conjecture be well founded, there is something of sadness about it. Love might well have inspired Robert Emmet to some solid work and achievement, might have led him to see that there are better ways of serving one's country than by back-yard conspiracies. But it may also have suggested to his rather emotional, theatrical nature some romantic, dazzling coup which would present him to Sarah Curran and to her father in the rôle of youthful hero.

To her father he had written earlier : " When I first addressed your daughter *I expected that in another week my fate would be decided.* I know that in case of success, many others ought to look on me differently from what they did at that moment. I spoke to your daughter, neither expecting nor, in fact, under these circumstances, wishing that there should be a return of attachment. I received no encouragement whatever. I staid away till the time had elapsed *when I found that the event to which I allude was to be postponed.* Afterwards I had reason to suppose that discoveries were made, and that I should be obliged to quit the kingdom immediately ; and I came to make a renunciation of any approach to friendship that might have been formed. On that day she herself spoke to me to discontinue my visits. That I have written to your daughter since an unfortunate event has taken place, was an additional breach of propriety for which I have suffered well."

If the first words here italicised refer to the rising of July 23, it is impossible not to judge Robert Emmet rather hardly. A young man who proposes within a week to stir up civil war, to attempt to subvert the established Government of his country, to run a very definite risk of swinging on a scaffold, is surely very much to blame if he at that moment declares himself to a young girl, asks her to be his wife. Whatever his feelings, he has no moral right at such a conjuncture to ask a woman to intertwine her life with his own. Some later passages are very obscure. To what *postponement* does he allude ? And the fear that " discoveries have been made," that he may be " obliged to quit the kingdom immediately," can scarcely be referred to the actual events of July 23. There was no question of ' discovery ' : the plot was open, exposed for all to see. There was no question of his being obliged to quit the kingdom : he was a hunted fugitive, and quitting the kingdom was the only means, if there were any means, of saving his neck. There is something very saddening in the words, " others might look on me differently from what they did at that moment." Was it the general opinion that young Emmet was an idler, a dreamer ? And did the poor boy dream of rehabilitating himself in the opinion of his friends by some wild, spasmodic effort rather than by honest, solid, humdrum work ?

William Curran in his life of his father gives this account of the matter : " The projector of the late insurrection, Mr Robert Emmet, who was a young gentleman of a highly respectable family, of very striking talents and interesting manners, was in the habit of visiting at Mr Curran's house : here he soon formed an attachment for Mr Curran's youngest daughter. Of the progress of that attachment, and of the period and occasion of his divulging it to her, Mr Emmet's letters, inserted hereafter, contain all that is to be told. It is necessary, however, to add, as indeed will sufficiently appear from those letters, that her father remained in total ignorance of the motive of Mr Emmet's visits, until subsequent events made it known to all. As the period, however, of the intended insurrection approached, Mr Curran began to suspect from minute indications, which probably would have escaped a less skilful observer, that his young visitor was actuated by some strong passions, which it cost him a perpetual effort to conceal ; and in consequence, without assigning to these appearances any precise motive, or giving to the subject much attention, he, in general terms, recommended to his family not to allow what at present was only a casual acquaintance to ripen into a greater degree of intimacy."

Here we may leave the matter for the moment. Whatever the beginning, the end was sad ; and possibly sadder for the girl than for the man.

Robert Emmet went abroad ; he was accompanied by, or fell into the company of, two men, John Allen and William Dowdall. Allen seems to have been personally a likeable kind of man : he was brave, gay, and, as his later life showed, in his way industrious. But, like a good many Irishmen of his day, he had a bee in his bonnet, or rather two bees. These bees were England and the English Administration in Ireland : they were the bees which, for every reason, it was desirable to get *out of* Emmet's bonnet, at least until Emmet reached a riper age, achieved a more dispassionate outlook on men and measures. Allen must have helped, perhaps unwittingly, to get the bees *in*.

He had been arrested in the company of Arthur O'Connor and the priest Quigley, and with them he had been tried at Maidstone for high treason. With O'Connor he was acquitted ; how he occupied himself for the next five years is not altogether clear ; but in 1803 he was concerned in Emmet's insurrection. His coolness and audacity, seconded by the coolness of a friend named Hickson, enabled him to escape, and he carried Dowdall with him to safety. When the hue and cry was out, Allen disguised himself as a British officer : he despatched Dowdall and Hickson a little in advance to a port where a ship lay ready to sail for France : he followed a little in the rear. Dowdall and Hickson, as he had anticipated, fell in with a patrol of soldiers : luckily for them there was no officer in command. The two were stopped ; they gave what explanation they could devise ; their explanation was not altogether satisfactory ; and the soldiers told them that they must consider themselves for the time in custody. At this moment Allen approached. Hickson good-humouredly told the soldiers that he had no wish to cause unpleasantness, but that, if they persisted in detaining him and his friend, he must appeal to the officer who was now coming on the scene. Allen, coming up, laughed; he assured the soldiers that he knew the gentlemen quite well, and that there was no need for them to trouble themselves. The soldiers saluted respectfully and went their way: Allen and Dowdall strolled calmly aboard the waiting vessel, and so to France. Hickson, presumably an inconspicuous individual, returned to his everyday avocations.

Allen entered French service, and in course of time rose to the rank of colonel. He was at Ciudad Rodrigo, and was taken prisoner, luckily for him by the Spaniards. With other French officers he was interned at Corunna; and at some later time he was exchanged or liberated. He served Napoleon faithfully through good and evil days; and he answered the Emperor's call on the return from Elba. After Waterloo the English, with rather unnecessary vindictiveness, demanded his extradition; and the Bourbon king, with quite inexcusable servility, acceded to the demand. Allen was despatched under military escort to the frontier. On the way the soldiers, more chivalrous than their masters, explained to M. le Colonel a way by which he could escape, and ventured to hope that M. le Colonel would *not* make use of it. This obvious wink to a by no means blind horse was understood: Colonel Allen faded out of the picture, while his escort thoughtfully contemplated the horizon. He returned to France; he was no more molested; and he lived to be an old man. It seems unfortunate that a man so brave and hardy could find no better way of serving Ireland than by conspiring against England.

Dowdall was a much less attractive personality. He was the illegitimate son of Walter Hussy Burgh, famous for his simile of England sowing her laws like dragon's teeth to spring up as armed men. He was a young man of good education and pleasant manner ; but he seems to have been somewhat of a wastrel. He was perpetually hanging about the edges of conspiracies ; but as a conspirator he lacked ' guts.' He talked a great deal, but he was as a rule quite sufficiently wary to avoid *doing* anything that would put his neck into a noose. After the arrest of Arthur O'Connor in '98—really Arthur O'Connor seems to have started a sort of ' fashion ' in this respect—Dowdall was arrested. There was nothing proved or provable against him : he had simply talked too much. He was liberated, and he made his way to London, where he fell in with one Colonel Despard. And this is the starting point of a curiously obscure ramification in the affairs of Robert Emmet.

Despard was an Irishman of an older generation : he was some thirty years senior to Robert Emmet. He entered the British army as an ensign at the age of sixteen ; he became a military engineer ; and he proved himself to be the possessor of very considerable talents. He served against the Spaniards in Honduras with great distinction ; later he was charged with the construction of public works in Jamaica, and by his skill and devotion to duty he won the formal thanks of the Governor of the island and of the

British Government. But somehow his fortunes began to go awry : what exactly had been his fault (if any) is not clear ; but apparently certain allegations were made, whispers to his detriment were heard. No formal, open censure or punishment was inflicted on him : he was placed on the unemployed list ; and his remonstrances, his petitions, his demands for inquiry were disregarded. Despard became that most lamentable of all beings, " a man with a grievance " ; and it can scarcely be disputed that perpetual brooding over his grievance undermined his reason.

He formed some extraordinary design of killing the King and of starting a revolution in England. He proposed to a soldier named Wood (who gave evidence against him) that Wood, while on duty at Windsor, should load ' the great gun ' and fire it at the King's carriage as the King drove forth. The King thus slain—the possibility that Wood might miss his mark does not seem to have occurred to Despard—the outbreak of the revolution was to be notified to the country by the stopping of all mail coaches. All this was to happen on November 24, 1802. What the end of the whole business would be or could be, Despard in all probability never considered. Naturally the crazy scheme leaked out ; and Despard with several others was arrested. In modern days he would have been placed in a criminal lunatic asylum : at the opening of the nineteenth century Governments paid little heed to a plea or pretence of insanity. Despard and half a dozen others were charged with high treason, convicted and hanged.

Dowdall was cognisant, in some measure at least, of Despard's crazy plottings. On the arrest of Despard he fled to France. It seems that at some time or other he communicated the plot to Robert Emmet, and that Emmet took this utter imbecility quite seriously. Up to the very last moment the unhappy boy seems to have believed that behind his bungling, amateur attempts at insurrection there was, or would be, some powerful supporting agency. For from the dock he addressed these strange words to his Judges : " I have been charged with that importance in the efforts to emancipate my country as to be considered the keystone of the combination of Irishmen, or, as it has been expressed, the life and blood of the conspiracy. You do me honour overmuch ; you have given to the subaltern all the credit of the superior. There are men concerned in this conspiracy who are not only superior to me, but even to your own conceptions of yourself, my Lord ; men before the splendour of whose genius and virtues I should bow with respectful deference." Poor Emmet ! what a child he was, a child attacking a tiger with a toy gun. It is a curious reflection that there was one man who, had he been alive in September 1803, might have had pity, might have bidden the boy go in peace and be a fool no more. But John Fitzgibbon was in his grave.

While the insurrection was preparing, a bomb in one of Emmet's depots exploded by accident. The futile Dowdall fled shrieking. Later, as has been described, by clinging to John Allen's coat tails he got away to France. He was a most unlucky friend or associate for Emmet.

Old Dr Emmet died a few months after his son's return to Ireland. By his father's death Robert Emmet came in for a sum of money estimated at between two and three thousand pounds. This inheritance proved his sincerity, and in the end, it is to be feared, proved to be his undoing. For he at once invested all his fortune in his revolution ; and undoubtedly he thus gathered about him a certain number of men whose one thought it was to live on his bounty. The reproach is not applicable to all. Among Emmet's adherents were Thomas Russell, the " P.P. Clerk of this Parish " of Wolfe Tone, and James Hope, a Belfast weaver, who seems to have been a man of fine and determined character. In a humbler station there was Owen Kirwan. Poor Russell paid for his allegiance with his life, as did Kirwan. But ' P.P.' now as ever proved to be a feckless conspirator. He was cheerful, enthusiastic, irresponsible ; he suggests irresistibly the actor who is always sure that " everything will be all right on the night." And the passing of the years had not taught him economy : his fondness for good wine was a sore drain on Emmet's exchequer.

Emmet's plan was simply an insurrection in Dublin : he would attack and seize simultaneously the Castle, the Pigeon House Fort at the entrance to the Liffey, and the Park Battery. The Castle, of course, was the chief object of attack : that once seized, the Viceroy and the Commander-in-Chief in Ireland could be held as

hostages pending developments. Emmet's conceptions do not seem to have gone much further.
It could scarcely be expected that the mere
temporary success of a mob would at once cause
England to abandon all hope of holding Ireland ;
and for meeting the inevitable counter-stroke
Emmet seems to have formed no plan.

He drew up a Proclamation addressed to the
People of Ireland : this Proclamation in itself
is illustrative of his curiously unpractical mind.
A revolutionary leader who thus addresses himself to the people must so address himself that
his readers can at once understand his intentions,
his point of view. Emmet's Proclamation was
an elaborate dissertation on politics, and it ran
to about the length of a ' Quarterly Review '
article. It closes with certain definite and
indefinite propositions. Church tithes were to be
at once abolished. Apparently all tenants of
land were to continue paying their rents as
heretofore. Banking transactions and the sale
of securities were to be prohibited for an un-
specified period. For the rest, " the Irish Generals " (whoever they might be) were to ad-
minister the country until some other form of
administration could be devised. The practical
James Hope warned Emmet that the land question
was then, as it always has been, the pivot on which
Irish politics turned : Emmet replied that he
could not contemplate undertaking an economic
change of such magnitude. And he congratulated
himself on the fact that no " leading Catholic "
was committed to his conspiracy. To attempt
a revolution in Ireland, and to leave out of

account land and religion, just the two things which most interested the majority of the people, was surely foolish.

The best account of the project as it appeared to Robert Emmet's mind (alas, the reality was far different) is to be found in the Diary kept by Thomas Emmet in Paris. " In the evening of Tuesday, May 31st, I went to Paris, and there saw Gallagher who brought accounts from Ireland. The purport of these accounts was that an organisation on a new and closer plan had been carried out to a great extent among the United Irishmen ; that a communication between North and South had been thoroughly established ; that very proper and respectable men had come forward, particularly in the North where it was least expected ; that the counties of Kildare, Wicklow and some others were in a very forward state ; that they had considerable depots in Dublin ; for instance, in one depot 2500 pikes were ready handled, and 1000 with the handles ready ; that Dwyer had pledged himself to come in and bring that county [Wicklow] with him, if any depot was attacked, which was to be the signal for the beginning ; that delegates from the people had been spoken to, who wished to know when they would be called out." This, no doubt, is a quite fair report of the information brought from Ireland by Gallagher. But in the light of after knowledge some criticisms at once suggest themselves. Communication with and assistance from the North of Ireland were certainly to be desired. But the sympathy and readiness of the North were assumed on the report of the enthusiastic ' P.P.' : in fact, the North never raised a finger in support. Dwyer's pledge of assistance " if any depot was attacked " was a singularly vague promise : in an insurrection all depends on the insurgents striking the first blow. Further reference will be made to Dwyer : he is a rather interesting personage. And the phrases " very proper and respectable men," and " delegates of the people " have really very little meaning.

Ere he returned to Ireland Robert Emmet had spoken with his brother in France. It would have been well had that slow-thinking but sagacious man disclosed to the impetuous boy the thoughts which were shaping themselves in his mind. Thomas Emmet saw that a rising in Ireland unsupported by France could have no chance of success. Robert Emmet in his speech from the dock declared, no doubt quite sincerely, that he would never have accepted French assistance on any terms which might have left France mistress of Ireland. Thomas Emmet was beginning to realise that Bonaparte, who for all practical purposes *was* France, would intervene in Ireland on no other terms. It is clear that two thoughts, later put into words by John Curran, were presenting themselves to Thomas Emmet. Curran spoke of " the fatuity of those who imagined that a revolution achieved by the assistance of France could have any other effect than subjecting Ireland to the merciless control of that power." And sarcastically Curran asked of the Irish people whether they could suppose " that the perfidy and treason of

surrendering your country to an invader would,
to your new master, be any pledge of your
allegiance ? "

And certain other reflections or suppositions
were beginning to give Thomas Emmet pause :
he was beginning to understand the hard, logical,
unsentimental mind of Bonaparte, of the French
people. Warned by the fate of Tone, Thomas
Emmet was insistent that Bonaparte should
issue his commissions to the Irish adventurers
who accompanied the French invading force,
and insist, by threat of reprisals, that England
should respect these commissions. Bonaparte
flatly refused to do anything of the kind : he
answered grimly that " *he never knew what
insurrections might be attempted against himself.*"
And ominous, and perhaps to the general reader
not very clear references to " Georges " and
" General Georges " appear in Thomas Emmet's
Diary. This " Georges " was George Cadoudal.
George Cadoudal was a Breton, a man of gigantic
strength and reckless bravery, a fanatical royalist,
and avowedly in intention an assassin. He made
no secret of his purpose of murdering Bonaparte ;
and quite obviously Bonaparte was very much
afraid that Cadoudal would accomplish his purpose. Cadoudal was in England ; and it undoubtedly was in Bonaparte's mind to offer a
surrender of any United Irishmen whom England
might be disposed to claim in exchange for England's surrender of George Cadoudal. Cadoudal
was a self-styled ' General ' ; quite possibly
he held a commission from the Bourbon family.
Bonaparte saw quite clearly that if he were to

insist on the Irish revolutionaries from France being treated as prisoners of war, he would probably be called upon to extend the same treatment to General George Cadoudal. In the end sundry Irishmen invading Ireland from France were hanged : George Cadoudal invading France from England was guillotined.

Meanwhile Robert Emmet was making his preparations in Ireland. He established arms depots, the principal depots being in Thomas Street and Patrick Street, both reasonably near to Dublin Castle. Here men worked at the making of arms and munitions. A principal arm was the pike ; and of this Emmet devised an ingenious variant. The pike handle was hinged ; and so a man wearing the rather long coat of the Irish country folk could fold up his pike and carry it unobserved beneath his coat. The rockets, one of which so frightened Dowdall, were lengths of iron tube filled with some explosive mixture, to be fired by a fuse. Hand grenades were manufactured by filling inkbottles with slugs and scraps of metal, and wrapping them about with layers of cloth and wadding. To hamper the attack of the Government troops, especially of the cavalry, long planks were studded with spikes : those planks were to be thrown down in the streets or somehow fastened to the roadway. Emissaries were despatched to beat up adherents without Dublin. In Emmet's Proclamation the following passage is found : " We have brought our plans to the moment when they are ripe for execution ; and in the promptitude with which nineteen counties will come forward at once to execute them it will be found that neither confidence nor communication are wanting to the people of Ireland." "*Will come forward*," "*will* be found " : alas, successful revolutions are not made in the future tense.

But—the question is inevitable—did the Government of Ireland know nothing of all this; were preparations for rebellion carried on under the Administration's unsuspecting nose ? Later there was an acrimonious discussion in the English House of Commons as to the alleged ignorance and unpreparedness of the Viceroy and Commander-in-Chief. Probably the true answer is that these highly placed dignitaries may have known very little, but that their underlings may have known a great deal. Indeed it has been imputed as a crime to the Administration that this conspiracy was allowed to come to a head. To speak so is to ignore hard facts, the harder side of human nature. Sirr and Swan were still alert and indefatigable ; and they had an efficient collaborator at headquarters in the person of one Edward Marsden, an Under-Secretary at the Castle. But the great experiment of the Union was still in its infancy ; all England wished that it should succeed ; and subordinates who asserted that all was not well needed to be sure of their facts before they spoke. Probably Sirr, Swan, Marsden and their like had no intention of giving a premature alarm which might indeed be true, but which might easily be represented by a dexterous politician as ill-founded. The representation would have been to the disadvantage of those who gave the alarm : hawks will not pick out hawks' eyes is a proverb which scarcely applies in the service of a Government.

On July 16 there was an accidental explosion at the Patrick Street depot. Considerable damage was done ; attention was attracted ; Major Sirr paid a visit to the place. Poor Emmet had a passion for the technique of conspiracy : as a boy he had contrived fantastic trapdoors and secret passages in his father's villa at Glenskeagh, outside Dublin. For his arms depot he had devised much the same apparatus : he flattered himself that Sirr had seen nothing, and had gone away unsuspecting. In all probability Sirr had seen all that he desired to see.

July 23 was the day fixed for the insurrection. To all appearances Dublin was quiet ; the Castle gates lay invitingly open. But did they invite the insurgents to come in and conquer, or did they invite poor foolish mice to walk into a trap ?

The tale of the rising is soon told. It was a a pitiful fiasco. The North never stirred : " P.P.'s " stories of the Northerns straining at the leash in all probability were but the product of his own exuberant imagination. A contingent of Kildare men did come to town : as they made their way towards the trysting place a trusty messenger (probably provided by Swan and Sirr) met them and whispered that all had been postponed to a more convenient season. Some returned, some pushed on to the depots. Those who pushed on found that at the depots nothing was really ready : of the rockets and hand grenades, on which much reliance had been placed, some had fuses, some had not. And the munition makers had mixed them up ! For some of the attacks scaling ladders were needed : none were ready. Angrily the Kildare men exclaimed that they had been misled by a foolish boy : they turned and made the best of their way to their homes.

Wicklow was to rise under the leadership of Dwyer. This Dwyer had been ' out ' in '98, and for nearly five years had been ' on his keeping.' Evidently he was a man of considerable intelligence and force of character—his after life proved this—for the people had confidence in him and affection for him. There was a price on his head ; yet he was never detected or betrayed. And he bore an irremovable identification mark : the thumb of his left hand had been blown away in a gunshot accident. That he failed Emmet on this occasion was through no fault of his own. A messenger was despatched to inform him that all was ready, to give him the ' zero hour ' for attack : this man took the message from Emmet and—did no more about it.

An advance party was sent to secure a footing in the Castle. The party drove in half a dozen hackney carriages ; they drove into the Castle yard ; an officer challenged them ; the leader of the party fired a shot from a pistol ; then all bolted.

As evening drew in it became apparent that all had gone awry. This is the description of a sympathiser : " On that night sixteen of the

leaders were supping with Hevey in St Thomas'
Court where the fray began. In fact, when they
ought to have been with their men they were
carousing with Hevey." The wretched Emmet
was now desperate of success ; yet he resolved
to do, at least to *try*, some stroke. He arrayed
himself—the pitiful tomfoolery of it all!—in a
green coat richly laced and with gold epaulets,
white waistcoat and pantaloons, top-boots and
a plumed hat. With threats and entreaties he
gathered together a rabble numbering about
eighty, and strove to make them march in some
semblance of order towards the Castle. And
then occurred the hideous tragedy of the whole
imbecile business.

A carriage drove in from the western side of
the city ; in it were an old man, a clergyman
and a lady. Emmet's followers stopped the
carriage and demanded the names of the travellers. "It is I—Kilwarden," said the old man
mildly : the clergyman was his nephew, the lady
his daughter.

Arthur Wolfe, later Lord Kilwarden, had been
the kindliest of the Irish Law Officers, the most
humane of the Irish Judges. "Are you ready
to help hang these traitors ?" once brutally
inquired of him a Judge in Court. "No, my
Lord," answered Wolfe defiantly, and addressed
himself to the Counsel defending twenty-four
prisoners. The Judge had defeated his own
object : Wolfe was no legal murderer. In-
tentionally and avowedly he so conducted the
prosecution that he saved the lives of twenty-
three of the accused. He was the Judge to whom

old Peter Tone had applied for a stay of the execution of his son ; and Wolfe, now Lord Kilwarden, had not failed him. When the Superintendent of the jail and the Provost-Marshal demurred to his order to produce the body of Wolfe Tone in his Court, Kilwarden sharply ordered the arrest of both. And now the mob dragged him and his nephew from their carriage and stabbed both to death. Kilwarden was carried still breathing to a neighbouring house. " We'll hang those fellows, my Lord," an officer savagely assured him. The dying man raised himself : " No, no," he whispered, " let no man suffer but by fair trial according to the laws of his country."

The murder of Kilwarden was the end of the business. By this time the tramp of troops approaching was heard : the mob broke and fled. Emmet tore off his fantastic finery and fled likewise. He made his way to a cottage at Rathfarnham which he had rented for a time. Anne Devlin, the servant at the house, received him with bitter words : " Bad welcome to you ; you coward, to lead people to destruction, and then to leave them." ' Fool,' would have been a better word : Robert Emmet was not a coward. "Don't blame me, Anne," he moaned. Blame him or not, Anne would not betray him. Sirr offered her a fortune for a woman in her station : she refused it contemptuously. He swung her up from a beam and half-choked her : she refused to utter a word.

Emmet was taken about a month later by Sirr at a house at Harold's Cross. There had been a great number of arrests ; and it is more than probable that some of those arrested ' squeaked.' Sirr searched his prisoner : in his breast pocket were some letters in a woman's writing. " Ah," said Sirr venomously.

The identity of the writer was suspected but not known : the letters were either unsigned, or signed by some ' pet name.' So extremely simple and artless was the wording that some hidden and important meaning was surmised. Emmet was brought before a Committee of the Privy Council and questioned. He declared that he would answer nothing : he had not the wit to realise that to make his declaration good he must utterly hold his tongue. Standish O'Grady, the Attorney-General, engaged him in seemingly casual conversation : Emmet did not disclose the lady's name ; but, as was almost inevitable, he disclosed *something*. He was taken to Kilmainham jail ; there he formed the futile plan, already described, of escaping ; and in a moment of utter foolishness he suborned his jailor to carry a letter for him. The letter he addressed openly to Sarah Curran : the jailor handed it to the Superintendent of the jail. For this the vials of patriotic wrath have been poured on the jailor's head : it should be remembered that those who tempt a servant to prove false to his duty have no great cause for complaint should that servant prove false to them.

For poor Sarah Curran the consequences were calamitous. Her father, for all his *bonhomie* at the Bar, was a hard man in his home ; and now he was beside himself with anger. He had, indeed, much cause for anger. He found his name dragged into what he described as "a drunken, riotous insurrection"; it can scarcely be denied that Emmet had in a measure abused his hospitality, that his daughter had in a measure deceived him. He acted promptly. He placed his papers under seal; then waited on the Attorney-General and informed him that he held himself entirely at the disposal of Government. For himself the matter proved to be little more than a formality. Some bundles of his papers, sealed by himself, were taken away; and he was asked to appear before the Privy Council. He was accompanied by the Attorney-General; he was assured that no suspicion of complicity in this unfortunate affair could possibly rest on him; when he asked for his papers, they were returned to him with his own seals unbroken. It was, of course, now clearly impossible that he should appear professionally on behalf of Emmet.

Robert Emmet was brought to trial on September 18. Three Judges sat on the Bench: Lord Norbury, better known in Irish history as John Toler, presided. Norbury has been described as a "hanging Judge," an Irish edition of the Scottish Lord Braxfield; but he seems to have conducted the trial of Emmet with dignity and humanity. Once, indeed, he uttered some words which might better have been left unsaid; but it must be admitted that he spoke under provocation. Day and George, J.J., were his fellow Judges.

For the Crown there naturally appeared the Attorney-General (O'Grady) and the Solicitor-

General (M'Clelland). ' With them ' was William
Conyngham Plunket, later Lord Chancellor of
Ireland. His appearance in the case then pro-
voked comment, and now incites speculation.
Leonard M'Nally led for Emmet : with him was
Peter Burrowes.

The Attorney-General opened the Crown case
in a rather dry, formal tone ; then he called and
examined his witnesses. M'Nally did not cross-
examine ; and when the last Crown witness had
been heard, he announced that he would neither
call evidence nor address the jury. Plunket
then rose. M'Nally promptly objected. By
custom, he said, when no defence was offered,
the Crown case could be no further urged. The
Attorney-General argued the point : there was a
difference, he said, between opening a case and
speaking to the evidence. It was his particular
desire that Mr Plunket be heard. Lord Norbury
held that, while as a general rule the Crown did
not speak when the prisoner put forward no
defence, a prisoner, nevertheless, could not enforce silence on the Crown by the simple expedient
of remaining silent himself. Mr Plunket then
addressed the jury.

It was a very curious business, and explanation
can only be conjectural. M'Nally was an arch-
scoundrel ; but it is unreasonable to suppose
that he deliberately betrayed Emmet in Court,
allowed the case to go by default. For one thing
he stated that he took his course in accordance
with his client's express instructions : for another,
this was not his mode of betrayal. He would
disclose to the Crown the defence which his

clients proposed to set up ; but no man ever fought harder for his clients in Court. It may be that he claimed reciprocity, and so justified himself to his own twisted soul. Let the Crown disclose their attack to him : he would disclose his defence to the Crown. Then let the jury judge between them.

Against Plunket the vilest insinuations were made. Changes in the legal establishment of the Crown were impending : it was alleged that to earn the Solicitor-Generalship he undertook the duty of hounding Emmet to death. Else why should he, but a few years before a stout opponent of the Union, now appear against an Irish patriot ? Plunket's whole life gives the lie to the allegation ; and the question is wholly illogical. Plunket had opposed the Union ; but his opposition had not prevailed. Is it unreasonable to suppose that he had accepted the decision, that he was unwilling that a great Constitutional issue should now be left to the decision of a drunken mob ?

There is a possible explanation. Emmet believed himself to be an eloquent man, and, it is to be feared, he was a vain man. He may have thought that he could do better than M'Nally. He may also have argued with a certain shrewdness that his one chance of escape lay in an *ad captandum* appeal to the Court : where the professional eloquence of M'Nally would be discounted, the eloquence of a young man pleading for his own life might be acceptable. For, whatever might be said fairly or unfairly of the blood-lust of the Bench, Irishmen, even Irish

Judges, have always been soft-hearted, susceptible to sentimental eloquence. This plan M'Nally may have betrayed to the Crown lawyers ; and the Crown may have determined that, should Emmet lay stress on his moral innocence, the most eloquent man in Ireland should lay a corresponding stress on the measure of Emmet's moral guilt. There were certainly in England many ready to discredit each and every action of the Irish Executive : that Executive were not minded to submit, unheard, to the condemnation of politicians.

This hypothesis—it is nothing more—receives some support from what followed. The jury returned their verdict : it could only be a verdict of ' Guilty.' Lord Norbury asked the prisoner whether he had anything to say why the sentence of the Law should not be pronounced. Emmet spoke : the length of his speech and the elaboration of his phrasing forbid the supposition that the speech was impromptu, unpremeditated.

Emmet's speech from the dock has been handed down and admired as a classic of Irish eloquence. But in the sober light of reason much of it seems to be fustian. " Where is the boasted freedom of your institutions, if an unfortunate prisoner, whom your policy, not justice, is about to deliver into the hands of the executioner, is not allowed to explain his motives ? " Emmet had consistently denied that the institutions of England were free, he had been guilty of armed rebellion against the established Government of the land. He had lost the game : is it altogether unreasonable to claim that the loser must pay ?

" If I stand at the Bar of the Court, and dare not vindicate my character, what a farce is your justice." Could he clear away, did he attempt to clear away from his character the stain of the brutal and unprovoked murder of Arthur Wolfe, Lord Kilwarden ?

On two or three occasions Lord Norbury interrupted the speaker. His interruptions were, for the most part, but reminders to the prisoner that his words must be kept within the bounds of relevance. Once he spoke harshly : he reminded the prisoner that his father had held an honoured position in the life of Dublin, that his brothers had enjoyed the esteem of their fellow members of the Irish Bar, that he himself had sunk to be the associate of a base rabble. These words were in a measure true ; but still they had better been left unsaid. Yet Norbury did not speak without provocation : he had heard these words addressed to himself by a man responsible for the murder of one of his judicial colleagues, " there are men concerned in this conspiracy *who would not disgrace themselves by shaking your bloodstained hand.*" Did the blood of Kilwarden leave no stain on Emmet's hand ?

At length Emmet was silent. Lord Norbury pronounced the death sentence. Next morning Emmet was brought forth to die. He had been taken from the Court-room to the Newgate prison : the spot appointed for his hanging was nearly opposite the Church of St Catherine at the meeting of Thomas Street and Bridgefoot Street. Ere he left the prison he wrote, as has been described, to John and Richard Curran : he also wrote to a secretary to Government a letter which contained the following passage : " It was my intention not only to acknowledge the delicacy with which I have been personally treated, but also to have done the most public justice to the mildness of the present Administration of this country." And yet he had endeavoured violently to overturn that Administration. Why ?

There was one more strange cue in the tragicomedy. Emmet stood on the scaffold with the rope about his neck. " Are you ready, sir ? " asked the hangman ; " Not yet," was the reply. Twice the hangman repeated his question : twice the reply was the same. Then the hangman knocked away the prop which supported the scaffold. This was the end. It would be unjust to attribute to Emmet in his last moment on earth a spasm of craven, futile fear. There is some reason to suppose that he expected up to the very last an attempt by the people to rescue him.

The body hung for about an ˋour : it was then taken down, and the head was severed from the body. Where the mangled trunk was laid no one now knows, seemingly no one then cared to learn.

The stories of some fellow actors in this sad play may be completed. However justifiable John Curran's anger, no one can justify his conduct to his unhappy daughter. The shock of her lover's arrest and execution for a time deprived the wretched girl of her reason : when she came to her wits, her father informed her that her presence was no longer welcome in his house. Sarah Curran found refuge with a Quaker family named Penrose, who lived near Cork. Here she attracted the admiration of a kindly, chivalrous soldier, one Captain Stourgen. He asked her to be his wife : she consented. Sarah spent a few years with her husband on foreign service ; when her husband was ordered home, she was expecting to become a mother. Their ship was caught in a storm : the violent plunging and tossing brought on travail prematurely, and Sarah did not survive the birth of her child.

Thomas Emmet remained in Paris for about a year longer. He still plotted, and still unceasingly quarrelled with Arthur O'Connor. It is clear that in the end the French became extremely distasteful to him, and that he became a wearisome bore to the French. He sailed for America ; he meddled no more with Irish politics ; he rose to an honoured position in the practice of the Law.

Dwyer, the Wicklow outlaw whom Emmet's message failed to reach, was taken by the police. He was sentenced to transportation for life, and shipped to Botany Bay. He was set at liberty wellnigh immediately ; he entered the public service of the colony ; he sent to Ireland for his wife and family. He was informed that he was quite at liberty to return to his native land if he so desired : he smiled and shook his head. He died, an honoured citizen of his new country, at a good age. Allen, O'Connor, Thomas Emmet, Dwyer—the list might be made wellnigh endless —all Irishmen finding work, usefulness, honour in other lands. Once more, is Ireland the

Upas tree in whose shade no Irishman can prosper?

Anne Devlin, who had half suffered death for Emmet's sake, died in old age and in extreme poverty. No patriot seemingly thought her heroism worthy of a copper or a crust.

One little touch of irony rounds off the story. Nearly a hundred years after Robert Emmet's death a descendant of his brother sought piously to discover the patriot's last resting place. The search was vain. But he examined what had been once the cemetery of St Peter's Church: in this had been the vault of the Emmet family. The cemetery when used had been well below the level of the adjoining street: it had long been closed to burials, and had been artificially raised by the heaping of earth upon it. No trace of any grave or tomb remained; but a few old tombstones lay battered and uncared for in a corner. Idly the younger Emmet turned one over, and read the wellnigh obliterated inscription. He was looking at the tombstone of—John Fitzgibbon.

BIBLIOGRAPHICAL NOTE.

ON bibliographies I look with a certain suspicion : frequently, I fear, they are used to suggest a width of reading to which the writer has no real claim. Nevertheless it is at once ungrateful and discourteous not to acknowledge one's obligations.

The standard English authorities for eighteenth century Ireland are Froude (' The English in Ireland ') and Lecky (' Ireland in the Eighteenth Century '). With these I am familiar. There are many general histories of Ireland : I prefer the larger edition of Mr Stephen Gwynn's ' History of Ireland.' Dr Madden's many volumes are a mine well worth digging in ; so are Sir Jonah Barrington's several ' Recollections.' Teeling's ' Personal Narrative,' so far as it goes, is interesting ; so is Fitzpatrick's ' Secret Service under Pitt.' And there are the officially recorded debates of the Irish Parliament.

O'Flanagan has written a memoir of John Fitzgibbon ; and his ' Lives of the Irish Chancellors ' throws a good deal of light on the legal world of Fitzgibbon's day.

For Wolfe Tone the chief authorities are his own ' Autobiographical Narrative ' and his inimitable ' Journal ' (he himself calls it his ' Giurnal '). There are several editions : I prefer that of Mr Barry O'Brien.

Moore was the first biographer of Lord Edward

Fitzgerald. There are other interesting works by Ida Taylor, Gerald Campbell, and Katharine Tynan.

Moore has written also of Robert Emmet: so has Mr R. W. Postgate. There is a good deal of information about Emmet in Mr W. H. Curran's 'Life' of his father, the famous advocate John Philpot Curran. Emmet's elder brother kept a Diary: much of it is reproduced in Dr T. A. Emmet's much later 'Ireland under English Rule.'

If I have omitted any due acknowledgment, I must plead inadvertence, not intention, as my excuse.